The Works

OF

Arthur
Schopenhauer

*The Wisdom of Life
and Other Essays*

BLACK'S READERS SERVICE
ROSLYN, NEW YORK

CONTENTS

THE WISDOM OF LIFE

THE ART OF LITERATURE

STUDIES IN PESSIMISM

AUTHOR'S PREFACE

In these pages I shall speak of *The Wisdom of Life* in the common meaning of the term, as the art, namely, of ordering our lives so as to obtain the greatest possible amount of pleasure and success; an art the theory of which may be called *eudæmonology*, for it teaches us how to lead a happy existence. Such an existence might perhaps be defined as one which, looked at from a purely objective point of view, or, rather, after cool and mature reflection—for the question necessarily involves subjective considerations,—would be decidedly preferable to non-existence; implying that we should cling to it for its own sake, and not merely from the fear of death; and further, that we should never like it to come to an end.

Now whether human life corresponds, or could possibly correspond, to this conception of existence, is a question to which, as is' well-known, my philosophical system returns a negative answer. On the eudæmonistic hypothesis, however, the question must be answered in the affirmative; and I have shown, in the second volume of my chief work (ch. 49), that this hypothesis is based upon a fundamental mistake. Accordingly, in elaborating the scheme of a happy existence, I have had to make a complete surrender of the higher metaphysical and ethical standpoint to which my own theories lead; and everything I shall say here will to some extent rest upon a compromise; in so far, that is, as I take the common standpoint of every day, and embrace the error which is at the bottom of it. My remarks, therefore, will possess only a qualified value, for the very word *eudæmonology* is a euphemism. Further, I make no claims to completeness; partly because the subject is inexhaustible, and partly because I should otherwise have to say over again what has been already said by others.

The only book composed, as far as I remember, with a like purpose to that which animates this collection of aphorisms, is Cardan's *De utilitate ex adversis capienda,* which is well worth reading, and may be used to supplement the present work. Aristotle, it is true, has a few words on eudæmonology in the fifth chapter of the first book of his *Rhetoric;* but what he says does not come to very much. As compilation is not my business, I have made no use of these predecessors; more especially because in the process of compiling, individuality of view is lost, and individuality of view is the kernel of works of this kind. In general, indeed, the wise in all ages have always said the same thing, and the fools, who at all times form the immense majority, have in their way too acted alike, and done just the opposite; and so it will continue. For, as Voltaire says, *we shall leave this world as foolish and as wicked as we found it on our arrival.*

INTRODUCTION

When a son and heir was born to Heinrich Floris Schopenhauer and his wife Johanna Henrietta Trosiener, in the free city of Danzig on February 22, 1788, the child was christened Arthur, because he was destined to be a merchant, and his father thought that a name which remains practically unchanged in all European languages would be advantageous to a man of international business. That he would be not merely a merchant but a successful one, there was little doubt, for he had a firm foundation on which to build and a distinguished tradition to uphold. If the Schopenhauers were not quite merchant princes, they were surely aristocrats of the commercial world. It was in their house, then proudly inhabited by Arthur's great-grandfather, that Peter the Great and Catherine of Russia had lodged as visitors to Danzig. Arthur's grandfather had known how to augment his inheritance of wealth and honor; and Heinrich Floris had proved, so far at least, a worthy bearer of the Schopenhauer name and a competent custodian of the family fortune. From his youthful mother, daughter of Senator Trosiener, Arthur inherited Danzig's bluest blood. A prophet could not have hesitated long: the boy's destiny pointed plainly to the heights of the practical world, where he would move as an equal among men of substance and power. And, that there might be no mistake as to his first step along that road, his father placed him when he was only ten in the home of a business correspondent at Havre, there to master French and begin his reading in "the book of the world."

When, after two years of France, Arthur entered school at Hamburg, to which city his parents had removed after Prussia's seizure of Danzig, the boy had his first real taste of learning; and one sip of that heady brew was fatal to the paternal ambitions. The scion of the Schopenhauers then knew what he wanted, and it was not money but knowledge. Two years of schooling decided him; he would be a scholar, in precisely what field he was not yet sure, but his work would be done with hard facts and elusive ideas rather than with counting-house gold and cautious contracts. He must learn and learn. But Heinrich Floris, who could not dissociate scholarship from starvation, was a man of resource, and the bribe of two years' European travel, given with the stipulation that Arthur should enter business at the end of it, was enough to lure the boy away from school. The bribe was paid in full; Arthur kept his promise, and found himself staring at his father's ledgers. He was barely seventeen.

How long his revolt would have been postponed, had his father lived, there is no saying; but it was a bright day for philosophy when Heinrich Floris fell or threw himself from an attic window into the canal at Hamburg in the spring of 1805. His son was immediately free, and assured of an income that made that freedom complete. He was free to attend the gymnasium at Gotha, where he concentrated on classical studies; free to sojourn in Weimar, where his sprightly mother was one of the satellites that circled around the luminous figure of Goethe; free to enter the University of Göttingen, where, studying philosophy and the natural sciences, he submitted to the influences of Plato and Kant, and the more immediate influence of Schelling; free to visit Berlin, in 1811, to sit somewhat irreverently at the feet of Fichte and Schleiermacher; free to retire to Rudolstadt, where he wrote his first work, "On the Fourfold Root of the Principle of Sufficient Reason," which he successfully presented at Jena as the dissertation for his doctor's degree; free to break with his unsympathetic mother forever, to settle in Dresden, and there to compose his master work, "The World as Will and Idea," which, published when he was only thirty, was the complete and rounded expression of his philosophy.

Yes, he was free; and the use that he made of his freedom

was swift and enduringly fruitful. But recognition of his
work lagged far behind the work itself. Nor is it strange that
the university philosophers should have had little use for the
thinker who had no use for them, for the man who could
write: "There is no Philosophy in the period between Kant
and myself; only mere University charlatanism." There
was another reason, too, why the professors should mistrust
him. A philosopher who writes in language that the average
man can understand is always suspect in the eyes of his pro-
fessionally incomprehensible fellows, while a philosopher who
is capable of wit is doubly suspect. Schopenhauer moved
under the twin cloud, and it was slow in lifting. During years
of European wandering and of obscurity in Frankfurt, where
he finally settled and remained until his death in 1860, years
that were busy with additions to the main body of his work,
the neglect that he suffered fortified his temperamental pessimism, and confirmed his philosophic conviction that "earthly
happiness is destined to be frustrated or recognized as an
illusion." But fortune smiled at last, and it is one of fate's
engaging ironies that the closing decade of the arch-pessi-
mist's life was a happy period in which he welcomed fame and
adulation with the innocent joy of a child.

"Suffering," he wrote, "is a condition of the power of genius.
Would Shakespeare and Goethe have written, Plato philoso-
phized, Kant criticized Pure Reason, if they had found satisfaction in the actual world, had felt at home in it and had
their desires fulfilled?" Perhaps not. But if Schopenhauer's
genius was conditioned by suffering, he did not refuse to
delight in the rewards of genius. And those rewards were
fully merited, for if this philosopher who wrote with a lucidity
that has proved the despair of commentators, since none can
explain him so easily as he explained himself, boasted ex-
cessively when he declared, "I have lifted the veil of truth
higher than any mortal before me," still he could justly claim
that no mortal had ever been more passionately devoted to
the pursuit of truth, and we can testify that few thinkers have
proved so stimulating in that quest which has no end. It is

a cry straight from the heart to which we listen when we read: "For if anything in the world is worth wishing for—so well worth wishing that even the ignorant and dull herd in its more reflective moments would prize it more than silver and gold—it is that a ray of light should fall on the obscurity of our being, and that we should gain some explanation of our mysterious existence, in which nothing is clear but its misery and vanity." The search for light was Arthur Schopenhauer's whole existence.

BEN RAY REDMAN.

The Wisdom of Life

CHAPTER I

DIVISION OF THE SUBJECT

ARISTOTLE[1] divides the blessings of life into three classes—those which come to us from without, those of the soul, and those of the body. Keeping nothing of this division but the number, I observe that the fundamental differences in human lot may be reduced to three distinct classes:

(1) What a man is: that is to say, personality, in the widest sense of the word; under which are included health, strength, beauty, temperament, moral character, intelligence, and education.

(2) What a man has: that is, property and possessions of every kind.

(3) How a man stands in the estimation of others: by which is to be understood, as everybody knows, what a man is in the eyes of his fellowmen, or, more strictly, the light in which they regard him. This is shown by their opinion of him; and their opinion is in its turn manifested by the honor in which he is held, and by his rank and reputation.

The differences which come under the first head are those which Nature herself has set between man and man; and from this fact alone we may at once infer that they influence the happiness or unhappiness of mankind in a much more vital and radical way than those contained under the two following heads, which are merely the effect of human arrangements. Compared with *genuine personal advantages,* such as a great mind or a great heart, all the

[1] *Eth. Nichom.,* I. 8.

1

privileges of rank or birth, even of royal birth, are but as kings on the stage, to kings in real life. The same thing was said long ago by Metrodorus, the earliest disciple of Epicurus, who wrote as the title of one of his chapters, *The happiness we receive from ourselves is greater than that which we obtain from our surroundings.*[2] And it is an obvious fact, which cannot be called in question, that the principal element in a man's well-being,—indeed, in the whole tenor of his existence,—is what he is made of, his inner constitution. For this is the immediate source of that inward satisfaction or dissatisfaction resulting from the sum total of his sensations, desires and thoughts; whilst his surroundings, on the other hand, exert only a mediate or indirect influence upon him. This is why the same external events or circumstances affect no two people alike; even with perfectly similar surroundings every one lives in a world of his own. For a man has immediate apprehension only of his own ideas, feelings and volitions; the outer world can influence him only in so far as it brings these to life. The world in which a man lives shapes itself chiefly by the way in which he looks at it, and so it proves different to different men; to one it is barren, dull, and superficial; to another rich, interesting, and full of meaning. On hearing of the interesting events which have happened in the course of a man's experience, many people will wish that similar things had happened in their lives too, completely forgetting that they should be envious rather of the mental aptitude which lent those events the significance they possess when he describes them; to a man of genius they were interesting adventures; but to the dull perceptions of an ordinary individual they would have been stale, every-day occurrences. This is in the highest degree the case with many of Goethe's and Byron's poems, which are obviously founded upon actual facts; where it is open

[2] Cf. Clemens Alex. Strom. II., 21.

to a foolish reader to envy the poet because so many delightful things happened to him, instead of envying that mighty power of phantasy which was capable of turning a fairly common experience into something so great and beautiful.

In the same way, a person of melancholy temperament will make a scene in a tragedy out of what appears to the sanguine man only in the light of an interesting conflict, and to a phlegmatic soul as something without any meaning;—all of which rests upon the fact that every event, in order to be realized and appreciated, requires the co-operation of two factors, namely, a subject and an object, although these are as closely and necessarily connected as oxygen and hydrogen in water. When therefore the objective or external factor in an experience is actually the same, but the subjective or personal appreciation of it varies, the event is just as much a different one in the eyes of different persons as if the objective factors had not been alike; for to a blunt intelligence the fairest and best object in the world presents only a poor reality, and is therefore only poorly appreciated,—like a fine landscape in dull weather, or in the reflection of a bad *camera obscura*. In plain language, every man is pent up within the limits of his own consciousness, and cannot directly get beyond those limits any more than he can get beyond his own skin; so external aid is not of much use to him. On the stage, one man is a prince, another a minister, a third a servant or a soldier or a general, and so on,—mere external differences: the inner reality, the kernel of all these appearances is the same—a poor player, with all the anxieties of his lot. In life it is just the same. Differences of rank and wealth give every man his part to play, but this by no means implies a difference of inward happiness and pleasure; here, too, there is the same being in all—a poor mortal, with his hardships and troubles. Though these may, indeed, in every case proceed from dissimilar causes, they are in their essential nature much the same in all their forms, with degrees of intensity which vary, no doubt, but in no wise correspond to the part a man .1as to play, to the presence or absence of position and wealth. Since everything which exists or happens for a man exists only in his consciousness and happens for it alone, the most essential thing for a man is the constitution of this consciousness, which is in most cases far more important than the circumstances which go to form its contents. All the pride and pleasure of the world mirrored in the dull consciousness of a fool, are poor indeed compared with the imagination of Cervantes writing his *Don Quixote* in a miserable prison. The objective half of life and reality is in the hand of fate, and accordingly takes various forms in different cases: the subjective half is ourself, and in essentials it always remains the same.

Hence the life of every man is stamped with the same character throughout, however much his external circumstances may alter; it is like a series of variations on a single theme. No one can get beyond his own individuality. An animal, under whatever circumstances it is placed, remains within the narrow limits to which nature has irrevocably consigned it; so that our endeavors to make a pet happy must always keep within the compass of its nature, and be restricted to what it can feel. So it is with man; the measure of the happiness he can attain is determined beforehand by his individuality. More especially is this the case with the mental powers, which fix once for all his capacity for the higher kinds of pleasure. If these powers are small, no efforts from without, nothing that his fellowmen or that fortune can do for him, will suffice to raise him above the ordinary degree of human happiness and pleasure, half animal though it be; his only resources are his sensual appetite,—a cozy and cheerful family life at the most,—low company and vulgar pastime;

even education, on the whole, can avail little, if anything, for the enlargement of his horizon. For the highest, most varied and lasting pleasures are those of the mind, however much our youth may deceive us on this point; and the pleasures of the mind turn chiefly on the powers of the mind. It is clear, then, that our happiness depends in a great degree upon what we *are*, upon our individuality, whilst lot or destiny is generally taken to mean only what we *have*, or our *reputation*. Our lot, in this sense, may improve; but we do not ask much of it if we are inwardly rich: on the other hand, a fool remains a fool, a dull blockhead, to his last hour, even though he were surrounded by houris in paradise. This is why Goethe, in the *Westöstlichen Divan*, says that every man, whether he occupies a low position in life, or emerges as its victor, testifies to personality as the greatest factor in happiness:—

> *Volk und Knecht und Überwinder*
> *Sie gestehen, zu jeder Zeit,*
> *Höchtes Glück der Erdenkinder*
> *Sei nur die Persönlichkeit.*

Everything confirms the fact that the subjective element in life is incomparably more important for our happiness and pleasure than the objective, from such sayings as *Hunger is the best sauce*, and *Youth and Age cannot live together*, up to the life of the Genius and the Saint. Health outweighs all other blessings so much that one may really say that a healthy beggar is happier than an ailing king. A quiet and cheerful temperament, happy in the enjoyment of a perfectly sound physique, an intellect clear, lively, penetrating and seeing things as they are, a moderate and gentle will, and therefore a good conscience—these are privileges which no rank or wealth can make up for or replace. For what a man is in himself, what accompanies him when he is alone, what no one can give or take away, is obviously more essential to him than every-

thing he has in the way of possessions, or even what he
may be in the eyes of the world. An intellectual man in
complete solitude has excellent entertainment in his own
thoughts and fancies, while no amount of diversity or social
pleasure, theatres, excursions and amusements, can ward
off boredom from a dullard. A good, temperate, gentle
character can be happy in needy circumstances, whilst a
covetous, envious and malicious man, even if he be the
richest in the world, goes miserable. Nay more; to one
who has the constant delight of a special individuality,
with a high degree of intellect, most of the pleasures which
are run after by mankind are simply superfluous; they
are even a trouble and a burden. And so Horace says of
himself, that, however many are deprived of the fancy-
goods of life, there is one at least who can live without them:—

> *Gemmas, marmor, ebur, Tyrrhena sigilla, tabellas,*
> *Argentum, vestes, Gœtulo murice tinctas*
> *Sunt qui non habeant, est qui non curat habere;*

and when Socrates saw various articles of luxury spread
out for sale, he exclaimed: *How much there is in the
world I do not want*.

So the first and most essential element in our life's happiness is what we are,—our personality, if for no other
reason than that it is a constant factor coming into play
under all circumstances: besides, unlike the blessings which
are described under the other two heads, it is not the sport
of destiny and cannot be wrested from us;—and, so far,
it is endowed with an absolute value in contrast to the
merely relative worth of the other two. The consequence
of this is that it is much more difficult than people commonly suppose to get a hold on a man from without. But
here the all-powerful agent, Time, comes in and claims its
rights, and before its influence physical and mental advantages gradually waste away. Moral character alone re-

mains inaccessible to it. In view of the destructive effect
of time, it seems, indeed, as if the blessings named under
the other two heads, of which time cannot directly rob
us, were superior to those of the first. Another advantage
might be claimed for them, namely, that being in their
very nature objective and external, they are attainable,
and every one is presented with the possibility, at least,
of coming into possession of them; whilst what is subjective
is not open to us to acquire, but making its entry by a
kind of *divine right,* it remains for life, immutable, inalien-
able, an inexorable doom. Let me quote those lines in
which Goethe describes how an unalterable destiny is assigned to every man at the hour of his birth, so that he
can develop only in the lines laid down for him, as it were,
by the conjunctions of the stars; and how the Sybil and
the prophets declare that *himself* a man can never escape,
nor any power of time avail to change the path on which
his life is cast:—

> *Wie an dem Tag, der dich der Welt verliehen,*
> *Die Sonne stand zum Grusse der Planeten,*
> *Bist alsobald und fort und fort gediehen,*
> *Nach dem Gesetz, wonach du angetreten.*
> *So musst du sein, dir kannst du nicht entfliehen,*
> *So tagten schon Sybillen und Propheten;*
> *Und keine Zeit, und keine Macht zerstückelt*
> *Geprägte Form, die lebend sich entwickelt.*

The only thing that stands in our power to achieve, is
to make the most advantageous use possible of the personal qualities we possess, and accordingly to follow such
pursuits only as will call them into play, to strive after
the kind of perfection of which they admit and to avoid
every other; consequently, to choose the position, occupation and manner of life which are most suitable for their
development.

Imagine a man endowed with herculean strength who
is compelled by circumstances to follow a sedentary occu-

pation, some minute exquisite work of the hands, for example, or to engage in study and mental labor demanding quite other powers, and just those which he has not got,—compelled, that is, to leave unused the powers in which he is pre-eminently strong; a man placed like this will never feel happy all his life through. Even more miserable will be the lot of the man with intellectual powers of a very high order, who has to leave them undeveloped and unemployed, in the pursuit of a calling which does not require them, some bodily labor, perhaps, for which his strength is insufficient. Still, in a case of this kind, it should be our care, especially in youth, to avoid the precipice of presumption, and not ascribe to ourselves a superfluity of power which is not there.

Since the blessings described under the first head decidedly outweigh those contained under the other two, it is manifestly a wiser course to aim at the maintenance of our health and the cultivation of our faculties, than at the amassing of wealth; but this must not be mistaken as meaning that we should neglect to acquire an adequate supply of the necessaries of life. Wealth, in the strict sense of the word, that is, great superfluity, can do little for our happiness; and many rich people feel unhappy just because they are without any true mental culture or knowledge, and consequently have no objective interests which would qualify them for intellectual occupations. For beyond the satisfaction of some real and natural necessities, all that the possession of wealth can achieve has a very small influence upon our happiness, in the proper sense of the word; indeed, wealth rather disturbs it, because the preservation of property entails a great many unavoidable anxieties. And still men are a thousand times more intent on becoming rich than on acquiring culture, though it is quite certain that what a man *is* contributes much more to his happiness than what he *has*. So you

may see many a man, as industrious as an ant, ceaselessly
occupied from morning to night in the endeavor to increase his heap of gold. Beyond the narrow horizon of
means to this end, he knows nothing; his mind is a blank,
and consequently unsusceptible to any other influence.
The highest pleasures, those of the intellect, are to him
inaccessible, and he tries in vain to replace them by the
fleeting pleasures of sense in which he indulges, lasting
but a brief hour and at tremendous cost. And if he is
lucky, his struggles result in his having a really great pile
of gold, which he leaves to his heir, either to make it still
larger, or to squander it in extravagance. A life like this,
though pursued with a sense of earnestness and an air
of importance, is just as silly as many another which has
a fool's cap for its symbol.

What a man has in himself is, then, the chief element in
his happiness. Because this is, as a rule, so very little,
most of those who are placed beyond the struggle with
penury feel at bottom quite as unhappy as those who are
still engaged in it. Their minds are vacant, their imagination dull, their spirits poor, and so they are driven to
the company of those like them—for *similis simili gaudet*—
where they make common pursuit of pastime and entertainment, consisting for the most part in sensual pleasure,
amusement of every kind, and finally, in excess and libertin-
ism. A young man of rich family enters upon life with
a large patrimony, and often runs through it in an incred-
ibly short space of time, in vicious extravagance; and
why? Simply because, here too, the mind is empty and
void, and so the man is bored with existence. He was
sent forth into the world outwardly rich but inwardly
poor, and his vain endeavor was to make his external
wealth compensate for his inner poverty, by trying to
obtain everything *from without,* like an old man who seeks
to strengthen himself as King David or Maréchal de Rex

tried to do. And so in the end one who is inwardly poor comes to be also poor outwardly.

I need not insist upon the importance of the other two kinds of blessings which make up the happiness of human life; now-a-days the value of possessing them is too well known to require advertisement. The third class, it is true, may seem, compared with the second, of a very ethereal character, as it consists only of other people's opinions. Still every one has to strive for reputation, that is to say, a good name. Rank, on the other hand, should be aspired to only by those who serve the state, and fame by very few indeed. In any case, reputation is looked upon as a priceless treasure, and fame as the most precious of all the blessings a man can attain,—the Golden Fleece, as it were, of the elect; whilst only fools will prefer rank to property. The second and third classes, moreover, are reciprocally cause and effect; so far, that is, as Petronius' maxim, *habes habeberis*, is true; and conversely, the favor of others, in all its forms, often puts us in the way of getting what we want.

CHAPTER II

PERSONALITY, OR WHAT A MAN IS

WE have already seen, in general, that what a man *is* contributes much more to his happiness than what he *has*, or how he is regarded by others. What a man is, and so what he has in his own person, is always the chief thing to consider; for his individuality accompanies him always and everywhere, and gives its color to all his experiences. In every kind of enjoyment, for instance, the pleasure depends principally upon the man himself. Every one admits this in regard to physical, and how much truer it is of intellectual, pleasure. When we use that English expression, "to enjoy one's self," we are employing a very striking and appropriate phrase; for observe—one says, not "he enjoys Paris," but "he enjoys himself in Paris." To a man possessed of an ill-conditioned individuality, all pleasure is like delicate wine in a mouth made bitter with gall. Therefore, in the blessings as well as in the ills of life, less depends upon what befalls us than upon the way in which it is met, that is, upon the kind and degree of our general susceptibility. What a man is and has in himself,—in a word personality, with all it entails, is the only immediate and direct factor in his happiness and welfare. All else is mediate and indirect, and its influence can be neutralized and frustrated; but the influence of personality never. This is why the envy which personal qualities excite is the most implacable of all,—as it is also the most carefully dissembled.

Further, the constitution of our consciousness is the ever present and lasting element in all we do or suffer;

our individuality is persistently at work, more or less at
every moment of our life: all other influences are tem-
poral, incidental, fleeting, and subject to every kind of
chance and change. This is why Aristotle says: *It is not
wealth but character that lasts.*[1]

—ἡ γὰρ φύσις βέβαιον, οὐ τὰ χρήματα.

And just for the same reason we can more easily bear a
misfortune which comes to us entirely from without, than
one which we have drawn upon ourselves; for fortune may
always change, but not character. Therefore, subjective
blessings,—a noble nature, a capable head, a joyful temperament, bright spirits, a well-constituted, perfectly sound
physique, in a word, *mens sana in corpore sano,* are the
first and most important elements in happiness; so that
we should be more intent on promoting and preserving
such qualities than on the possession of external wealth
and external honor.

And of all these, the one which makes us the most
directly happy is a genial flow of good spirits; for this
excellent quality is its own immediate reward. The man
who is cheerful and merry has always a good reason for
being so,—the fact, namely, that he is so. There is nothing
which, like this quality, can so completely replace the loss
of every other blessing. If you know anyone who is young,
handsome, rich and esteemed, and you want to know, further, if he is happy, ask, Is he cheerful and genial?—and
if he is, what does it matter whether he is young or old,
straight or humpbacked, poor or rich?—he is happy. In
my early days I once opened an old book and found these
words: *If you laugh a great deal, you are happy; if you
cry a great deal, you are unhappy;*—a very simple remark, no doubt; but just because it is so simple I have
never been able to forget it, even though it is in the last

[1] Eth. Eud., vii. 2. 37:

degree a truism. So if cheerfulness knocks at our door, we should throw it wide open, for it never comes inopportunely; instead of that, we often make scruples about letting it in. We want to be quite sure that we have every reason to be contented; then we are afraid that cheerfulness of spirit may interfere with serious reflections or weighty cares. Cheerfulness is a direct and immediate gain,—the very coin, as it were, of happiness, and not, like all else, merely a cheque upon the bank; for it alone makes us immediately happy in the present moment, and that is the highest blessing for beings like us, whose existence is but an infinitesimal moment between two eternities. To secure and promote this feeling of cheerfulness should be the supreme aim of all our endeavors after happiness.

Now it is certain that nothing contributes so little to cheerfulness as riches, or so much, as health. Is it not in the lower classes, the so-called working classes, more especially those of them who live in the country, that we see cheerful and contented faces? And is it not amongst the rich, the upper classes, that we find faces full of ill-humor and vexation? Consequently we should try as much as possible to maintain a high degree of health; for cheerfulness is the very flower of it. I need hardly say what one must do to be healthy—avoid every kind of excess, all violent and unpleasant emotion, all mental overstrain, take daily exercise in the open air, cold baths and such like hygienic measures. For without a proper amount of daily exercise no one can remain healthy; all the processes of life demand exercise for the due performance of their functions, exercise not only of the parts more immediately concerned, but also of the whole body. For, as Aristotle rightly says, *Life is movement;* it is its very essence. Ceaseless and rapid motion goes on in every part of the organism. The heart, with its complicated double systole and diastole, beats strongly and untiringly; with

twenty-eight beats it has to drive the whole of the blood
through arteries, veins and capillaries; the lungs pump
like a steam-engine, without intermission; the intestines
are always in peristaltic action; the glands are all constantly absorbing and secreting; even the brain has a
double motion of its own, with every beat of the pulse
and every breath we draw. When people can get no
exercise at all, as is the case with the countless numbers
who are condemned to a sedentary life, there is a glaring
and fatal disproportion between outward inactivity and
inner tumult. For this ceaseless internal motion requires
some external counterpart, and the want of it produces
effects like those of emotion which we are obliged to suppress. Even trees must be shaken by the wind, if they
are to thrive. The rule which finds its application here
may be most briefly expressed in Latin: *omnis motis, quo
celerior, eo magis motus.*

How much our happiness depends upon our spirits, and
these again upon our state of health, may be seen by comparing the influence which the same external circumstances
or events have upon us when we are well and strong with
the effects which they have when we are depressed and
troubled with ill-health. It is not what things are objectively and in themselves, but what they are for us, in our
way of looking at them, that makes us happy or the reverse. As Epictetus says, *Men are not influenced by things,
but by their thoughts about things.* And, in general, nine-
tenths of our happiness depends upon health alone. With
health, everything is a source of pleasure; without it,
nothing else, whatever it may be, is enjoyable; even the
other personal blessings—a great mind, a happy temperament—are degraded and dwarfed for want of it. So it
is really with good reason that, when two people meet, the
first thing they do is to inquire after each other's health,
and to express the hope that it is good; for good health

is by far the most important element in human happiness. It follows from all this that the greatest of follies is to sacrifice health for any other kind of happiness, whatever it may be, for gain, advancement, learning or fame, let alone, then, for fleeting sensual pleasures. Everything else should rather be postponed to it.

But however much health may contribute to that flow of good spirits which is so essential to our happiness, good spirits do not entirely depend upon health; for a man may be perfectly sound in his physique and still possess a melancholy temperament and be generally given up to sad thoughts. The ultimate cause of this is undoubtedly to be found in innate, and therefore unalterable, physical constitution, especially in the more or less normal relation of a man's sensitiveness to his muscular and vital energy. Abnormal sensitiveness produces inequality of spirits, a predominating melancholy, with periodical fits of unrestrained liveliness. A genius is one whose nervous power or sensitiveness is largely in excess; as Aristotle [2] has very correctly observed, *Men distinguished in philosophy, politics, poetry or art appear to be all of a melancholy temperament.* This is doubtless the passage which Cicero has in his mind when he says, as he often does, *Aristotles ait omnes ingeniosos melancholicos esse.* [3] Shakespeare has very neatly expressed this radical and innate diversity of temperament in those lines in *The Merchant of Venice:*

> *Nature has framed strange fellows in her time;*
> *Some that will evermore peep through their eyes,*
> *And laugh, like parrots at a bag-piper;*
> *And others of such vinegar aspect,*
> *That they'll not show their teeth in way of smile,*
> *Though Nestor swear the jest be laughable.*

[2] Probl. xxx., ep. 1.
[3] Tusc. i., 33.

This is the difference which Plato draws between εὔκολος and δύσκολος — the man of *easy,* and the man of *difficult* disposition—in proof of which he refers to the varying degrees of susceptibility which different people show to pleasurable and painful impressions; so that one man will laugh at what makes another despair. As a rule, the stronger the susceptibility to unpleasant impressions, the weaker is the susceptibility to pleasant ones, and *vice versa.* If it is equally possible for an event to turn out well or ill, the δύσκολος will be annoyed or grieved if the issue is unfavorable, and will not rejoice, should it be happy. On the other hand, the εὔκολος will neither worry nor fret over an unfavorable issue, but rejoice if it turns out well. If the one is successful in nine out of ten undertakings, he will not be pleased, but rather annoyed that one has miscarried; whilst the other, if only a single one succeeds, will manage to find consolation in the fact and remain cheerful. But here is another instance of the truth, that hardly any evil is entirely without its compensation; for the misfortunes and sufferings which the υσκόλοι, that is, people of gloomy and anxious character, have to overcome, are, on the whole, more imaginary and therefore less real than those which befall the gay and careless; for a man who paints everything black, who constantly fears the worst and takes measures accordingly, will not be disappointed so often in this world, as one who always looks upon the bright side of things. And when a morbid affection of the nerves, or a derangement of the digestive organs, plays into the hands of an innate tendency to gloom, this tendency may reach such a height that permanent discomfort produces a weariness of life. So arises an inclination to suicide, which even the most trivial unpleasantness may actually bring about; nay, when the tendency attains its worst form, it may be occasioned by nothing in particular, but a man may resolve to put an end to his existence, simply because he is permanently unhappy, and then coolly and firmly carry out his determination; as may be seen by the way in which the sufferer, when placed under supervision, as he usually is, eagerly waits to seize the first unguarded moment, when, without a shudder, without a struggle or recoil, he may use the now natural and welcome means of effecting his release.[4] Even the healthiest, perhaps even the most cheerful man, may resolve upon death under certain circumstances; when, for instance, his sufferings, or his fears of some inevitable misfortune, reach such a pitch as to outweigh the terrors of death. The only difference lies in the degree of suffering necessary to bring about the fatal act, a degree which will be high in the case of a cheerful, and low in that of a gloomy man. The greater the melancholy, the lower need the degree be; in the end, it may even sink to zero. But if a man is cheerful, and his spirits are supported by good health, it requires a high degree of suffering to make him lay hands upon himself. There are countless steps in the scale between the two extremes of suicide, the suicide which springs merely from a morbid intensification of innate gloom, and the suicide of the healthy and cheerful man, who has entirely objective grounds for putting an end to his existence.

Beauty is partly an affair of health. It may be reckoned as a personal advantage; though it does not, properly speaking, contribute directly to our happiness. It does so indirectly, by impressing other people; and it is no unimportant advantage, even in man. Beauty is an open letter of recommendation, predisposing the heart to favor the person who presents it. As is well said in these lines of Homer, the gift of beauty is not lightly to be thrown away,

[4] For a detailed description of this condition of mind *Cf.* Esquirol, *Des maladies mentales.*

that glorious gift which none can bestow save the gods alone—

οὔτοι ἀπόβλητ' ἐπὶ θεῶν ἐρικυδέα δῶρα,
ὅσσα κεν αὐτοὶ δῶσιν, ἑκὼν δ'οὐκ ἄν τις ἕλοιτο.[5]

The most general survey shows us that the two foes of human happiness are pain and boredom. We may go further, and say that in the degree in which we are fortunate enough to get away from the one, we approach the other. Life presents, in fact, a more or less violent oscillation between the two. The reason of this is that each of these two poles stands in a double antagonism to the other, external or objective, and inner or subjective. Needy surroundings and poverty produce pain; while, if a man is more than well off, he is bored. Accordingly, while the lower classes are engaged in a ceaseless struggle with need, in other words, with pain, the upper carry on a constant and often desperate battle with boredom.[6] The inner or subjective antagonism arises from the fact that, in the individual, susceptibility to pain varies inversely with susceptibility to boredom, because susceptibility is directly proportionate to mental power. Let me explain. A dull mind is, as a rule, associated with dull sensibilities, nerves which no stimulus can affect, a temperament, in short, which does not feel pain or anxiety very much, however great or terrible it may be. Now, intellectual dullness is at the bottom of that *vacuity of soul* which is stamped on so many faces, a state of mind which betrays itself by a constant and lively attention to all the trivial circumstances in the external world. This is the true source of boredom—a continual panting after excitement,

[5] *Iliad* 3, 65.

[6] And the extremes meet; for the lowest state of civilization, a nomad or wandering life, finds its counterpart in the highest, where everyone is at times a tourist. The earlier stage was a case of necessity; the latter is a remedy for boredom.

in order to have a pretext for giving the mind and spirits something to occupy them. The kind of things people choose for this purpose shows that they are not very particular, as witness the miserable pastimes they have recourse to, and their ideas of social pleasure and conversation: or again, the number of people who gossip on the doorstep or gape out of the window. It is mainly because of this inner vacuity of soul that people go in quest of society, diversion, amusement, luxury of every sort, which lead many to extravagance and misery. Nothing is so good a protection against such misery as inward wealth, the wealth of the mind, because the greater it grows, the less room it leaves for boredom. The inexhaustible activity of thought! finding ever new material to work upon in the multifarious phenomena of self and nature, and able and ready to form new combinations of them,—there you have something that invigorates the mind, and apart from moments of relaxation, sets it far above the reach of boredom.

But, on the other hand, this high degree of intelligence is rooted in a high degree of susceptibility, greater strength of will, greater passionateness; and from the union of these qualities comes an increased capacity for emotion, an enhanced sensibility to all mental and even bodily pain, greater impatience of obstacles, greater resentment of interruption;—all of which tendencies are augmented by the power of the imagination, the vivid character of the whole range of thought, including what is disagreeable. This applies, in various degrees, to every step in the long scale of mental power, from the veriest dunce to the greatest genius that ever lived. Therefore the nearer anyone is, either from a subjective or from an objective point of view, to one of those sources of suffering in human life, the farther he is from the other. And so a man's natural bent will lead him to make his objective world conform to his subjective as much as possible; that is to say, he will take the greatest measures against that form of suffering to which he is most liable. The wise man will, above all, strive after freedom from pain and annoyance, quiet and leisure, consequently a tranquil, modest life, with as few encounters as may be; and so, after a little experience of his so-called fellowmen, he will elect to live in retirement, or even, if he is a man of great intellect, in solitude. For the more a man has in himself, the less he will want from other people,—the less, indeed, other people can be to him. This is why a high degree of intellect tends to make a man unsocial. True, if *quality* of intellect could be made up for by quantity, it might be worth while to live even in the great world; but unfortunately, a hundred fools together will not make one wise man.

But the individual who stands at the other end of the scale is no sooner free from the pangs of need than he endeavors to get pastime and society at any cost, taking up with the first person he meets, and avoiding nothing so much as himself. For in solitude, where every one is thrown upon his own resources, what a man has in himself comes to light; the fool in fine raiment groans under the burden of his miserable personality, a burden which he can never throw off, whilst the man of talent peoples the waste places with his animating thoughts. Seneca declares that folly is its own burden,—*omnis stultitia laborat fastido sui*,—a very true saying, with which may be compared the words of Jesus, the son of Sirach, *The life of a fool is worse than death.*[7] And, as a rule, it will be found that a man is sociable just in the degree in which he is intellectually poor and generally vulgar. For one's choice in this world does not go much beyond solitude on one side and vulgarity on the other. It is said that the most so-

[7] Ecclesiasticus, xxii. 11.

ciable of all people are the negroes; and they are at the bottom of the scale in intellect. I remember reading once in a French paper [8] that the blacks in North America, whether free or enslaved, are fond of shutting themselves up in large numbers in the smallest space, because they cannot have too much of one another's snub-nosed company.

The brain may be regarded as a kind of parasite of the organism, a pensioner, as it were, who dwells with the body: and leisure, that is, the time one has for the free enjoyment of one's consciousness or individuality, is the fruit or produce of the rest of existence, which is in general only labor and effort. But what does most people's leisure yield?—boredom and dullness; except, of course, when it is occupied with sensual pleasure or folly. How little such leisure is worth may be seen in the way in which it is spent: and, as Ariosto observes, how miserable are the idle hours of ignorant men!—*ozio lungo d'uomini ignoranti.* Ordinarily people think merely how they shall *spend* their time; a man of any talent tries to *use* it. The reason why people of limited intellect are apt to be bored is that their intellect is absolutely nothing more than the means by which the motive power of the will is put into force: and whenever there is nothing particular to set the will in motion, it rests, and their intellect takes a holiday, because, equally with the will, it requires something external to bring it into play. The result is an awful stagnation of whatever power a man has—in a word, boredom. To counteract this miserable feeling, men run to trivialities which please for the moment they are taken up, hoping thus to engage the will in order to rouse it to action, and so set the intellect in motion; for it is the latter which has to give effect to these motives of the will. Compared with real and natural motives, these are but as paper

[8] *Le Commerce,* Oct. 19th, 1837.

money to coin; for their value is only arbitrary—card games and the like, which have been invented for this very purpose. And if there is nothing else to be done, a man will twirl his thumbs or beat the devil's tattoo; or a cigar may be a welcome substitute for exercising his brains. Hence, in all countries the chief occupation of society is card-playing,[9] and it is the gauge of its value, and an outward sign that it is bankrupt in thought. Because people have no thoughts to deal in, they deal cards, and try and win one another's money. Idiots! But I do not wish to be unjust; so let me remark that it may certainly be said in defence of card-playing that it is a preparation for the world and for business life, because one learns thereby how to make a clever use of fortuitous but unalterable circumstances (cards, in this case), and to get as much out of them as one can: and to do this a man must learn a little dissimulation, and how to put a good face upon a bad business. But, on the other hand, it is exactly for this reason that card-playing is so demoralizing, since the whole object of it is to employ every kind of trick and machination in order to win what belongs to another. And a habit of this sort, learnt at the card-table, strikes root and pushes its way into practical life; and in the affairs of every day a man gradually comes to regard *meum* and *tuum* in much the same light as cards, and to consider that he may use to the utmost whatever advantages he possesses, so long as he does not come within the arm of the law. Examples of what I mean are of daily occurrence in mercantile life. Since, then, leisure is the flower, or rather the fruit, of existence, as it puts a man into possession of himself, those are happy indeed who possess

[9] *Translator's Note.*—Card-playing to this extent is now, no doubt, a thing of the past, at any rate amongst the nations of northern Europe. The present fashion is rather in favor of a dilettante interest in art or literature.

something real in themselves. But what do you get from most people's leisure?—only a good-for-nothing fellow, who is terribly bored and a burden to himself. Let us, therefore rejoice, dear brethren, for *we are not children of the bondwoman, but of the free.*

Further, as no land is so well off as that which requires few imports, or none at all, so the happiest man is one who has enough in his own inner wealth, and requires little or nothing from outside for his maintenance, for imports are expensive things, reveal dependence, entail danger, occasion trouble, and when all is said and done, are a poor substitute for home produce. No man ought to expect much from others, or, in general, from the external world. What one human being can be to another is not a very great deal: in the end every one stands alone, and the important thing is *who* it is that stands alone. Here, then, is another application of the general truth which Goethe recognizes in *Dichtung und Wahreit* (Bk. III.), that in everything a man has ultimately to appeal to himself; or, as Goldsmith puts it in *The Traveller:*

> *Still to ourselves in every place consign'd*
> *Our own felicity we make or find.*

Himself is the source of the best and most a man can be or achieve. The more this is so—the more a man finds his sources of pleasure in himself—the happier he will be. Therefore, it is with great truth that Aristotle[10] says, *To be happy means to be self-sufficient.* For all other sources of happiness are in their nature most uncertain, precarious, fleeting, the sport of chance; and so even under the most favorable circumstances they can easily be exhausted; nay, this is unavoidable, because they are not always within reach. And in old age these sources of happiness must necessarily dry up:—love leaves us then, and wit, desire

[10] Eth. Eud., vii. 2.

to travel, delight in horses, aptitude for social intercourse; friends and relations, too, are taken from us by death. Then more than ever, it depends upon what a man has in himself; for this will stick to him longest; and at any period of life it is the only genuine and lasting source of happiness. There is not much to be got anywhere in the world. It is filled with misery and pain; and if a man escapes these, boredom lies in wait for him at every corner. Nay more; it is evil which generally has the upper hand, and folly makes the most noise. Fate is cruel, and mankind is pitiable. In such a world as this, a man who is rich in himself is like a bright warm, happy room at Christmastide, while without are the frost and snow of a December night. Therefore, without doubt, the happiest destiny on earth is to have the rare gift of a rich individuality, and more especially to be possessed of a good endowment of intellect; this is the happiest destiny, though it may not be, after all, a very brilliant one.

There was a great wisdom in that remark which Queen Christina of Sweden made, in her nineteenth year, about Descartes, who had then lived for twenty years in the deepest solitude in Holland, and, apart from report, was known to her only by a single essay: *M. Descartes*, she said, *is the happiest of men, and his condition seems to me much to be envied.*[11] Of course, as was the case with Descartes, external circumstances must be favorable enough to allow a man to be master of his life and happiness; or, as we read in *Ecclesiastes*,[12]—*Wisdom is good together with an inheritance, and profitable unto them that see the sun.* The man to whom nature and fate have granted the blessing of wisdom, will be most anxious and careful to keep open the fountains of happiness which he has in himself; and for this, independence and leisure are

[11] *Vie de Descartes*, par Baillet. Liv. vii., ch. 10.
[12] vii. 12.

necessary. To obtain them, he will be willing to moderate
his desires and harbor his resources, all the more because
he is not, like others, restricted to the external world for
his pleasures. So he will not be misled by expectations
of office, or money, or the favor and applause of his fellowmen, into surrendering himself in order to conform to low
desires and vulgar tastes; nay, in such a case he will follow
the advice that Horace gives in his epistle to Mæcenas.[13]

> *Nec somnum plebis laudo, satur altilium, neo*
> *Otia divitiis Arabum liberrima muto.*

It is a great piece of folly to sacrifice the inner for the
outer man, to give the whole or the greater part of one's
quiet, leisure and independence for splendor, rank, pomp,
titles and honor. This is what Goethe did. My good luck
drew me quite in the other direction.

The truth which I am insisting upon here, the truth,
namely, that the chief source of human happiness is internal, is confirmed by that most accurate observation of
Aristotle in the *Nichomachean Ethics*,[14] that every pleasure
presupposes some sort of activity, the application of some
sort of power, without which it cannot exist. The doctrine of Aristotle's, that a man's happiness consists in the
free exercise of his highest faculties, is also enunciated by
Strobæus in his exposition of the Peripatetic philosophy[15]:
happiness, he says, *means vigorous and successful activity
in all your undertakings;* and he explains that by vigor
ἀρετη he means *mastery* in any thing, whatever it be.
Now, the original purpose of those forces with which nature has endowed man is to enable him to struggle against
the difficulties which beset him on all sides. But if this
struggle comes to an end, his unemployed forces become
a burden to him; and he has to set to work and play

[13] Lib. 1., ep. 7.
[14] i. 7 and vii. 13, 14.
[15] Ecl. et. ii. ch. 7.

with them,—to use them, I mean, for no purpose at all,
beyond avoiding the other source of human suffering, boredom, to which he is at once exposed. It is the upper
classes, people of wealth, who are the greatest victims of
boredom. Lucretius long ago described their miserable
state, and the truth of his description may be still recognized today, in the life of every great capital—where the
rich man is seldom in his own halls, because it bores him
to be there, and still he returns thither, because he is no
better off outside;—or else he is away in post-haste to
his house in the country, as if it were on fire; and he is
no sooner arrived there, than he is bored again, and seeks
to forget everything in sleep, or else hurries back to town
once more.

> *Exit saepe foras magnis ex œdibus ille,*
> *Esse domi quem pertaesum est, subitoque reventat,*
> *Quippe foris nihilo melius qui sentiat esse.*
> *Currit, agens mannos, ad villam precipitanter,*
> *Auxilium tectis quasi ferre ordentibus instans:*
> *Oscitat extemplo, tetigit quum limina villae;*
> *Aut abit in somnum gravis, atque oblivia quaerit;*
> *Aut etiam properans urbem petit atque revisit.*[16]

In their youth, such people must have had a superfluity
of muscular and vital energy,—powers which, unlike those
of the mind, cannot maintain their full degree of vigor
very long; and in later years they either have no mental
powers at all, or cannot develop any for want of employ-
ment which would bring them into play; so that they are
in a wretched plight. *Will*, however, they still possess, for
this is the only power that is inexhaustible; and they try
to stimulate their will by passionate excitement, such as
games of chance for high stakes—undoubtedly a most degrading form of vice. And one may say generally that if
a man finds himself with nothing to do, he is sure to choose
some amusement suited to the kind of power in which he

[16] III 1073.

excels,—bowls, it may be, or chess; hunting or painting; horse-racing or music; cards, or poetry, heraldry, philosophy, or some other dilettante interest. We might classify these interests methodically, by reducing them to expressions of the three fundamental powers, the factors, that is to say, which go to make up the physiological constitution of man; and further, by considering these powers by themselves, and apart from any of the definite aims which they may subserve, and simply as affording three sources of possible pleasure, out of which every man will choose what suits him, according as he excels in one direction or another.

First of all come the pleasures of *vital energy*, of food, drink, digestion, rest and sleep; and there are parts of the world where it can be said that these are characteristic and national pleasures. Secondly, there the pleasures of *muscular energy*, such as walking, running, wrestling, dancing, fencing, riding and similar athletic pursuits, which sometimes take the form of sport, and sometimes of a military life and real warfare. Thirdly, there are the pleasures of sensibility, such as observation, thought, feeling, or a taste for poetry or culture, music, learning, reading, meditation, invention, philosophy and the like. As regards the value, relative worth and duration of each of these kinds of pleasure, a great deal might be said, which, however, I leave the reader to supply. But every one will see that the nobler the power which is brought into play, the greater will be the pleasure which it gives; for pleasure always involves the use of one's own powers, and happiness consists in a frequent repetition of pleasure. No one will deny that in this respect the pleasures of sensibility occupy a higher place than either of the other two fundamental kinds; which exist in an equal, nay, in a greater degree in brutes; it is this preponderating amount' of sensibility which distinguishes man from other animals.

Now, our mental powers are forms of sensibility, and therefore a preponderating amount of it makes us capable of that kind of pleasure which has to do with mind, so-called intellectual pleasure; and the more sensibility predominates, the greater the pleasure will be.[17]

The normal, ordinary man takes a vivid interest in anything only in so far as it excites his will, that is to say, is a matter of personal interest to him. But constant ex-

[17] Nature exhibits a continual progress, starting from the mechanical and chemical activity of the inorganic world, proceeding to the vegetable, with its dull enjoyment of self, from that to the animal world, where intelligence and consciousness begin, at first very weak, and only after many intermediate stages attaining its last great development in man, whose intellect is Nature's crowning point, the goal of all her efforts, the most perfect and difficult of all her works. And even within the range of the human intellect, there are a great many observable differences of degree, and it is very seldom that intellect reaches its highest point, intelligence properly so-called, which in this narrow and strict sense of the word, is Nature's most consummate product, and so the rarest and most precious thing of which the world can boast. The highest product of Nature is the clearest degree of consciousness, in which the world mirrors itself more plainly and completely than anywhere else. A man endowed with this form of intelligence is in possession of what is noblest and best on earth; and accordingly, he has a source of pleasure in comparison with which all others are small. From his surroundings he asks nothing but leisure for the free enjoyment of what he has got, time, as it were, to polish his diamond. All other pleasures that are not of the intellect are of a lower kind; for they are, one and all, movements of will—desires, hopes, fears and ambitions, no matter to what directed: they are always satisfied at the cost of pain, and in the case of ambition, generally with more or less of illusion. With intellectual pleasure, on the other hand, truth becomes clearer and clearer. In the realm of intelligence pain has no power. Knowledge is all in all. Further, intellectual pleasures are accessible entirely and only through the medium of the intelligence, and are limited by its capacity. *For all the wit there is in the world is useless to him who has none.* Still this advantage is accompanied by a substantial disadvantage; for the whole of Nature shows that with the growth of intelligence comes increased capacity for pain, and it is only with the highest degree of intelligence that suffering reaches its supreme point.

citement of the will is never an unmixed good, to say the least; in other words, it involves pain. Card-playing, that universal occupation of "good society" everywhere, is a device for providing this kind of excitement, and that, too, by means of interests so small as to produce slight and momentary, instead of real and permanent, pain. Card-playing is, in fact, a mere tickling of the will.[18]

On the other hand, a man of powerful intellect is capable of taking a vivid interest in things in the way of mere *knowledge*, with no admixture of *will*; nay, such an interest is a necessity to him. It places him in a sphere where pain is an alien,—a diviner air, where the gods live serene.

θεοὶ 'ρεῖα ζώοντες.[19]

Look on these two pictures—the life of the masses, one long, dull record of struggle and effort entirely devoted to the petty interests of personal welfare, to misery in all its forms, a life beset by intolerable boredom as soon as ever

---

[18] *Vulgarity* is, at bottom, the kind of consciousness in which the will completely predominates over the intellect, where the latter does nothing more than perform the service of its master, the will. Therefore, when the will makes no demands, supplies no motives, strong or weak, the intellect entirely loses its power, and the result is complete vacancy of mind. Now *will without intellect* is the most vulgar and common thing in the world, possessed by every blockhead, who, in the gratification of his passions, shows the stuff of which he is made. This is the condition of mind called *vulgarity*, in which the only active elements are the organs of sense, and that small amount of intellect which is necessary for apprehending the data of sense. Accordingly, the vulgar man is constantly open to all sorts of impressions, and immediately perceives all the little trifling things that go on in his environment: the lightest whisper, the most trivial circumstance, is sufficient to rouse his attention; he is just like an animal. Such a man's mental condition reveals itself in his face, in his whole exterior; and hence that vulgar, repulsive appearance, which is all the more offensive, if, as is usually the case, his will—the only factor in his consciousness—is a base, selfish and altogether bad one.

[19] Odyssey IV., 805.

those aims are satisfied and the man is thrown back upon
himself, whence he can be roused again to some sort of
movement only by the wild fire of passion. On the other
side you have a man endowed with a high degree of
mental power, leading an existence rich in thought and full
of life and meaning, occupied by worthy and interesting
objects as soon as ever he is free to give himself to them,
bearing in himself a source of the noblest pleasure. What
external promptings he wants come from the works of
nature, and from the contemplation of human affairs and
the achievements of the great of all ages and countries,
which are thoroughly appreciated by a man of this type
alone, as being the only one who can quite understand
and feel with them. And so it is for him alone that those
great ones have really lived; it is to him that they make
their appeal; the rest are but casual hearers who only
half understand either them or their followers. Of course,
this characteristic of the intellectual man implies that he
has one more need than the others, the need of reading,
observing, studying, meditating, practising, the need, in
short, of undisturbed leisure. For, as Voltaire has very
rightly said, *there are no real pleasures without real needs;*
and the need of them is why to such a man pleasures are
accessible which are denied to others,—the varied beauties
of nature and art and literature. To heap these pleasures
round people who do not want them and cannot appreciate
them, is like expecting gray hairs to fall in love. A man
who is privileged in this respect leads two lives, a personal and an intellectual life; and the latter gradually
comes to be looked upon as the true one, and the former
as merely a means to it. Other people make this shallow,
empty and troubled existence an end in itself. To the life
of the intellect such a man will give the preference over all
his other occupations: by the constant growth of insight
and knowledge, this intellectual life, like a slowly-forming

work of art, will acquire a consistency, a permanent intensity, a unity which becomes ever more and more complete; compared with which, a life devoted to the attainment of personal comfort, a life that may broaden indeed, but can never be deepened, makes but a poor show: and yet, as I have said, people make this baser sort of existence an end in itself.

The ordinary life of every day, so far as it is not moved by passion, is tedious and insipid; and if it is so moved, it soon becomes painful. Those alone are happy whom nature has favored with some superfluity of intellect, something beyond what is just necessary to carry out the behests of their will; for it enables them to lead an intellectual life as well, a life unattended by pain and full of vivid interests. Mere leisure, that is to say, intellect unoccupied in the service of the will, is not of itself sufficient: there must be a real superfluity of power, set free from the service of the will and devoted to that of the intellect; for, as Seneca says, *otium sine litteris mors est et vivi hominis sepulture*—illiterate leisure is a form of death, a living tomb. Varying with the amount of the superfluity, there will be countless developments in this second life, the life of the mind; it may be the mere collection and labelling of insects, birds, minerals, coins, or the highest achievements of poetry and philosophy. The life of the mind is not only a protection against boredom; it also wards off the pernicious effects of boredom; it keeps us from bad company, from the many dangers, misfortunes, losses and extravagances which the man who places his happiness entirely in the objective world is sure to encounter. My philosophy, for instance, has never brought me in a six-pence; but it has spared me many an expense.

The ordinary man places his life's happiness in things external to him, in property, rank, wife and children, friends, society, and the like, so that when he loses them or finds them disappointing, the foundation of his happiness is destroyed. In other words, his centre of gravity is not in himself; it is constantly changing its place, with every wish and whim. If he is a man of means, one day it will be his house in the country, another buying horses, or entertaining friends, or traveling,—a life, in short, of general luxury, the reason being that he seeks his pleasure in things outside him. Like one whose health and strength are gone, he tries to regain by the use of jellies and drugs, instead of by developing his own vital power, the true source of what he has lost. Before proceeding to the opposite, let us compare with this common type the man who comes midway between the two, endowed, it may be, not exactly with distinguished powers of mind, but with somewhat more than the ordinary amount of intellect. He will take a dilettante interest in art, or devote his attention to some branch of science—botany, for example, or physics, astronomy, history, and find a great deal of pleasure in such studies, and amuse himself with them when external forces of happiness are exhausted or fail to satisfy him any more. Of a man like this it may be said that his centre of gravity is partly in himself. But a dilettante interest in art is a very different thing from creative activity; and an amateur pursuit of science is apt to be superficial and not to penetrate to the heart of the matter. A man cannot entirely identify himself with such pursuits, or have his whole existence so completely filled and permeated with them that he loses all interest in everything else. It is only the highest intellectual power, what we call *genius*, that attains to this degree of intensity, making all time and existence its theme, and striving to express its peculiar conception of the world, whether it contemplates life as the subject of poetry or of philosophy. Hence, undisturbed occupation with himself, his own thoughts and works, is a matter of urgent necessity to such a man; solitude is welcome, leisure is the highest good, and everything else is unnecessary, nay, even burdensome.

This is the only type of man of whom it can be said that his centre of gravity is entirely in himself; which explains why it is that people of this sort—and they are very rare—no matter how excellent their character may be, do not show that warm and unlimited interest in friends, family, and the community in general, of which others are so often capable; for if they have only themselves they are not inconsolable for the loss of everything else. This gives an isolation to their character, which is all the more effective since other people never really quite satisfy them, as being, on the whole, of a different nature: nay more, since this difference is constantly forcing itself upon their notice they get accustomed to move about amongst mankind as alien beings, and in thinking of humanity in general, to say *they* instead of *we*.

So the conclusion we come to is that the man whom nature has endowed with intellectual wealth is the happiest; so true it is that the subjective concerns us more than the objective; for whatever the latter may be, it can work only indirectly, secondly, and through the medium of the former—a truth finely expressed by Lucian:—

Πλοῦτος ὁ τῆς ψυχῆς πλοῦτος μόνος ἐστὶν ἀληθής
Τἄλλα δ' ἔχει ἄτην πλείονα τῶν κτεάνων—[20]

the wealth of the soul is the only true wealth, for with all other riches comes a bane even greater than they. The man of inner wealth wants nothing from outside but the negative gift of undisturbed leisure, to develop and mature his intellectual faculties, that is, to enjoy his wealth; in short, he wants permission to be himself, his whole life long, every day and every hour. If he is destined to impress the character of his mind upon a whole race, he has

[20] Epigrammata, 12.

only one measure of happiness or unhappiness—to succeed or fail in perfecting his powers and completing his work. All else is of small consequence. Accordingly, the greatest minds of all ages have set the highest value upon undisturbed leisure, as worth exactly as much as the man himself. *Happiness appears to consist in leisure,* says Aristotle;[21] and Diogenes Laertius reports that *Socrates praised leisure as the fairest of all possessions.* So, in the *Nichomachean Ethics,* Aristotle concludes that a life devoted to philosophy is the happiest; or, as he says in the *Politics,*[22] *the free exercise of any power, whatever it may be, is happiness.* This again, tallies with what Goethe says in *Wilhelm Meister: The man who is born with a talent which he is meant to use, finds his greatest happiness in using it.*

But to be in possession of undisturbed leisure, is far from being the common lot; nay, it is something alien to human nature, for the ordinary man's destiny is to spend life in procuring what is necessary for the subsistence of himself and his family; he is a son of struggle and need, not a free intelligence. So people as a rule soon get tired of undisturbed leisure, and it becomes burdensome if there are no fictitious and forced aims to occupy it, play, pastime and hobbies of every kind. For this very reason it is full of possible danger, and *difficilis in otio quies* is a true saying,—it is difficult to keep quiet if you have nothing to do. On the other hand, a measure of intellect far surpassing the ordinary, is as unnatural as it is abnormal. But if it exists, and the man endowed with it is to be happy, he will want precisely that undisturbed leisure which the others find burdensome or pernicious; for without it he is a Pegasus in harness, and consequently unhappy. If these two unnatural circumstances, external, and internal, un-

[21] Eth. Nichom. x. 7.
[22] iv. 11.

disturbed leisure and great intellect, happen to coincide in the same person, it is a great piece of fortune; and if the fate is so far favorable, a man can lead the higher life, the life protected from the two opposite sources of human suffering, pain and boredom, from the painful struggle for existence, and the incapacity for enduring leisure (which is free existence itself)—evils which may be escaped only by being mutually neutralized.

But there is something to be said in opposition to this view. Great intellectual gifts mean an activity preeminently nervous in its character, and consequently a very high degree of susceptibility to pain in every form. Further, such gifts imply an intense temperament, larger and more vivid ideas, which, as the inseparable accompaniment of great intellectual power, entail on its possessor a corresponding intensity of the emotions, making them incomparably more violent than those to which the ordinary man is a prey. Now, there are more things in the world productive of pain than of pleasure. Again, a large endowment of intellect tends to estrange the man who has it from other people and their doings; for the more a man has in himself, the less he will be able to find in them; and the hundred things in which they take delight, he will think shallow and insipid. Here, then, perhaps, is another instance of that law of compensation which makes itself felt everywhere. How often one hears it said, and said, too, with some plausibility, that the narrow-minded man is at bottom the happiest, even though his fortune is unenviable. I shall make no attempt to forestall the reader's own judgment on this point; more especially as Sophocles himself has given utterance to two diametrically opposite opinions:—

Πολλῷ τὸ φρονεῖν εὐδαιμονίας
πρῶτον ὑπάρχε'.[23]

[23] Antigone, 1347-8.

he says in one place—wisdom is the greatest part of happiness; and again, in another passage, he declares that the life of the thoughtless is the most pleasant of all—

'Εν τῷ φρονεῖν γὰρ μηδὲν ἥδιστος βίος.[24]

The philosophers of the *Old Testament* find themselves in a like contradiction.

The life of a fool is worse than death [25]

and—

In much wisdom is much grief;
and he that increasesth knowledge increaseth sorrow. [26]

I may remark, however, that a man who has no mental needs, because his intellect is of the narrow and normal amount, is, in the strict sense of the word, what is called a *philistine*—an expression at first peculiar to the German language, a kind of slang term at the Universities, afterwards used, by analogy, in a higher sense, though still in its original meaning, as denoting one who is not a *Son of the Muses*. A philistine is and remains ἀμούσος ἄνηρ. I should prefer to take a higher point of view, and apply the term *philistine* to people who are always seriously occupied with realities which are no realities; but as such a definition would be a transcendental one, and therefore not generally intelligible, it would hardly be in place in the present treatise, which aims at being popular. The other definition can be more easily elucidated, indicating, as it does, satisfactorily enough, the essential nature of all those qualities which distinguish the philistine. He is defined to be *a man without mental needs*. From this it follows, firstly, *in relation to himself*, that he has *no intellectual pleasures*; for, as was remarked before, there are no real

[24] Ajax, 554.
[25] Ecclesiasticus, xxii. 11.
[26] Ecclesiastes, i. 18.

pleasures without real needs.   The philistine's life is
animated by no desire to gain knowledge and insight for
their own sake, or to experience that true æsthetic pleasure which is so nearly akin to them.   If pleasures of this
kind are fashionable, and the philistine finds himself compelled to pay attention to them, he will force himself to
do so, but he will take as little interest in them as possible.
His only real pleasures are of a sensual kind, and he thinks
that these indemnify him for the loss of the others.   To
him oysters and champagne are the height of existence;
the aim of his life is to procure what will contribute to his
bodily welfare, and he is indeed in a happy way if this
causes him some trouble.   If the luxuries of life are heaped
upon him, he will inevitably be bored, and against boredom he has a great many fancied remedies, balls, theatres,
parties, cards, gambling, horses, women, drinking, traveling
and so on; all of which can not protect a man from being
bored, for where there are no intellectual needs, no intellectual pleasures are possible.   The peculiar characteristic of the philistine is a dull, dry kind of gravity, akin to
that of animals.   Nothing really pleases, or excites, or
interests him, for sensual pleasure is quickly exhausted, and
the society of philistines soon becomes burdensome, and
one may even get tired of playing cards.   True, the pleasures of vanity are left, pleasures which he enjoys in his
own way, either by feeling himself superior in point of
wealth, or rank, or influence and power to other people,
who thereupon pay him honor; or, at any rate, by going
about with those who have a superfluity of these blessings,
sunning himself in the reflection of their splendor—what
the English call a *snob*.

From the essential nature of the philistine it follows,
secondly, *in regard to others*, that, as he possesses no intellectual, but only physical need, he will seek the society
of those who can satisfy the latter, but not the former.

The last thing he will expect from his friends is the possession of any sort of intellectual capacity; nay, if he chances to meet with it, it will rouse his antipathy and even hatred; simply because in addition to an unpleasant sense of inferiority, he experiences, in his heart, a dull kind of envy, which has to be carefully concealed even from himself. Nevertheless, it sometimes grows into a secret feeling of rancor. But for all that, it will never occur to him to make his own ideas of worth or value conform to the standard of such qualities; he will continue to give the preference to rank and riches, power and influence, which in his eyes seem to be the only genuine advantages in the world; and his wish will be to excel in them himself. All this is the consequence of his being a man *without intellectual needs*. The great affliction of all philistines is that they have no interest in *ideas*, and that, to escape being bored, they are in constant need of *realities*. But realities are either unsatisfactory or dangerous; when they lose their interest, they become fatiguing. But the ideal world is illimitable and calm,

> *something afar*
> *From the sphere of our sorrow.*

NOTE.—In these remarks on the personal qualities which go to make happiness, I have been mainly concerned with the physical and intellectual nature of man. For an account of the direct and immediate influence of *morality* upon happiness, let me refer to my prize essay on *The Foundation of Morals* (Sec. 22.)

CHAPTER III

PROPERTY, OR WHAT A MAN HAS

EPICURUS divides the needs of mankind into three classes, and the division made by this great professor of happiness is a true and a fine one. First come natural and necessary needs, such as, when not satisfied, produce pain, —food and clothing, *victus et amictus,* needs which can easily be satisfied. Secondly, there are those needs which, though natural, are not necessary, such as the gratification of certain of the senses. I may add, however, that in the report given by Diogenes Laertius, Epicurus does not mention which of the senses he means; so that on this point my account of his doctrine is somewhat more definite and exact than the original. These are needs rather more difficult to satisfy. The third class consists of needs which are neither natural nor necessary, the need of luxury and prodigality, show and splendor, which never come to an end, and are very hard to satisfy.[1]

It is difficult, if not impossible, to define the limits which reason should impose on the desire for wealth; for there is no absolute or definite amount of wealth which will satisfy a man. The amount is always relative, that is to say, just so much as will maintain the proportion between what he wants and what he gets; for to measure a man's happiness only by what he gets, and not also by what he expects to get, is as futile as to try and express a fraction which shall have a numerator but no denominator. A man

[1] Cf. Diogenes Laertius, Bk. x., ch. xxvii., pp. 127 and 149; also Cicero *de finibus,* i., 13.

never feels the loss of things which it never occurs to him
to ask for; he is just as happy without them; whilst
another, who may have a hundred times as much, feels
miserable because he has not got the one thing he wants.
In fact, here too, every man has an horizon of his own,
and he will expect as much as he thinks it is possible for
him to get. If an object within his horizon looks as though
he could confidently reckon on getting it, he is happy; but
if difficulties come in the way, he is miserable. What lies
beyond his horizon has no effect at all upon him. So it is
that the vast possessions of the rich do not agitate the
poor, and conversely, that a wealthy man is not consoled
by all his wealth for the failure of his hopes. Riches, one
may say, are like sea-water; the more you drink the
thirstier you become; and the same is true of fame. The
loss of wealth and prosperity leaves a man, as soon as the
first pangs of grief are over, in very much the same
habitual temper as before; and the reason of this is, that
as soon as fate diminishes the amount of his possessions,
he himself immediately reduces the amount of his claims.
But when misfortune comes upon us, to reduce the amount
of our claims is just what is most painful; once that we
have done so, the pain becomes less and less, and is felt no
more; like an old wound which has healed. Conversely,
when a piece of good fortune befalls us, our claims mount
higher and higher, as there is nothing to regulate them; it
is in this feeling of expansion that the delight of it lies.
But it lasts no longer than the process itself, and when the
expansion is complete, the delight ceases; we have become
accustomed to the increase in our claims, and consequently
indifferent to the amount of wealth which satisfies them.
There is a passage in the *Odyssey* [2] illustrating this truth,
of which I may quote the last two lines:

[2] xviii., 130-7.

Τοῶς γὰρ νόος ἐστὶν ἐπιχθονίων ἀνθρώπων
Οἶον ἐφ ἦμαρ ἄγει πατὴρ ἀνδρῶν τε θεῶν τε.

—the thoughts of man that dwells on the earth are as the
day granted him by the father of gods and men. Discontent springs from a constant endeavor to increase the
amount of our claims, when we are powerless to increase
the amount which will satisfy them.

When we consider how full of needs the human race is,
how its whole existence is based upon them, it is not a
matter for surprise that *wealth* is held in more sincere
esteem, nay, in greater honor, than anything else in the
world; nor ought we to wonder that gain is made the only
good of life, and everything that does not lead to it pushed
aside or thrown overboard—philosophy, for instance, by
those who profess it. People are often reproached for
wishing for money above all things, and for loving it more
than anything else; but it is natural and even inevitable
for people to love that which, like an unwearied Proteus, is
always ready to turn itself into whatever object their
wandering wishes or manifold desires may for the moment
fix upon. Everything else can satisfy only *one* wish, *one*
need: food is good only if you are hungry; wine, if you
are able to enjoy it; drugs, if you are sick; fur for the
winter; love for youth, and so on. These are all only
relatively good, ἀγαθα πρός τι. Money alone is absolutely
good, because it is not only a concrete satisfaction of one
need in particular; it is an abstract satisfaction of all.

If a man has an independent fortune, he should regard
it as a bulwark against the many evils and misfortunes
which he may encounter; he should not look upon it as
giving him leave to get what pleasure he can out of the
world, or as rendering it incumbent upon him to spend it
in this way. People who are not born with a fortune, but
end by making a large one through the exercise of whatever talents they possess, almost always come to think

that their talents are their capital, and that the money they
have gained is merely the interest upon it; they do not
lay by a part of their earnings to form a permanent capital,
but spend their money much as they have earned it.
Accordingly, they often fall into poverty; their earnings
decreased, or come to an end altogether, either because their
talent is exhausted by becoming antiquated,—as, for instance, very often happens in the case of fine art; or else
it was valid only under a special conjunction of circumstances which has now passed away. There is nothing to
prevent those who live on the common labor of their
hands from treating their earnings in that way if they like;
because their kind of skill is not likely to disappear, or, if
it does, it can be replaced by that of their follow-work-
men; morever, the kind of work they do is always in demand, so that what the proverb says is quite true, *a useful
trade is a mine of gold*. But with artists and professionals
of every kind the case is quite different, and that is the
reason why they are well paid. They ought to build up a
capital out of their earnings; but they recklessly look upon
them as merely interest, and end in ruin. On the other
hand, people who inherit money know, at least, how to
distinguish between capital and interest, and most of them
try to make their capital secure and not encroach upon
it; nay, if they can, they put by at least an eighth of their
interests in order to meet future contingencies. So most of
them maintain their position. These few remarks about
capital and interest are not applicable to commercial life,
for merchants look upon money only as a means of further gain, just as a workman regards his tools; so even if
their capital has been entirely the result of their own
efforts, they try to preserve and increase it by using it.
Accordingly, wealth is nowhere so much at home as in the
merchant class.

It will generally be found that those who know what it is

to have been in need and destitution are very much less afraid of it, and consequently more inclined to extravagance, than those who know poverty only by hearsay. People who have been born and bred in good circumstances are as a rule much more careful about the future, more economical, in fact, than those who, by a piece of good luck, have suddenly passed from poverty to wealth. This looks as if poverty were not really such a very wretched thing as it appears from a distance. The true reason, however, is rather the fact that the man who has been born into a position of wealth comes to look upon it as something without which he could no more live than he could live without air; he guards it as he does his very life; and so he is generally a lover of order, prudent and economical. But the man who has been born into a poor position looks upon it as the natural one, and if by any chance he comes in for a fortune, he regards it as a superfluity, something to be enjoyed or wasted, because, if it comes to an end, he can get on just as well as before, with one anxiety the less; or, as Shakespeare says in Henry VI.,[3]

> . . . . *the adage must be verified*
> *That beggars mounted run their horse to death.*

But it should be said that people of this kind have a firm and excessive trust, partly in fate, partly in the peculiar means which have already raised them out of need and poverty,—a trust not only of the head, but of the heart also; and so they do not, like the man born rich, look upon the shallows of poverty as bottomless, but console themselves with the thought that once they have touched ground again, they can take another upward flight. It is this trait in human character which explains the fact that women who were poor before their marriage often make greater claims, and are more extravagant, than

[3] Part III., Act 1., Sc. 4.

those who have brought their husbands a rich dowry; because, as a rule, rich girls bring with them, not only a fortune, but also more eagerness, nay, more of the inherited instinct, to preserve it, than poor girls do. If anyone doubts the truth of this, and thinks that it is just the opposite, he will find authority for his view in Ariosto's first Satire; but, on the other hand, Dr. Johnson agrees with my opinion. *A woman of fortune,* he says, *being used to the handling of money, spends it judiciously; but a woman who gets the command of money for the first time upon her marriage, has such a gusto in spending it, that she throws it away with great profusion.*[4] And in any case let me advise anyone who marries a poor girl not to leave her the capital but only the interest, and to take especial care that she has not the management of the children's fortune.

I do not by any means think that I am touching upon a subject which is not worth my while to mention when I recommend people to be careful to preserve what they have earned or inherited. For to start life with just as much as will make one independent, that is, allow one to live comfortably without having to work—even if one has only just enough for oneself, not to speak of a family— is an advantage which cannot be over-estimated; for it means exemption and immunity from that chronic disease of penury, which fastens on the life of man like a plague; it is emancipation from that forced labor which is the natural lot of every mortal. Only under a favorable fate like this can a man be said to be born free, to be, in the proper sense of the word, *sui juris,* master of his own time and powers, and able to say every morning, *This day is my own.* And just for the same reason the difference between the man who has a hundred a year and the man who has a thousand, is infinitely smaller than the difference between the former and a man who has nothing at all. But

[4] Boswell's Life of Johnson: ann: 1776, ætat: 67.

inherited wealth reaches its utmost value when it falls to the individual endowed with mental powers of a high order, who is resolved to pursue a line of life not compatible with the making of money; for he is then doubly endowed by fate and can live for his genius; and he will pay his debt to mankind a hundred times, by achieving what no other could achieve, by producing some work which contributes to the general good, and redounds to the honor of humanity at large.   Another, again, may use his wealth to further philanthropic schemes, and make himself well-deserving of his fellowmen.   But a man who does none of these things, who does not even try to do them, who never attempts to learn the rudiments of any branch of knowledge so that he may at least do what he can towards promoting it—such a one, born as he is into riches, is a mere idler and thief of time, a contemptible fellow.   He will not even be happy, because, in his case, exemption from need delivers him up to the other extreme of human suffering, boredom, which is such martyrdom to him, that he would have been better off if poverty had given him something to do.   And as he is bored he is apt to be extravagant, and so lose the advantage of which he showed himself unworthy.   Countless numbers of people find themselves in want, simply because, when they had money, they spent it only to get momentary relief from the feeling of boredom which oppressed them.

It is quite another matter if one's object is success in political life, where favor, friends and connections are all-important, in order to mount by their aid step by step on the ladder of promotion, and perhaps gain the topmost rung.   In this kind of life, it is much better to be cast upon the world without a penny; and if the aspirant is not of noble family, but is a man of some talent, it will redound to his advantage to be an absolute pauper.   For what every one most aims at in ordinary contact with his fellows is to prove them inferior to himself; and how much more is this the case in politics. Now, it is only an absolute pauper who has such a thorough conviction of his own complete, profound and positive inferiority from every point of view, of his own utter insignificance and worthlessness, that he can take his place quietly in the political machine.[5] He is the only one who can keep on bowing low enough, and even go right down upon his face if necessary; he alone can submit to everything and laugh at it; he alone knows the entire worthlessness of merit; he alone uses his loudest voice and his boldest type whenever he has to speak or write of those who are placed over his head, or occupy any position of influence; and if they do a little scribbling, he is ready to applaud it as a masterwork. He alone understands how to beg, and so betimes, when he is hardly out of his boyhood, he becomes a high priest of that hidden mystery which Goethe brings to light.

> *Über's Niederträchtige*
> *Niemand sich beklage:*
> *Denn es ist das Mächtige*
> *Was man dir auch sage:*

—it is no use to complain of low aims; for, whatever people may say, they rule the world.

On the other hand, the man who is born with enough to live upon is generally of a somewhat independent turn of mind; he is accustomed to keep his head up; he has not learned all the arts of the beggar; perhaps he even presumes a little upon the possession of talents which, as he ought to know, can never compete with cringing medioc-

[5] *Translator's Note.*—Schopenhauer is probably here making one of his most virulent attacks upon Hegel; in this case on account of what he thought to be the philosopher's abject servility to the government of his day. Though the Hegelian system has been the fruitful mother of many liberal ideas, there can be no doubt that Hegel's influence, in his own lifetime, was an effective support of Prussian bureaucracy.

rity; in the long run he comes to recognize the inferiority
of those who are placed over his head, and when they try
to put insults upon him, he becomes refractory and shy.
This is not the way to get on in the world. Nay, such a
man may at least incline to the opinion freely expressed by
Voltaire: *We have only two days to live; it is not worth
our while to spend them* in cringing to contemptible rascals.
But alas! let me observe by the way, that *contemptible
rascal* is an attribute which may be predicated of an abominable number of people. What Juvenal says—it is difficult to rise if your poverty is greater than your talent—

> *Haud facile emergunt quorum virtutibus obstat*
> *Res angusta domi—*

is more applicable to a career of art and literature than
to a political and social ambition.

Wife and children I have not reckoned amongst a man's
possessions: he is rather in their possession. It would be
easier to include friends under that head; but a man's
friends belong to him not a whit more than he belongs to
them.

CHAPTER IV.

POSITION, OR A MAN'S PLACE IN THE ESTIMATION OF OTHERS

Section 1.—Reputation

By a peculiar weakness of human nature, people generally think too much about the opinion which others form of them; although the slightest reflection will show that this opinion, whatever it may be, is not in itself essential to happiness. Therefore it is hard to understand why everybody feels so very pleased when he sees that other people have a good opinion of him, or say anything flattering to his vanity. If you stroke a cat, it will purr; and, as inevitably, if you praise a man, a sweet expression of delight will appear on his face; and even though the praise is a palpable lie, it will be welcome, if the matter is one on which he prides himself. If only other people will applaud him, a man may console himself for downright misfortune or for the pittance he gets from the two sources of human happiness already discussed: and conversely, it is astonishing how infallibly a man will be annoyed, and in some cases deeply pained, by any wrong done to his feeling of self-importance, whatever be the nature, degree, or circumstances of the injury, or by any depreciation, slight, or disregard.

If the feeling of honor rests upon this peculiarity of human nature, it may have a very salutary effect upon the welfare of a great many people, as a substitute for morality; but upon their happiness, more especially upon that peace of mind and independence which are so essential to happiness, its effect will be disturbing and prejudicial rather than salutary. Therefore it is advisable, from our point of view, to set limits to this weakness, and duly to consider and rightly to estimate the relative value of advantages, and thus temper, as far as possible, this great susceptibility to other people's opinion, whether the opinion be one flattering to our vanity, or whether it causes us pain; for in either case it is the same feeling which is touched. Otherwise, a man is the slave of what other people are pleased to think,—and how little it requires to disconcert or soothe the mind that is greedy of praise:

Sic leve, sic parvum est, animum quod laudis avarum
Subruit ac reficit.[1]

Therefore it will very much conduce to our happiness if we duly compare the value of what a man is in and for himself with what he is in the eyes of others. Under the former comes everything that fills up the span of our existence and makes it what it is, in short, all the advantages already considered and summed up under the heads of personality and property; and the sphere in which all this takes place is the man's own consciousness. On the other hand, the sphere of what we are for other people is their consciousness, not ours; it is the kind of figure we make in their eyes, together with the thoughts which this arouses.[2] But this is something which has no direct and immediate existence for us, but can affect us only mediately and indirectly, so far, that is, as other people's behavior towards us is directed by it; and even then it ought to affect us only in so far as it can move us to modify *what we are in and for ourselves.* Apart from this, what goes on in other people's consciousness is, as such, a matter of indifference to us; and in time we get really indifferent to it, when we come to see how superficial and futile are most

[1] Horace, Epist: II., 1, 180.
[2] Let me remark that people in the highest positions in life, with all their brilliance, pomp, display, magnificence and general show, may well say:—Our happiness lies entirely outside us, for it exists only in the heads of others.

people's thoughts, how narrow their ideas, how mean their sentiments, how perverse their opinions, and how much of error there is in most of them; when we learn by experience with what depreciation a man will speak of his fellow, when he is not obliged to fear him, or thinks that what he says will not come to his ears. And if ever we have had an opportunity of seeing how the greatest of men will meet with nothing but slight from half-a-dozen blockheads, we shall understand that to lay great value upon what other people say is to pay them too much honor.

At all events, a man is in a very bad way, who finds no source of happiness in the first two classes of blessings already treated of, but has to seek it in the third; in other words, not in what he is in himself, but in what he is in the opinion of others. For, after all, the foundation of our whole nature, and, therefore, of our happiness, is our physique, the most essential factor in happiness is health, and, next in importance after health, the ability to maintain ourselves in independence and freedom from care. There can be no competition or compensation between these essential factors on the one side, and honor, pomp, rank and reputation on the other, however much value we may set upon the latter. No one would hesitate to sacrifice the latter for the former, if it were necessary. We should add very much to our happiness by a timely recognition of the simple truth that every man's chief and real existence is in his own skin, and not in other people's opinions; and, consequently, that the actual conditions of our personal life,—health, temperament, capacity, income, wife, children, friends, home, are a hundred times more important for our happiness that what other people are pleased to think of us: otherwise we shall be miserable. And if people insist that honor is dearer than life itself, what they really mean is that existence and well-being are as nothing compared with other people's opinions. Of course, this may be only an exaggerated way of stating the prosaic truth that reputation, that is, the opinion others have of us, is indispensable if we are to make any progress in the world; but I shall come back to that presently. When we see that almost everything men devote their lives to attain, sparing no effort and encountering a thousand toils and dangers in the process, has, in the end, no further object than to raise themselves in the estimation of others; when we see that not only offices, titles, decorations, but also wealth, nay, even knowledge [3] and art, are striven for only to obtain, as the ultimate goal of all effort, greater respect from one's fellowmen,—it not this a lamentable proof of the extent to which human folly can go? To set much too high a value on other people's opinion is a common error everywhere; an error, it may be, rooted in human nature itself, or the result of civilization, and social arrangements generally; but, whatever its source, it exercises a very immoderate influence on all we do, and is very prejudicial to our happiness. We can trace it from a timorous and slavish regard for what other people will say, up to the feeling which made Virginius plunge the dagger into his daughter's heart, or induces many a man to sacrifice quiet, riches, health and even life itself, for posthumous glory. Undoubtedly this feeling is a very convenient instrument in the hands of those who have the control or direction of their fellowmen; and accordingly we find that in every scheme for training up humanity in the way it should go, the maintenance and strengthening of the feeling of honor occupies an important place. But it is quite a different matter in its effect on human happiness, of which it is here our object to treat; and we should rather be careful to dissuade people from setting too much store

[3] *Scire tuum nihil est nisi te scire hoc sciat alter,* (Persius i. 27)—knowledge is no use unless others know that you have it.

by what others think of them. Daily experience shows us, however, that this is just the mistake people persist in making; most men set the utmost value precisely on what other people think, and are more concerned about it than about what goes on in their own consciousness, which is the thing most immediately and directly present to them. They reverse the natural order,—regarding the opinions of others as real existence and their own consciousness as something shadowy; making the derivative and secondary into the principal, and considering the picture they present to the world of more importance than their own selves. By thus trying to get a direct and immediate result out of what has no really direct or immediate existence, they fall into the kind of folly which is called *vanity* —the appropriate term for that which has no solid or instrinsic value. Like a miser, such people forget the end in their eagerness to obtain the means.

The truth is that the value we set upon the opinion of others, and our constant endeavor in respect of it, are each quite out of proportion to any result we may reasonably hope to attain; so that this attention to other people's attitude may be regarded as a kind of universal mania which every one inherits. In all we do, almost the first thing we think about is, what will people say; and nearly half the troubles and bothers of life may be traced to our anxiety on this score; it is the anxiety which is at the bottom of all that feeling of self-importance, which is so often mortified because it is so very morbidly sensitive. It is solicitude about what others will say that underlies all our vanity and pretension, yes, and all our show and swagger too. Without it, there would not be a tenth part of the luxury which exists. Pride in every form, *point d'honneur* and *punctilio*, however varied their kind or sphere, are at bottom nothing but this—anxiety about what others will say—and what sacrifices it costs! One

can see it even in a child; and though it exists at every
period of life, it is strongest in age; because, when the
capacity for sensual pleasure fails, vanity and pride have
only avarice to share their dominion. Frenchmen, perhaps, afford the best example of this feeling, and amongst
them it is a regular epidemic, appearing sometimes in the
most absurd ambition, or in a ridiculous kind of national
vanity and the most shameless boasting. However, they
frustrate their own gains, for other people make fun of
them and call them *la grande nation.*

By way of specially illustrating this perverse and
exuberant respect for other people's opinion, let me take
passage from the *Times* of March 31st, 1846, giving a detailed account of the execution of one Thomas Wix, an
apprentice who, from motives of vengeance had murdered
his master. Here we have very unusual circumstances
and an extraordinary character, though one very suitable
for our purpose; and these combine to give a striking picture of this folly, which is so deeply rooted in human nature, and allow us to form an accurate notion of the extent to which it will go. On the morning of the execution, says the report, *the rev. ordinary was early in at-
tendance upon him, but Wix, beyond a quiet demeanor,
betrayed no interest in his ministration, appearing to feel
anxious only to acquit himself "bravely" before the spectators of his ignominious end. . . . In the procession Wix
fell into his proper place with alacrity, and, as he entered
the Chapel-yard, remarked, sufficiently loud to be heard by
several persons near him, "Now, then, as Dr. Dodd said, I
shall soon know the grand secret." On reaching the scaffold, the miserable wretch mounted the drop without the
slightest assistance, and when he got to the centre, he
bowed to the spectators twice, a proceeding which called
forth a tremendous cheer from the degraded crowd be-
neath.*

This is an admirable example of the way in which a man, with death in the most dreadful form before his very eyes, and eternity beyond it, will care for nothing but the impression he makes upon a crowd of gapers, and the opinion he leaves behind him in their heads. There was much the same kind of thing in the case of Lecompte, who was executed at Frankfurt, also in 1846, for an attempt on the king's life. At the trial he was very much annoyed that he was not allowed to appear, in decent attire, before the Upper House; and on the day of the execution it was a special grief to him that he was not permitted to shave. It is not only in recent times that this kind of things has been known to happen. Mateo Aleman tells us, in the Introduction to his celebrated romance, *Juzman de Alfarache,* that many infatuated criminals, instead of devoting their last hours to the welfare of their souls, as they ought to have done, neglect this duty for the purpose of preparing and committing to memory a speech to be made from the scaffold.

I take these extreme cases as being the best illustrations to what I mean; for they give us a magnified reflection of our own nature. The anxieties of all of us, our worries, vexations, bothers, troubles, uneasy apprehensions and strenuous efforts are due, in perhaps the large majority of instances, to what other people will say; and we are just as foolish in this respect as those miserable criminals. Envy and hatred are very often traceable to a similar source.

Now, it is obvious that happiness, which consists for the most part in peace of mind and contentment, would be served by nothing so much as by reducing this impulse of human nature within reasonable limits,—which would perhaps make it one fiftieth part of what it is now. By doing so, we should get rid of a thorn in the flesh which is always causing us pain. But it is a very difficult task, because the impulse in question is a natural and innate perversity of human nature. Tacitus says, *The lust of fame is the*

last that a wise man shakes off.[4] The only way of putting
an end to this universal folly is to see clearly that it is a
folly; and this may be done by recognizing the fact that
most of the opinions in men's heads are apt to be false,
perverse, erroneous and absurd, and so in themselves unworthy of attention; further, that other people's opinions
can have very little real and positive influence upon us in
most of the circumstances and affairs of life. Again, this
opinion is generally of such an unfavorable character that
it would worry a man to death to hear everything that was
said of him, or the tone in which he was spoken of. And
finally, among other things, we should be clear about the
fact that honor itself has no really direct, but only an
indirect, value. If people were generally converted from
this universal folly, the result would be such an addition
to our peace of mind and cheerfulness as at present seems
inconceivable; people would present a firmer and more
confident front to the world, and generally behave with less
embarrassment and restraint. It is observable that a retired mode of life has an exceedingly beneficial influence
on our peace of mind, and this is mainly because we thus
escape having to live constantly in the sight of others, and
pay everlasting regard to their casual opinions; in a word,
we are able to return upon ourselves. At the same time
a good deal of positive misfortune might be avoided, which
we are now drawn into by striving after shadows, or, more
correctly, by indulging a mischievous piece of folly; and we
should consequently have more attention to give to solid
realities and enjoy them with less interruption than at present. But χαλέπα τὰ καλά—what is worth doing is hard to do.

Section 2.—Pride

The folly of our nature which we are discussing puts
forth three shoots, ambition, vanity and pride. The dif-
[4] Hist., iv., 6.

ference between the last two is this: *pride* is an established conviction of one's own paramount worth in some particular respect; while *vanity* is the desire of rousing such a conviction in others, and it is generally accompanied by the secret hope of ultimately coming to the same conviction oneself. Pride works *from within;* it is the direct appreciation of oneself. Vanity is the desire to arrive at this appreciation indirectly, *from without.* So we find that vain people are talkative, proud, and taciturn. But the vain person ought to be aware that the good opinion of others, which he strives for, may be obtained much more easily and certainly by persistent silence than by speech, even though he has very good things to say. Anyone who wishes to affect pride is not therefore a proud man; but he will soon have to drop this, as every other, assumed character.

It is only a firm, unshakeable conviction of pre-eminent worth and special value which makes a man proud in the true sense of the word,—a conviction which may, no doubt, be a mistaken one or rest on advantages which are of an adventitious and conventional character: still pride is not the less pride for all that, so long as it be present in real earnest. And since pride is thus rooted in conviction, it resembles every other form of knowledge in not being within our own arbitrament. Pride's worst foe,—I mean its greatest obstacle,—is vanity, which courts the applause of the world in order to gain the necessary foundation for a high opinion of one's own worth, whilst pride is based upon a pre-existing conviction of it.

It is quite true that pride is something which is generally found fault with, and cried down; but usually, I imagine, by those who have nothing upon which they can pride themselves. In view of the impudence and foolhardiness of most people, anyone who possesses any kind of superiority or merit will do well to keep his eyes fixed on it, if he does not want it to be entirely forgotten; for if a man is

good-natured enough to ignore his own privileges, and hob‑
nob with the generality of other people, as if he were quite
on their level, they will be sure to treat him, frankly and
candidly, as one of themselves. This is a piece of advice
I would specially offer to those whose superiority is of the
highest kind—real superiority, I mean, of a purely personal
nature—which cannot, like orders and titles, appeal to the
eye or ear at every moment; as, otherwise, they will find
that familiarity breeds contempt, or, as the Romans used
to say, *sus Minervam. Joke with a slave, and he'll soon
show his heels,* is an excellent Arabian proverb; nor ought
we to despise what Horace says,

> *Sume superbiam
> Quæsitam meritis.*

—usurp the fame you have deserved. No doubt, when
modesty was made a virtue, it was a very advantageous
thing for the fools; for everybody is expected to speak of
himself as if he were one. This is leveling down indeed;
for it comes to look as if there were nothing but fools in
the world.

The cheapest sort of pride is national pride; for if a man
is proud of his own nation, it argues that he has no qualities
of his own of which he can be proud; otherwise he would
not have recourse to those which he shares with so many
millions of his fellowmen. The man who is endowed with
important personal qualities will be only too ready to see
clearly in what respects his own nation falls short, since
their failings will be constantly before his eyes. But every
miserable fool who has nothing at all of which he can be
proud adopts, as a last resource, pride in the nation to
which he belongs; he is ready and glad to defend all its
faults and follies tooth and nail, thus reimbursing himself
for his own inferiority. For example, if you speak of the
stupid and degrading bigotry of the English nation with
the contempt it deserves, you will hardly find one English-

man in fifty to agree with you; but if there should be one, he will generally happen to be an intelligent man.

The Germans have no national pride, which shows how honest they are, as everybody knows! and how dishonest are those who, by a piece of ridiculous affectation, pretend that they are proud of their country—the *Deutsche Brüder* and the demagogues who flatter the mob in order to mislead it. I have heard it said that gunpowder was invented by a German. I doubt it. Lichtenberg asks, *Why is it that a man who is not a German does not care about pretending that he is one; and that if he makes any pretence at all, it is to be a Frenchman or an Englishman?*[5]

However that may be, individuality is a far more important thing than nationality, and in any given man deserves a thousand-fold more consideration. And since you cannot speak of national character without referring to large masses of people, it is impossible to be loud in your praises and at the same time honest. National character is only another name for the particular form which the littleness, perversity and baseness of mankind take in every country. If we become disgusted with one, we praise another, until we get disgusted with this too. Every nation mocks at other nations, and all are right.

The contents of this chapter, which treats, as I have said, of what we represent in the world, or what we are in the eyes of others, may be further distributed under three heads: honor, rank and fame.

Section 3.—Rank

Let us take rank first, as it may be dismissed in a few words, although it plays an important part in the eyes of

[5] *Translator's Note.*—It should be remembered that these remarks were written in the earlier part of the present century, and that a German philosopher now-a-days, even though he were as apt to say bitter things as Schopenhauer, could hardly write in a similar strain.

the masses and of the philistines, and is a most useful wheel
in the machinery of the State.

It has a purely conventional value. Strictly speaking, it
is a sham; its method is to exact an artificial respect, and,
as a matter of fact, the whole thing is a mere farce.

Orders, it may be said, are bills of exchange drawn on
public opinion, and the measure of their value is the credit
of the drawer. Of course, as a substitute for pensions,
they save the State a good deal of money; and, besides,
they serve a very useful purpose, if they are distributed
with discrimination and judgment. For people in general
have eyes and ears, it is true; but not much else, very
little judgment indeed, or even memory. There are many
services of the State quite beyond the range of their understanding; others, again, are appreciated and made much of
for a time, and then soon forgotten. It seems to me, therefore, very proper, that a cross or a star should proclaim to
the mass of people always and everywhere, *This man is
not like you; he has done something.* But orders lose their
value when they are distributed unjustly, or without due
selection, or in too great numbers: a prince should be as
careful in conferring them as a man of business is in signing
a bill. It is a pleonasm to inscribe on any order *for distinguished service;* for every order ought to be for distinguished service. That stands to reason.

Section 4.—Honor

Honor is a much larger question than rank, and more
difficult to discuss. Let us begin by trying to define it.

If I were to say *Honor is external conscience, and conscience is inward honor,* no doubt a good many people
would assent; but there would be more show than reality
about such a definition, and it would hardly go to the root
of the matter. I prefer to say, *Honor is, on its objective
side, other people's opinion of what we are worth; on its*

subjective side, it is the respect we pay to this opinion. From the latter point of view, to be *a man of honor* is to exercise what is often a very wholesome, but by no means a purely moral, influence.

The feelings of honor and shame exist in every man who is not utterly depraved, and honor is everywhere recognized as something particularly valuable. The reason of this is as follows. By and in himself a man can accomplish very little; he is like Robinson Crusoe on a desert island. It is only in society that a man's powers can be called into full activity. He very soon finds this out when his consciousness begins to develop, and there arises in him the desire to be looked upon as a useful member of society, as one, that is, who is capable of playing his part as a man—*pro parte virili*—thereby acquiring a right to the benefits of social life. Now, to be a useful member of society, one must do two things: firstly, what everyone is expected to do everywhere; and, secondly, what one's own particular position in the world demands and requires.

But a man soon discovers that everything depends upon his being useful, not in his own opinion, but in the opinion of others; and so he tries his best to make that favorable impression upon the world, to which he attaches such a high value. Hence, this primitive and innate characteristic of human nature, which is called the feeling of honor, or, under another aspect, the feeling of shame—*verecundia.* It is this which brings a blush to his cheeks at the thought of having suddenly to fall in the estimation of others, even when he knows that he is innocent, nay, even if his remissness extends to no absolute obligation, but only to one which he has taken upon himself of his own free will. Conversely, nothing in life gives a man so much courage as the attainment or renewal of the conviction that other people regard him with favor; because it means that everyone joins to give him help and protection, which is an infinitely stronger bulwark against the ills of life than anything he can do himself.

The variety of relations in which a man can stand to other people so as to obtain their confidence, that is, their good opinion, gives rise to a distinction between several kinds of honor, resting chiefly on the different bearings that *meum* may take to *tuum;* or, again, on the performance of various pledges; or finally, on the relation of sexes. Hence there are three main kinds of honor, each of which takes various forms—civic honor, official honor, and sexual honor.

Civic honor has the widest sphere of all. It consists in the assumption that we shall pay unconditional respect to the rights of others, and, therefore, never use any unjust or unlawful means of getting what we want. It is the condition of all peaceable intercourse between man and man; and it is destroyed by anything that openly and manifestly militates against his peaceable intercourse, anything, accordingly, which entails punishment at the hands of the law, always supposing that the punishment is a just one.

The ultimate foundation of honor is the conviction that moral character is unalterable: a single bad action implies that future actions of the same kind will, under similar circumstances, also be bad. This is well expressed by the English use of the word *character* as meaning credit, reputation, honor. Hence honor, once lost, can never be recovered; unless the loss rested on some mistake, such as may occur if a man is slandered or his actions viewed in a false light. So the law provides remedies against slander, libel, and even insult; for insult though it amounts to no more than mere abuse, is a kind of summary slander with a suppression of the reasons. What I mean may be well put in the Greek phrase—not quoted from any author— ἔστιν ἡ λοιδόρια διαβολὴ συντμος. It is true that if a man abuses another, he is simply showing that he has no real or true causes of complaint against him; as, otherwise, he would bring these forward as the premises, and rely upon his hearers to draw the conclusion themselves: instead of which, he gives the conclusion and leaves out the premises, trusting that people will suppose that he has done so only for the sake of being brief.

Civic honor draws its existence and name from the middle classes; but it applies equally to all, not excepting the highest. No man can disregard it, and it is a very serious thing, of which every one should be careful not to make light. The man who breaks confidence has for ever forfeited confidence, whatever he may do, and whoever he may be; and the bitter consequences of the loss of confidence can never be averted.

There is a sense in which honor may be said to have a *negative* character in opposition to the *positive* character of fame. For honor is not the opinion people have of particular qualities which a man may happen to possess exclusively: it is rather the opinion they have of the qualities which a man may be expected to exhibit, and to which he should not prove false. Honor, therefore, means that a man is not exceptional; fame, that he is. Fame is something which must be won; honor, only something which must not be lost. The absence of fame is obscurity, which is only a negative; but loss of honor is shame, which is a positive quality. This negative character of honor must not be confused with anything *passive;* for honor is above all things active in its working. It is the only quality which proceeds *directly* from the man who exhibits it; it is concerned entirely with what he does and leaves undone, and has nothing to do with the actions of others or the obstacles they place in his way. It is something entirely in our own power—$\tau\hat{\omega}\nu$ $\dot{\epsilon}\phi'\dot{\eta}\mu\omega\nu$. This distinction, as we shall see presently, marks off true honor from the sham honor of chivalry.

Slander is the only weapon by which honor can be attacked from without; and the only way to repel the attack is to confute the slander with the proper amount of publicity, and a due unmasking of him who utters it.

The reason why respect is paid to age is that old people have necessarily shown in the course of their lives whether or not they have been able to maintain their honor unblemished; while that of young people has not been put to the proof, though they are credited with the possession of it. For neither length of years,—equalled, as it is, and even excelled, in the case of the lower animals,—nor, again, experience, which is only a closer knowledge of the world's ways, can be any sufficient reason for the respect which the young are everywhere required to show towards the old: for if it were merely a matter of years, the weakness which attends on age would call rather for consideration than for respect. It is a remarkable fact that white hair always commands reverence—a reverence really innate and instinctive. Wrinkles—a much surer sign of old age—command no reverence at all; you never hear any one speak of *venerable wrinkles;* but *venerable white hair* is a common expression.

Honor has only an indirect value. For, as I explained at the beginning of this chapter, what other people think of us, if it affects us at all, can affect us only in so far as it governs their behavior towards us, and only just so long as we live with, or have to do with, them. But it is to society alone that we owe that safety which we and our possessions enjoy in a state of civilization; in all we do we need the help of others, and they, in their turn, must have confidence in us before they can have anything to do with us. Accordingly, their opinion of us is, indirectly, a matter of great importance; though I cannot see how it can have a direct or immediate value. This is an opinion also held by Cicero. *I quite agree,* he writes, *with what Chrysippus and Diogenes used to say, that a good reputation is not worth raising a finger to obtain, if it were not*

that it is so useful.[6] This truth has been insisted upon at
great length by Helvetius in his chief work *De l'Esprit*,[7]
the conclusion of which is that *we love esteem not for its
own sake, but solely for the advantages which it brings.*
And as the means can never be more than the end, that
saying, of which so much is made, *Honor is dearer than
life itself*, is, as I have remarked, a very exaggerated statement. So much then, for civic honor.

Official honor is the general opinion of other people that
a man who fills any office really has the necessary qualities
for the proper discharge of all the duties which appertain
to it. The greater and more important the duties a man
has to discharge in the State, and the higher and more in-
fluential the office which he fills, the stronger must be the
opinion which people have of the moral and intellectual
qualities which render him fit for his post. Therefore,
the higher his position, the greater must be the degree of
honor paid to him, expressed, as it is, in titles, orders and
the generally subservient behavior of others towards him.
As a rule, a man's official rank implies the particular degree
of honor which ought to be paid to him, however much
this degree may be modified by the capacity of the masses
to form any notion of its importance. Still, as a matter of
fact, greater honor is paid to a man who fulfills special
duties than to the common citizen, whose honor mainly consists in keeping clear of dishonor.

Official honor demands, further, that the man who occupies an office must maintain respect for it, for the sake
both of his colleagues and of those who will come after him.
This respect an official can maintain by a proper observance
of his duties, and by repelling any attack that may be made
upon the office itself or upon its occupant: he must not, for
instance, pass over unheeded any statement to the effect

[6] *De finibus* iii., 17.
[7] *Disc:* iii. 17.

that the duties of the office are not properly discharged, or that the office itself does not conduce to the public welfare. He must prove the unwarrantable nature of such attacks by enforcing the legal penalty for them.

Subordinate to the honor of official personages comes that of those who serve the State in any other capacity, as doctors, lawyers, teachers, anyone, in short, who, by graduating in any subject, or by any other public declaration that he is qualified to exercise some special skill, claims to practice it; in a word, the honor of all those who take any public pledges whatever. Under this head comes military honor, in the true sense of the word, the opinion that people who have bound themselves to defend their country really possess the requisite qualities which will enable them to do so, especially courage, personal bravery and strength, and that they are perfectly ready to defend their country to the death, and never and under any circumstances desert the flag to which they have once sworn allegiance. I have here taken official honor in a wider sense than it is generally used, namely, the respect due by citizens to an office itself.

In treating of *sexual honor* and the principles on which it rests, a little more attention and analysis are necessary; and what I shall say will support my contention that all honor really rests upon a utilitarian basis. There are two natural divisions of the subject—the honor of women and the honor of men, in either side issuing in a well-understood *esprit de corps*. The former is by far the more important of the two, because the most essential feature in woman's life is her relation to man.

Female honor is the general opinion in regard to a girl that she is pure, and in regard to a wife that she is faithful. The importance of this opinion rests upon the following considerations. Women depend upon men in all the relations of life; men upon women, it might be said, in one only. So an arrangement is made for mutual interdependence—man undertaking responsibility for all woman's needs and also for the children that spring from their union—an arrangement on which is based the welfare of the whole female race. To carry out this plan, women have to band together with a show of *esprit de corps,* and present one undivided front to their common enemy, man,—who possesses all the good things of the earth, in virtue of his superior physical and intellectual power,—in order to lay siege to and conquer him, and so get possession of him and a share of those good things. To this end the honor of all women depends upon the enforcement of the rule that no woman should give herself to a man except in marriage, in order that every man may be forced, as it were, to surrender and ally himself with a woman; by this arrangement provision is made for the whole of the female race. This is a result, however, which can be obtained only by a strict observance of the rule; and, accordingly, women everywhere show true *esprit de corps* in carefully insisting upon its maintenance. Any girl who commits a breach of the rule betrays the whole female race, because its welfare would be destroyed if every woman were to do likewise; so she is cast out with shame as one who has lost her honor. No woman will have anything more to do with her; she is avoided like the plague. The same doom is awarded to a woman who breaks the marriage tie; for in so doing she is false to the terms upon which the man capitulated; and as her conduct is such as to frighten other men from making a similar surrender, it imperils the welfare of all her sisters. Nay, more; this deception and coarse breach of troth is a crime punishable by the loss, not only of personal, but also of civic honor. This is why we minimize the shame of a girl, but not of a wife; because, in the former case, marriage can restore honor, while in the latter, no atonement can be made for the breach of contract.

Once this *esprit de corps* is acknowledged to be the

foundation of female honor, and is seen to be a wholesome, nay, a necessary arrangement, as at bottom a matter of prudence and interest, its extreme importance for the welfare of women will be recognized. But it does not possess anything more than a relative value. It is no absolute end, lying beyond all other aims of existence and valued above life itself. In this view, there will be nothing to applaud in the forced and extravagant conduct of a Lucretia or a Virginius—conduct which can easily degenerate into tragic farce, and produce a terrible feeling of revulsion. The conclusion of *Emilia Galotti*, for instance, makes one leave the theatre completely ill at ease; and, on the other hand, all the rules of female honor cannot prevent a certain sympathy with Clara in *Egmont*. To carry this principle of female honor too far is to forget the end in thinking of the means—and this is just what people often do; for such exaggeration suggests that the value of sexual honor is absolute; while the truth is that it is more relative than any other kind. One might go so far as to say that its value is purely conventional, when one sees from Thomasius how in all ages and countries, up to the time of the Reformation, irregularities were permitted and recognized by law, with no derogation to female honor,—not to speak of the temple of Mylitta at Babylon.[8]

There are also of course certain circumstances in civil life which make external forms of marriage impossible, especially in Catholic countries, where there is no such thing as divorce. Ruling princes everywhere, would, in my opinion, do much better, from a moral point of view, to dispense with forms altogether rather than contract a morganatic marriage, the descendants of which might raise claims to the throne if the legitimate stock happened to die out; so that there is a possibility, though, perhaps, a remote one, that a morganatic marriage might produce a civil war.

[8] Herodotus, i. 199.

And, besides, such a marriage, concluded in defiance of all
outward ceremony, is a concession made to women and
priests—two classes of persons to whom one should be most
careful to give as little tether as possible. It is further to
be remarked that every man in a country can marry the
woman of his choice, except one poor individual, namely,
the prince. His hand belongs to his country, and can be
given in marriage only for reasons of State, that is, for the
good of the country. Still, for all that, he is a man; and,
as a man, he likes to follow whither his heart leads. It
is an unjust, ungrateful and priggish thing to forbid, or to
desire to forbid, a prince from following his inclinations in
this matter; of course, as long as the lady has no influence
upon the Government of the country. From her point of
view she occupies an exceptional position, and does not
come under the ordinary rules of sexual honor; for she has
merely given herself to a man who loves her, and whom she
loves but cannot marry. And in general, the fact that the
principle of female honor has no origin in nature, is shown
by the many bloody sacrifices which have been offered to
it,—the murder of children and the mother's suicide. No
doubt a girl who contravenes the code commits a breach
of faith against her whole sex; but this faith is one which
is only secretly taken for granted, and not sworn to. And
since, in most cases, her own prospects suffer most immediately, her folly is infinitely greater than her crime.

The corresponding virtue in men is a product of the one
I have been discussing. It is their *esprit de corps,* which
demands that, once a man has made that surrender of
himself in marriage which is so advantageous to his con-
queror, he shall take care that the terms of the treaty are
maintained; both in order that the agreement itself may
lose none of its force by the permission of any laxity in its
observance, and that men, having given up everything,
may, at least, be assured of their bargain, namely, exclu-

sive possession. Accordingly, it is part of a man's honor to resent a breach of the marriage tie on the part of his wife, and to punish it, at the very least by separating from her. If he condones the offence, his fellowmen cry shame upon him; but the shame in this case is not nearly so foul as that of the woman who has lost her honor; the stain is by no means of so deep a dye—*levioris notæ macula;*—because a man's relation to woman is subordinate to many other and more important affairs in his life. The two great dramatic poets of modern times have each taken man's honor as the theme of two plays; Shakespeare in *Othello* and *The Winter's Tale,* and Calderon in *El medico de su honra,* (The Physician of his Honor,) and *A secreto agravio secreta venganza,* (for Secret Insult Secret Vengeance). It should be said, however, that honor demands the punishment of the wife only; to punish her paramour too, is a work of supererogation. This confirms the view I have taken, that a man's honor originates in *esprit de corps.*

The kind of honor which I have been discussing hitherto has always existed in its various forms and principles amongst all nations and at all times; although the history of female honor shows that its principles have undergone certain local modifications at different periods. But there is another species of honor which differs from this entirely, a species of honor of which the Greeks and Romans had no conception, and up to this day it is perfectly unknown amongst Chinese, Hindoos or Mohammedans. It is a kind of honor which arose only in the Middle Age, and is indigenous only to Christian Europe, nay, only to an extremely small portion of the population, that is to say, the higher classes of society and those who ape them. It is *knightly honor,* or *point d'honneur.* Its principles are quite different from those which underlie the kind of honor I have been treating until now, and in some respects are even opposed to them. The sort I am referring to produces the *cavalier;* the other kind creates the *man of honor.* As this is so, I shall give an explanation of its principles, as a kind of code or mirror of knightly courtesy.

(1) To begin with, honor of this sort consists, not in other people's opinion of what we are worth, but wholly and entirely in whether they express it or not, no matter whether they really have any opinion at all, let alone whether they know of reasons for having one. Other people may entertain the worst opinion of us in consequence of what we do, and may despise us as much as they like; so long as no one dares to give expression to his opinion, our honor remains untarnished. So if our actions and qualities compel the highest respect from other people, and they have no option but to give this respect,—as soon as anyone, no matter how wicked or foolish he may be, utters something depreciatory of us, our honor is offended, nay, gone for ever, unless we can manage to restore it. A superfluous proof of what I say, namely, that knightly honor depends, not upon what people think, but upon what they say, is furnished by the fact that insults can be withdrawn, or, if necessary, form the subject of an apology, which makes them as though they had never been uttered. Whether the opinion which underlays the expression has also been rectified, and why the expression should ever have been used, are questions which are perfectly unimportant: so long as the statement is withdrawn, all is well. The truth is that conduct of this kind aims, not at earning respect, but at extorting it.

(2) In the second place, this sort of honor rests, not on what a man does, but on what he suffers, the obstacles he encounters; differing from the honor which prevails in all else, in consisting, not in what he says or does himself, but in what another man says or does. His honor is thus at the mercy of every man who can talk it away on the tip of his tongue; and if he attacks it, in a moment it is gone

for ever,—unless the man who is attacked manages to wrest it back again again by a process which I shall mention presently, a process which involves danger to his life, health, freedom, property and peace of mind. A man's whole conduct may be in accordance with the most righteous and noble principles, his spirit may be the purest that ever breathed, his intellect of the very highest order; and yet his honor may disappear the moment that anyone is pleased to insult him, anyone at all who has not offended against this code of honor himself, let him be the most worthless rascal or the most stupid beast, an idler, gambler, debtor, a man, in short, of no account at all. It is usually this sort of fellow who likes to insult people; for, as Seneca[*] rightly remarks, *ut quisque contemtissimus et ludibrio est, ita solutissimæ est,* the more contemptible and ridiculous a man is,—the readier he is with his tongue. His insults are most likely to be directed against the very kind of man I have described, because people of different tastes can never be friends, and the sight of pre-eminent merit is apt to raise the secret ire of a ne'er-do-well. What Goethe says in the *Westöstlicher Divan* is quite true: it is useless to complain against your enemies for they can never become your friends, if your whole being is a standing reproach to them:—

> *Was klagst du über Feinde?*
> *Sollten Solche je werden Freunde*
> *Denen das Wesen, wie du bist,*
> *Im stillen ein ewiger Vorwurf ist?*

It is obvious that people of this worthless description have good cause to be thankful to the principle of honor, because it puts them on a level with people who in every other respect stand far above them. If a fellow likes to insult any one, attribute to him, for example, some bad quality, this is taken *prima facie* as a well-founded opinion, true in fact; a decree, as it were, with all the force of law;

[*] *De Constantia,* 11.

nay, if it is not at once wiped out in blood, it is a judgment which holds good and valid to all time. In other words, the man who is insulted remains—in the eyes of all *honorable people*—what the man who uttered the insult—even though he were the greatest wretch on earth—was pleased to call him; for he has *put up with* the insult—the technical term, I believe. Accordingly, all *honorable people* will have nothing more to do with him, and treat him like a leper, and, it may be, refuse to go into any company where he may be found, and so on.

This wise proceeding may, I think, be traced back to the fact that in the Middle Age, up to the fifteenth century, it was not the accuser in any criminal process who had to prove the guilt of the accused, but the accused who had to prove his innocence.[10] This he could do by swearing he was not guilty; and his backers—*consacramentales*—had to come and swear that in their opinion he was incapable of perjury. If he could find no one to help him in this way, or the accuser took objection to his backers, recourse was had to trial by *the Judgment of God,* which generally meant a duel. For the accused was now *in disgrace,*[11] and had to clear himself. Here, then, is the origin of the notion of disgrace, and of that whole system which prevails now-a-days amongst *honorable people*—only that the oath is omitted. This is also the explanation of that deep feeling of indignation which *honorable people* are called upon to show if they are given the lie; it is a reproach which they say must be wiped out in blood. It seldom comes to this pass, however, though lies are of common occurrence; but in England, more than elsewhere, it is a superstition which

[10] See C. G. von Wächter's *Beiträge zur deutschen Geschichte,* especially the chapter on criminal law.

[11] *Translator's Note.*—It is true that this expression has another special meaning in the technical terminology of Chivalry, but it is the nearest English equivalent which I can find for the German—*ein Bescholtener.*

has taken very deep root. As a matter of order, a man who threatens to kill another for telling a lie should never have told one himself. The fact is, that the criminal trial of the Middle Age also admitted of a shorter form. In reply to the charge, the accused answered: *That is a lie;* whereupon it was left to be decided by *the Judgment of God.* Hence, the code of knightly honor prescribes that, when the lie is given, an appeal to arms follows as a matter of course. So much, then, for the theory of insult.

But there is something even worse than insult, something so dreadful that I must beg pardon of all *honorable people* for so much as mentioning it in this code of knightly honor; for I know they will shiver, and their hair will stand on end, at the very thought of it—the *summum molum,* the greatest evil on earth, worse than death and damnation. A man may give another—*horrible dictu!*—a slap or a blow. This is so awful, and so utterly fatal to all honor, that, while any other species of insult may be healed by blood-letting, this can be cured only by the *coup-de-grâce.*

(3) In the third place, this kind of honor has absolutely nothing to do with what a man may be in and for himself; or, again, with the question whether his moral character can ever become better or worse, and all such pedantic inquiries. If your honor happens to be attacked, or to all appearances gone, it can very soon be restored in its entirety if you are only quick enough in having recourse to the one universal remedy—*a duel.* But if the aggressor does not belong to the classes which recognize the code of knightly honor, or has himself once offended against it, there is a safer way of meeting any attack upon your honor, whether it consists in blows, or merely in words. If you are armed, you can strike down your opponent on the spot, or perhaps later. This will restore your honor.

But if you wish to avoid such an extreme step, from fear of any unpleasant consequences arising therefrom, or from uncertainty as to whether the aggressor is subject to the laws of knightly honor or not, there is another means of making your position good, namely, the *Avantage*. This consists in returning rudeness with still greater rudeness; and if insults are no use, you can try a blow, which forms a sort of climax in the redemption of your honor; for instance, a box on the ear may be cured by a blow with a stick, and a blow with a stick by a thrashing with a horse-whip; and, as the approved remedy for this last, some people recommend you to spit at your opponent.[12] If all these means are of no avail, you must not shrink from drawing blood. And the reason for these methods of wiping out insult is, in this code, as follows:

(4) To receive an insult is disgraceful; to give one, honorable. Let me take an example. My opponent has truth, right and reason on his side. Very well. I insult him. Thereupon right and honor leave him and come to me, and, for the time being, he has lost them—until he gets them back, not by the exercise of right or reason, but by shooting and sticking me. Accordingly, rudeness is a quality which, in point of honor, is a substitute for any other and outweighs them all. The rudest is always right. What more do you want? However stupid, bad or wicked a man may have been, if he is only rude into the bargain, he condones and legitimizes all his faults. If in any discussion or conversation, another man shows more knowledge, greater love of truth, a sounder judgment, better understanding than we, or generally exhibits intellectual qualities which cast ours into the shade, we can at once annul his superiority and our own shallowness, and in our turn be superior to him, by being insulting and offensive. For rudeness is better than any argument; it totally eclipses

[12] *Translator's Note.*—It must be remembered that Schopenhauer is here describing, or perhaps caricaturing the manners and customs of the German aristocracy of half a century ago. Now, of course, *nous avons changé tout cela!*

intellect. If our opponent does not care for our mode of attack, and will not answer still more rudely, so as to plunge us into the ignoble rivalry of the *Avantage,* we are the victors and honor is on our side. Truth, knowledge, understanding, intellect, wit, must beat a retreat and leave the field to this almighty insolence.

Honorable people immediately make a show of mounting their war-horse, if anyone utters an opinion adverse to theirs, or shows more intelligence than they can muster; and if in any controversy they are at a loss for a reply, they look about for some weapon of rudeness, which will serve as well and come readier to hand; so they retire masters of the position. It must now be obvious that people are quite right in applauding this principle of honor as having ennobled the tone of society. This principle springs from another, which forms the heart and soul of the entire code.

(5) Fifthly, the code implies that the highest court to which a man can appeal in any differences he may have with another on a point of honor is the court of physical force, that is, of brutality. Every piece of rudeness is, strictly speaking, an appeal to brutality; for it is a declaration that intellectual strength and moral insight are incompetent to decide, and that the battle must be fought out by physical force—a struggle which, in the case of man, whom Franklin defines as *a tool-making animal,* is decided by the weapons peculiar to the species; and the decision is irrevocable. This is the well-known principle of *right of might*—irony, of course, like *the wit of a fool,* a parallel phrase. The honor of a knight may be called the glory of might.

(6) Lastly, if, as we saw above, civic honor is very scrupulous in the matter of *meum* and *tuum,* paying great respect to obligations and a promise once made, the code we are here discussing displays, on the other hand, the

noblest liberality. There is only one word which may not be broken, *the word of honor*—upon my *honor,* as people say—the presumption being, of course, that every other form of promise may be broken. Nay, if the worst comes to the worst, it is easy to break even one's word of honor, and still remain honorable—again by adopting that universal remedy, the duel, and fighting with those who maintain that we pledged our word. Further, there is one debt, and one alone, that under no circumstances must be left unpaid—a gambling debt, which has accordingly been called *a debt of honor.* In all other kinds of debt you may cheat Jews and Christians as much as you like; and your knightly honor remains without a stain. The unprejudiced reader will see at once that such a strange, savage and ridiculous code of honor as this has no foundation in human nature, nor any warrant in a healthy view of human affairs. The extremely narrow sphere of its operation serves only to intensify the feeling, which is exclusively confined to Europe since the Middle Age, and then only to the upper classes, officers and soldiers, and people who imitate them. Neither Greeks nor Romans knew anything of this code of honor or of its principles; nor the highly civilized nations of Asia, ancient or modern. Amongst them no other kind of honor is recognized but that which I discussed first, in virtue of which a man is what he shows himself to be by his actions, not what any wagging tongue is pleased to say of him. They thought that what a man said or did might perhaps affect his own honor, but not any other man's. To them, a blow was but a blow—and any horse or donkey could give a harder one—a blow which under certain circumstances might make a man angry and demand immediate vengeance; but it had nothing to do with honor. No one kept account of blows or insulting words, or of the *satisfaction* which was demanded or omitted to be demanded. Yet in personal bravery and contempt of death, the ancients were certainly not inferior to the nations of Christian Europe. The Greeks and Romans were thorough heroes, if you like; but they knew nothing about *point d'honneur*. If they had any idea of a duel, it was totally unconnected with the life of the nobles; it was merely the exhibition of mercenary gladiators, slaves devoted to slaughter, condemned criminals, who, alternately with wild beasts, were set to butcher one another to make a Roman holiday. When Christianity was introduced, gladiatorial shows were done away with, and their place taken, in Christian times, by the duel, which was a way of settling difficulties by *the Judgment of God*.

If the gladiatorial fight was a cruel sacrifice to the prevailing desire for great spectacles, dueling is a cruel sacrifice to existing prejudices—a sacrifice, not of criminals, slaves and prisoners, but of the noble and the free.[13]

There are a great many traits in the character of the ancients which show that they were entirely free from these prejudices. When, for instance, Marius was summoned to a duel by a Teutonic chief, he returned answer to the effect that, if the chief were tired of his life, he might go and hang himself; at the same time he offered him a veteran gladiator for a round or two. Plutarch relates in his life of Themistocles that Eurybiades, who was in command of the fleet, once raised his stick to strike him; whereupon Themistocles, instead of drawing his sword, simply said: *Strike, but hear me.* How sorry the reader must be, if he is an *honorable* man, to find that we have no information that the Athenian officers refused in a body to serve any longer under Themistocles, if he acted like that! There is a modern French writer who declares that if anyone considers Demosthenes a man of honor, his

[13] *Translator's Note.*—These and other remarks on dueling will no doubt wear a belated look to English readers; but they are hardly yet antiquated for most parts of the Continent.

ignorance will excite a smile of pity; and that Cicero was
not a man of honor either![14] In a certain passage in
Plato's *Laws*,[15] the philosopher speaks at length of α'ικια
or *assault*, showing us clearly enough that the ancients had
no notion of any feeling of honor in connection with such
matters. Socrates' frequent discussions were often followed
by his being severely handled, and he bore it all mildly.
Once, for instance, when somebody kicked him, the patience
with which he took the insult surprised one of his friends.
Do you think, said Socrates, *that if an ass happened to
kick me, I should resent it?*[16] On another occasion, when
he was asked, *Has not that fellow abused and insulted you?*
No, was his answer, *what he says is not addressed to me.*[17]
Stobæus has preserved a long passage from Musonius, from
which we can see how the ancients treated insults. They
knew no other form of satisfaction than that which the
law provided, and wise people despised even this. If a
Greek received a box on the ear, he could get satisfaction
by the aid of the law; as is evident from Plato's *Gorgias*,
where Socrates' opinion may be found. The same thing
may be seen in the account given by Gellius of one Lucius
Veratius, who had the audacity to give some Roman citizens whom he met on the road a box on the ear, without
any provocation whatever; but to avoid any ulterior consequences, he told a slave to bring a bag of small money,
and on the spot paid the trivial legal penalty to the men
whom he had astonished by his conduct.

Crates, the celebrated Cynic philosopher, got such a box
on the ear from Nicodromus, the musician, that his face
swelled up and became black and blue; whereupon he put
a label on his forehead, with the inscription, *Nicodromus
fecit,* which brought much disgrace to the fluteplayer who

[14] *Soirées litteraires:* par C. Durand. Rouen, 1828.
[15] Bk. IX.
[16] Diogenes Laertius, ii., 21.
[17] *Ibid* 36.

had committed such a piece of brutality upon the man
whom all Athens honored as a household god.[18] And in a
letter to Melesippus, Diogenes of Sinope tells us that he
got a beating from the drunken sons of the Athenians; but
he adds that it was a matter of no importance.[19]   And
Seneca devotes the last few chapters of his *De Constantia*
to a lengthy discussion on insult—*contumelia;* in order to
show that a wise man will take no notice of it.   In Chapter
XIV, he says, *What shall a wise man do if he is given a
blow? What Cato did, when some one struck him on the
mouth;—not fire up or avenge the insult, or even return
the blow, but simply ignore it.*

Yes, you say, *but these men were philosophers.*—And
you are fools, eh?   Precisely.

It is clear that the whole code of knightly honor was
utterly unknown to the ancients; for the simple reason
that they always took a natural and unprejudiced view of
human affairs, and did not allow themselves to be influenced
by any such vicious and abominable folly.   A blow in the
face was to them a blow and nothing more, a trivial physical injury; whereas the moderns make a catastrophe out
of it, a theme for a tragedy; as, for instance, in the *Cid*
of Corneille, or in a recent German comedy of middle-class
life, called *The Power of Circumstance,* which should have
been entitled *The Power of Prejudice.*   If a member of the
National Assembly at Paris got a blow on the ear, it would
resound from one end of Europe to the other.   The examples which I have given of the way in which such an
occurrence would have been treated in classic times may
not suit the ideas of *honorable people;* so let me recommend to their notice, as a kind of antidote, the story of
Monsieur Desglands in Diderot's masterpiece, *Jacques le
fataliste.*   It is an excellent specimen of modern knightly

[18] Diogenes Laertius, vi. 87, and Apul: Flor: p. 126.
[19] Cf. Casaubon's Note, Diog. Laert., vi. 33.

honor, which, no doubt, they will find enjoyable and edifying.[20]

From what I have said it must be quite evident that the principle of knightly honor has no essential and spontaneous origin in human nature. It is an artificial product, and its source is not hard to find. Its existence obviously dates from the time when people used their fists more than their heads, when priestcraft had enchained the human intellect, the much bepraised Middle Age, with its system of chivalry. That was the time when people let the Almighty not only care for them but judge for them too; when difficult cases were decided by an ordeal, a *Judgment of God;* which, with few exceptions, meant a duel, not only where nobles were concerned, but in the case of ordinary citizens as well. There is a neat illustration of this in Shakespeare's Henry VI.[21] Every judicial sentence was subject to an appeal to arms—a court, as it were, of higher instance, namely, *the Judgment of God:* and this really meant that physical strength and activity, that is, our animal nature, usurped the place of reason on the judgment seat, deciding in matters of right and wrong, not by

[20] *Translator's Note.*—The story to which Schopenhauer here refers is briefly as follows: Two gentlemen, one of whom was named Desglands, were paying court to the same lady. As they sat at table side by side, with the lady opposite, Desglands did his best to charm her with his conversation; but she pretended not to hear him, and kept looking at his rival. In the agony of jealousy, Desglands, as he was holding a fresh egg in his hand, involuntarily crushed it; the shell broke, and its contents bespattered his rival's face. Seeing him raise his hand, Desglands seized it and whispered: *Sir, I take it as given.* The next day Desglands appeared with a large piece of black sticking-plaster upon his right cheek. In the duel which followed, Desglands severely wounded his rival; upon which he reduced the size of the plaster. When his rival recovered, they had another duel; Desglands drew blood again, and again made his plaster a little smaller; and so on for five or six times. After every duel Desglands' plaster grew less and less, until at last his rival was killed.

[21] Part II., Act 2, Sc. 3.

what a man had done, but by the force with which he was
opposed, the same system, in fact, as prevails to-day under
the principles of knightly honor. If any one doubts that
such is really the origin of our modern duel, let him read
an excellent work by J. B. Millingen, *The History of Dueling*.[22] Nay, you may still find amongst the supporters of
the system,—who are not usually the most educated or
thoughtful of men,—some who look upon the result of a duel
as constituting divine judgment in the matter in dispute; no
doubt in consequence of the traditional feeling on the subject.

But leaving aside the question of origin, it must now be
clear to us that the main tendency of the principle is to
use physical menace for the purpose of extorting an appearance of respect which is deemed too difficult or superfluous
to acquire in reality; a proceeding which comes to much
the same thing as if you were to prove the warmth of your
room by holding your hand on the thermometer and so
make it rise. In fact, the kernel of the matter is this:
whereas civic honor aims at peaceable intercourse, and
consists in the opinion of other people that *we deserve full
confidence*, because we pay unconditional respect to their
rights; knightly honor, on the other hand, lays down that
we are to be feared, as being determined at all costs to
maintain our own.

As not much reliance can be placed upon human integ-
rity, the principle that it is more essential to arouse fear
than to invite confidence would not, perhaps, be a false
one, if we were living in a state of nature, where every
man would have to protect himself and directly maintain
his own rights. But in civilized life, where the State under-
takes the protection of our person and property, the principle is no longer applicable: it stands, like the castles
and watch-towers of the age when might was right, a useless
and forlorn object, amidst well-tilled fields and frequented
roads, or even railways.

[22] Published in 1849.

Accordingly, the application of knightly honor, which still recognizes this principle, is confined to those small cases of personal assault which meet with but slight punishment at the hands of the law, or even none at all, for *de minimis non*,—mere trivial wrongs committed sometimes only in jest. The consequence of this limited application of the principle is that it has forced itself into an exaggerated respect for the value of the person,—a respect utterly alien to the nature, constitution or destiny of man—which it has elated into a species of sanctity: and as it considers that the State has imposed a very insufficient penalty on the commission of such trivial injuries, it takes upon itself to punish them by attacking the aggressor in life or limb. The whole thing manifestly rests upon an excessive degree of arrogant pride, which, completely forgetting what man really is, claims that he shall be absolutely free from all attack or even censure. Those who determine to carry out this principle by main force, and announce, as their rule of action, *whoever insults or strikes me shall die!* ought for their pains to be banished the country.[23]

[23] Knightly honor is the child of pride and folly, and it is *need*, not pride, which is the heritage of the human race. It is a very remarkable fact that this extreme form of pride should be found exclusively amongst the adherents of the religion which teaches the deepest humility. Still, this pride must not be put down to religion, but, rather, to the feudal system, which made every nobleman a petty sovereign who recognized no human judge, and learned to regard his person as sacred and inviolable, and any attack upon it, or any blow or insulting word, as an offence punishable with death. The principle of knightly honor and of the duel were at first confined to the nobles, and, later on, also to officers in the army, who, enjoying a kind of off-and-on relationship with the upper classes, though they were never incorporated with them, were anxious not to be behind them. It is true that duels were the product of the old ordeals; but the latter are not the foundation, but rather the consequence and application of the principle of honor: the man who recognized no human judge appealed to the divine. Ordeals, however, are not peculiar to Christendom: they may be found in great force among the Hindoos, especially of ancient times; and there are traces of them even now.

As a palliative to this rash arrogance, people are in the habit of giving way on everything. If two intrepid persons meet, and neither will give way, the slightest difference may cause a shower of abuse, then fisticuffs, and, finally, a fatal blow: so that it would really be a more decorous proceeding to omit the intermediate steps and appeal to arms at once. An appeal to arms has its own special formalities; and these have developed into a rigid and precise system of laws and regulations, together forming the most solemn farce there is—a regular temple of honor dedicated to folly! For if two intrepid persons dispute over some trivial matter, (more important affairs are dealt with by law,) one of them, the cleverer of the two, will of course yield; and they will agree to differ. That this is so is proved by the fact that common people,—or, rather, the numerous classes of the community who do not acknowledge the principle of knightly honor, let any dispute run its natural course. Amongst these classes homicide is a hundredfold rarer than amongst those—and they amount, perhaps, in all, to hardly one in a thousand,—who pay homage to the principle: and even blows are of no very frequent occurrence.

Then it has been said that the manners and tone of good society are ultimately based upon this principle of honor, which, with its systems of duels, is made out to be a bulwark against the assaults of savagery and rudeness. But Athens, Corinth and Rome could assuredly boast of good, nay, excellent society, and manners and tone of a high order, without any support from the bogey of knightly honor. It is true that women did not occupy that prominent place in ancient society which they hold now, when conversation has taken on a frivolous and trifling character, to the exclusion of that weighty discourse which distinguished the ancients. This change has certainly contributed a great deal to bring about the tendency, which is observ-

able in good society now-a-days, to prefer personal courage to the possession of any other quality. The fact is that
personal courage is really a very subordinate virtue,—
merely the distinguishing mark of a subaltern,—a virtue,
indeed, in which we are surpassed by the lower animals;
or else you would not hear people say, *as brave as a lion.*
Far from being the pillar of society, knightly honor affords
a sure asylum, in general for dishonesty and wickedness,
and also for small incivilities, want of consideration and
unmannerliness. Rude behavior is often passed over in
silence because no one cares to risk his neck in correcting it.

After what I have said, it will not appear strange that
the dueling system is carried to the highest pitch of sanguinary zeal precisely in that nation whose political and financial records show that they are not too honorable. What
that nation is like in its private and domestic life, is a
question which may be best put to those who are experienced in the matter. Their urbanity and social culture
have long been conspicuous by their absence.

There is no truth, then, in such pretexts. It can be urged
with more justice that as, when you snarl at a dog, he snarls
in return, and when you pet him, he fawns; so it lies in the
nature of men to return hostility by hostility, and to be
embittered and irritated at any signs of depreciatory treatment or hatred: and, as Cicero says, *there is something
so penetrating in the shaft of envy that even men of wisdom and worth find its wound a painful one;* and nowhere
in the world, except, perhaps, in a few religious sects, is
an insult or a blow taken with equanimity. And yet a
natural view of either would in no case demand anything
more than a requital proportionate to the offence, and
would never go to the length of assigning *death* as the
proper penalty for anyone who accuses another of lying or
stupidity or cowardice. The old German theory of *blood
for a blow* is a revolting superstition of the age of chivalry.

And in any case the return or requital of an insult is dictated by anger, and not by any such obligation of honor and duty as the advocates of chivalry seek to attach to it. The fact is that, the greater the truth, the greater the slander; and it is clear that the slightest hint of some real delinquency will give much greater offence than a most terrible accusation which is perfectly baseless: so that a man who is quite sure that he has done nothing to deserve a reproach may treat it with contempt, and will be safe in doing so. The theory of honor demands that he shall show a susceptibility which he does not possess, and take bloody vengeance for insults which he cannot feel. A man must himself have but a poor opinion of his own worth who hastens to prevent the utterance of an unfavorable opinion by giving his enemy a black eye.

True appreciation of his own value will make a man really indifferent to insult; but if he cannot help resenting it, a little shrewdness and culture will enable him to save appearances and dissemble his anger. If he could only get rid of this superstition about honor—the idea, I mean, that it disappears when you are insulted, and can be restored by returning the insult; if we could only stop people from thinking that wrong, brutality and insolence can be legalized by expressing readiness to give satisfaction, that is, to fight in defence of it, we should all soon come to the general opinion that insult and depreciation are like a battle in which the loser wins; and that, as Vincenzo Monti says, abuse resembles a church-procession, because it always returns to the point from which it set out. If we could only get people to look upon insult in this light, we should no longer have to say something rude in order to prove that we are in the right. Now, unfortunately, if we want to take a serious view of any question, we have first of all to consider whether it will not give offence in some way or other to the dullard, who generally shows alarm and resentment at the merest sign of intelligence; and it may easily happen that the head which contains the intelligent view has to be pitted against the noodle which is empty of everything but narrowness and stupidity. If all this were done away with, intellectual superiority could take the leading place in society which is its due—a place now occupied, though people do not like to confess it, by excellence of physique, mere fighting pluck, in fact; and the natural effect of such a change would be that the best kind of people would have one reason the less for withdrawing from society. This would pave the way for the introduction of real courtesy and genuinely good society, such as undoubtedly existed in Athens, Corinth and Rome. If anyone wants to see a good example of what I mean, I should like him to read Xenophon's *Banquet*.

The last argument in defence of knightly honor no doubt is, that, but for its existence, the world—awful thought!— would be a regular bear-garden. To which I may briefly reply that nine hundred and ninety-nine people out of a thousand who do not recognize the code have often given and received a blow without any fatal consequences: whereas amongst the adherents of the code a blow usually means death to one of the parties. But let me examine this argument more closely.

I have often tried to find some tenable, or at any rate, plausible basis—other than a merely conventional one— some positive reasons, that is to say, for the rooted conviction which a portion of mankind entertains, that a blow is a very dreadful thing; but I have looked for it in vain, either in the animal or in the rational side of human nature. A blow is, and always will be, a trivial physical injury which one man can do to another; proving, thereby, nothing more than his superiority in strength or skill, or that his enemy was off his guard. Analysis will carry us no further. The same knight who regards a blow from

the human hand as the greatest of evils, if he gets a ten
times harder blow from his horse, will give you the assurance, as he limps away in suppressed pain, that it is a
matter of no consequence whatever. So I have come to
think that it is the human hand which is at the bottom
of the mischief. And yet in a battle the knight may get
cuts and thrusts from the same hand, and still assure you
that his wounds are not worth mentioning. Now, I hear
that a blow from the flat of a sword is not by any means
so bad as a blow from a stick; and that, a short time ago,
cadets were liable to be punished by the one but not the
other, and that the very greatest honor of all is the
accolade. This is all the psychological or moral basis that
I can find; and so there is nothing left me but to pro-
nounce the whole thing an antiquated superstition that has
taken deep root, and one more of the many examples
which show the force of tradition. My view is confirmed
by the well-known fact that in China a beating with a bam-
boo is a very frequent punishment for the common people,
and even for officials of every class; which shows that
human nature, even in a highly civilized state, does not
run in the same groove here and in China.

On the contrary, an unprejudiced view of human nature
shows that it is just as natural for a man to beat as it
is for savage animals to bite and rend in pieces, or for
horned beasts to butt or push. Man may be said to be
the animal that beats. Hence it is revolting to our sense
of the fitness of things to hear, as we sometimes do, that
one man has bitten another; on the other hand, it is a natural and everyday occurrence for him to get blows or give
them. It is intelligible enough that, as we become educated, we are glad to dispense with blows by a system of
mutual restraint. But it is a cruel thing to compel a
nation or a single class to regard a blow as an awful misfortune which must have death and murder for its con-

sequences. There are too many genuine evils in the world to allow of our increasing them by imaginary misfortunes, which brings real ones in their train: and yet this is the precise effect of the superstition, which thus proves itself at once stupid and malign.

It does not seem to me wise of governments and legislative bodies to promote any such folly by attempting to do away with flogging as a punishment in civil or military life. Their idea is that they are acting in the interests of humanity; but, in point of fact, they are doing just the opposite; for the abolition of flogging will serve only to strengthen this inhuman and abominable superstition, to which so many sacrifices have already been made. For all offences, except the worst a "beating is the obvious, and therefore the natural penalty; and a man who will not listen to reason will yield to blows. It seems to me right and proper to administer corporal punishment to the man who possesses nothing and therefore cannot be fined, or cannot be put in prison because his master's interests would suffer by the loss of his service. There are really no arguments against it; only mere talk about *the dignity of man*—talk which proceeds, not from any clear notions on the subject, but from the pernicious superstition I have been describing. That it is a superstition which lies at the bottom of the whole business is proved by an almost laughable example. Not long ago, in the military discipline of many countries, the cat was replaced by the stick. In either case, the object was to produce physical pain; but the latter method involved no disgrace, and was not derogatory to honor.

By promoting this superstition, the State is playing into the hands of the principle of knightly honor, and therefore of the duel; while at the same time it is trying, or at any rate it pretends it is trying to abolish the duel by legislative enactment. As a natural consequence we find that this fragment of the theory that *might is right*, which has come down to us from the most savage days of the Middle Age, has still in this nineteenth century a good deal of life left in it—more shame to us! It is high time for the principle to be driven out bag and baggage. Now-a-days no one is allowed to set dogs or cocks to fight each other,—at any rate, in England it is a penal offence,—but men are plunged into deadly strife against their will, by the operation of this ridiculous, superstitious and absurd principle, which imposes upon us the obligation, as its narrow-minded supporters and advocates declare, of fighting with one another like gladiators, for any little trifle. Let me recommend our purists to adopt the expression *baiting*,[24] instead of *duel*, which probably comes to us, not from the Latin duellum, but from the Spanish *duelo*,—meaning suffering, nuisance, annoyance.

In any case, we may well laugh at the pedantic excess to which this foolish system has been carried. It is really revolting that this principle, with its absurd code, can form a power within the State—*imperium in imperio*—a power too easily put in motion, which, recognizing no right but might, tyrannizes over the classes which come within its range, by keeping up a sort of inquisition, before which any one may be haled on the most flimsy pretext, and there and then be tried on an issue of life and death between himself and his opponent. This is the lurking place from which every rascal, if he only belongs to the classes in question, may menace and even exterminate the noblest and best of men, who, as such, must of course be an object of hatred to him. Our system of justice and police-protection has made it impossible in these days for any scoundrel in the street to attack us with—*Your money or your life!* An end should be put to the burden which weighs upon the higher classes—the burden, I mean, of

[24] *Ritterhetze.*

having to be ready every moment to expose life and limb to the mercy of anyone who takes it into his rascally head to be coarse, rude, foolish or malicious. It is perfectly atrocious that a pair of silly, passionate boys should be wounded, maimed or even killed, simply because they have had a few words.

The strength of this tryrannical power within the State, and the force of the superstition, may be measured by the fact that people who are prevented from restoring their knightly honor by the superior or inferior rank of their aggressor, or anything else that puts the persons on a different level, often come to a tragic-comic end by committing suicide in sheer despair. You may generally know a thing to be false and ridiculous by finding that, if it is carried to its logical conclusion, it results in a contradiction; and here, too, we have a very glaring absurdity. For an officer is forbidden to take part in a duel; but if he is challenged and declines to come out, he is punished by being dismissed the service.

As I am on the matter, let me be more frank still. The important distinction, which is often insisted upon, between killing your enemy in a fair fight with equal weapons, and lying in ambush for him, is entirely a corollary of the fact that the power within the State, of which I have spoken, recognizes no other right than might, that is, the right of the stronger, and appeal to a *Judgment of God* as the basis of the whole code. For to kill a man in a fair fight, is to prove that you are superior to him in strength or skill; and to justify the deed, *you must assume that the right of the stronger is really a right.*

But the truth is that, if my opponent is unable to defend himself, it gives me the possibility, but not by any means the right, of killing him. The *right*, the *moral justification*, must depend entirely upon the *motives* which I have for taking his life. Even supposing that I have suffi-

cient motive for taking a man's life, there is no reason
why I should make his death depend upon whether I can
shoot or fence better than he. In such a case, it is imma-
terial in what way I kill him, whether I attack him from
the front or the rear. From a moral point of view, the
right of the stronger is no more convincing than the right
of the more skillful; and it is skill which is employed if
you murder a man treacherously. Might and skill are in
this case equally right; in a duel, for instance, both the
one and the other come into play; for a feint is only
another name for treachery. If I consider myself morally
justified in taking a man's life, it is stupid of me to try
first of all whether he can shoot or fence better than I;
as, if he can, he will not only have wronged me, but have
taken my life into the bargain.

It is Rousseau's opinion that the proper way to avenge
an insult is, not to fight a duel with your aggressor, but
to assassinate him,—an opinion, however, which he is cautious enough only to barely indicate in a mysterious note to
one of the books of his *Emile*. This shows the philosopher
so completely under the influence of the mediæval superstition of knightly honor that he considers it justifiable to
murder a man who accuses you of lying: whilst he must
have known that every man, and himself especially, has deserved to have the lie given him times without number.

The prejudice which justifies the killing of your adversary, so long as it is done in an open contest and with
equal weapons, obviously looks upon might as really right,
and a duel as the interference of God. The Italian who,
in a fit of rage, falls upon his aggressor wherever he finds
him, and despatches him without any ceremony, acts, at
any rate, consistently and naturally: he may be cleverer,
but he is not worse, than the duelist. If you say, I am
justified in killing my adversary in a duel, because he is
at the moment doing his best to kill me; I can reply that

it is your challenge which has placed him under the necessity of defending himself; by mutually putting it on the ground of self-defence, the combatants are seeking a plausible pretext for committing murder. I should rather justify the deed by the legal maxim *Volenti non fit injurio;* because the parties mutually agree to set their life upon the issue.

This argument may, however, be rebutted by showing that the injured party is not injured *volens;* because it is this tyrannical principle of knightly honor, with its absurd code, which forcibly drags one at least of the combatants before a bloody inquisition.

I have been rather prolix on the subject of knightly honor, but I had a good reason for being so, because the Augean stable of moral and intellectual enormity in this world can be cleaned out only with the besom of philosophy. There are two things which more than all else serve to make the social arrangements of modern life compare unfavorably with those of antiquity, by giving our age a gloomy, dark and sinister aspect, from which antiquity, fresh, natural, and, as it were, in the morning of life, is completely free; I mean modern honor and modern disease,—*par nobile fratum!*—which have combined to poison all the relations of life, whether public or private. The second of this noble pair extends its influence much farther than at first appears to be the case, as being not merely a physical, but also a moral disease. From the time that poisoned arrows have been found in Cupid's quiver, an estranging, hostile, nay, devilish element has entered into the relations of men and women, like a sinister thread of fear and mistrust in the warp and woof of their intercourse; indirectly shaking the foundations of human fellowship, and so more or less affecting the whole tenor of existence. But it would be beside my present purpose to pursue the subject further.

An influence analogous to this, though working on other

lines, is exerted by the principle of knightly honor,—that solemn farce, unknown to the ancient world, which makes modern society stiff, gloomy and timid, forcing us to keep the strictest watch on every word that falls. Nor is this all. The principle is a universal Minotaur; and the goodly company of the sons of noble houses which it demands in yearly tribute, comes, not from one country alone, as of old, but from every land in Europe. It is high time to make a regular attack upon this foolish system; and this is what I am trying to do now. Would that these two monsters of the modern world might disappear before the end of the century!

Let us hope that medicine may be able to find some means of preventing the one, also, by clearing our ideals, philosophy may put an end to the other: for it is only by clearing our ideas that the evil can be eradicated. Governments have tried to do so by legislation, and failed.

Still, if they are really concerned to stop the dueling system; and if the small success that has attended their efforts is really due only to their inability to cope with the evil, I do not mind proposing a law the success of which I am prepared to guarantee. It will involve no sanguinary measures, and can be put into operation without recourse either to the scaffold or the gallows, or to imprisonment for life. It is a small homeopathic pilule, with no serious after effects. If any man send or accept a challenge, let the corporal take him before the guard house, and there give him, in broad daylight, twelve strokes with a stick *à la Chinoise;* a non-commissioned officer or a private to receive six. If a duel has actually taken place, the usual criminal proceedings should be instituted.

A person with knightly notions might, perhaps, object that, if such a punishment were carried out, a man of honor would possibly shoot himself; to which I should answer that it is better for a fool like that to shoot himself rather than other people. However, I know very well that governments are not really in earnest about putting down dueling. Civil officials, and much more so, officers in the army, (except those in the highest positions), are paid most inadequately for the services they perform; and the deficiency is made up by honor, which is represented by titles and orders, and, in general, by the system of rank and distinction. The duel is, so to speak, a very serviceable extra-horse for people of rank; so they are trained in the knowledge of it at the universities. The accidents which happen to those who use it make up in blood for the deficiency of the pay.

Just to complete the discussion, let me here mention the subject of *national honor*. It is the honor of a nation as a unit in the aggregate of nations. And as there is no court to appeal to but the court of force; and as every nation must be prepared to defend its own interests, the honor of a nation consists in establishing the opinion, not only that it may be trusted (its credit), but also that it is to be feared. An attack upon its rights must never be allowed to pass unheeded. It is a combination of civic and knightly honor.

Section 5.—Fame

Under the heading of place in the estimation of the world we have put *Fame;* this we must now consider.

Fame and honor are twins; and twins, too, like Castor and Pollux, of whom the one was mortal and the other was not. Fame is the undying brother of ephemeral honor. I speak, of course, of the highest kind of fame, that is, of fame in the true and genuine sense of the word; for, to be sure, there are many sorts of fame, some of which last but a day. Honor is concerned merely with such qualities as everyone may be expected to show under similar circumstances; fame only of those which cannot be required of any man. Honor is of qualities which everyone has a right to attribute to himself; fame only of those which should be left to others to attribute. Whilst our honor extends as far as people have knowledge of us; fame runs in advance, and makes us known wherever it finds its way. Everyone can make a claim to honor; few to fame, as being attainable only in virtue of extraordinary achievements.

These achievements may be of two kinds, either *actions* or *works;* and so to fame there are two paths open. On the path of actions, a great heart is the chief recommendation; on that of works, a great head. Each of the two paths has its own peculiar advantages and detriments; and the chief difference between them is that actions are fleeting, while works remain. The influence of an action, be it ever so noble, can last but a short time; but a work of genius is a living influence, beneficial and ennobling throughout the ages. All that can remain of actions is a memory, and that becomes weak and disfigured by time— a matter of indifference to us, until at last it is extinguished altogether; unless, indeed, history takes it up, and presents it, fossilized, to posterity. Works are immortal in themselves, and once committed to writing, may live for ever. Of Alexander the Great we have but the name and the record; but Plato and Aristotle, Homer and Horace are alive, and as directly at work to-day as they were in their own life-time. The *Vedas,* and their *Upanishads,* are still with us: but of all contemporaneous actions not a trace has come down to us.[25]

[25] Accordingly it is a poor compliment, though sometimes a fashionable one, to try to pay honor to a work by calling it an action. For a work is something essentially higher in its nature. An action is always something based on motive, and, therefore, fragmentary and fleeting—a part, in fact, of that Will which is the universal and original element in the constitution of the world. But a great and beautiful work has a permanent character, as being of universal significance, and sprung from the

Another disadvantage under which actions labor is that they depend upon chance for the possibility of coming into existence; and hence, the fame they win does not flow entirely from their intrinsic value, but also from the circumstances which happened to lend them importance and lustre. Again, the fame of actions, if, as in war, they are purely personal, depends upon the testimony of fewer witnesses; and these are not always present, and even if present, are not always just or unbiased observers. This disadvantage, however, is counterbalanced by the fact that actions have the advantage of being of a practical character, and, therefore, within the range of general human intelligence; so that once the facts have been correctly reported, justice is immediately done; unless, indeed, the motive underlying the action is not at first properly understood or appreciated. No action can be really understood apart from the motive which prompted it.

It is just the contrary with works. Their inception does not depend upon chance, but wholly and entirely upon their author; and whoever they are in and for themselves, that they remain as long as they live. Further, there is a difficulty in properly judging them, which becomes all the harder, the higher their character; often there are no persons competent to understand the work, and often no unbiased or honest critics. Their fame, however, does

---

Intellect, which rises, like a perfume, above the faults and follies of the world of Will.

The fame of a great action has this advantage, that it generally starts with a loud explosion; so loud, indeed, as to be heard all over Europe: whereas the fame of a great work is slow and gradual in its beginnings; the noise it makes is at first slight, but it goes on growing greater, until at last, after a hundred years perhaps, it attains its full force; but then it remains, because the works remain, for thousands of years. But in the other case, when the first explosion is over, the noise it makes grows less and less, and is heard by fewer and fewer persons; until it ends by the action having only a shadowy existence in the pages of history.

not depend upon one judge only; they can enter an appeal to another. In the case of actions, as I have said, it is only their memory which comes down to posterity, and then only in the traditional form; but works are handed down themselves, and, except when parts of them have been lost, in the form in which they first appeared. In this case there is no room for any disfigurement of the facts; and any circumstance which may have prejudiced them in their origin, fall away with the lapse of time. Nay, it is often only after the lapse of time that the persons really competent to judge them appear—exceptional critics sitting in judgment on exceptional works, and giving their weighty verdicts in succession. These collectively form a perfectly just appreciation: and though there are cases where it has taken hundreds of years to form it, no further lapse of time is able to reverse the verdict; —so secure and inevitable is the fame of a great work.

Whether authors ever live to see the dawn of their fame depends upon the chance of circumstance; and the higher and more important their works are, the less likelihood there is of their doing so. That was an incomparably fine saying of Seneca's, that fame follows merit as surely as the body casts a shadow; sometimes falling in front, and sometimes behind. And he goes on to remark that *though the envy of contemporaries be shown by universal silence, there will come those who will judge without enmity or favor*. From this remark it is manifest that even in Seneca's age there were rascals who understood the art of suppressing merit by maliciously ignoring its existence, of concealing good work from the public to favor the bad: it is an art well understood in our day, too, manifesting itself, both then and now, in *an envious conspiracy of silence*.

As a general rule, the longer a man's fame is likely to last, the later it will be in coming; for all excellent products require time for their development. The fame which

lasts to posterity is like an oak, of very slow growth; and
that which endures but a little while, like plants which
spring up in a year and then die; whilst false fame is like
a fungus, shooting up in a night and perishing as soon.

And why? For this reason; the more a man belongs
to posterity, in other words, to humanity in general, the
more of an alien he is to his contemporaries; since his
work is not meant for them as such, but only for them in
so far as they form part of mankind at large; there is
none of that familiar local color about his productions
which would appeal to them; and so what he does, fails
of recognition because it is strange.

People are more likely to appreciate the man who serves
the circumstances of his own brief hour, or the temper of
the moment,—belonging to it, living and dying with it.

The general history of art and literature shows that the
highest achievements of the human mind are, as a rule, not
favorably received at first; but remain in obscurity until
they win notice from intelligence of a high order, by whose
influence they are brought into a position which they then
maintain, in virtue of the authority thus given them.

If the reason of this should be asked, it will be found
that ultimately, a man can really understand and appreciate those things only which are of like nature with himself. The dull person will like what is dull, and the common person what is common; a man whose ideas are mixed
will be attracted by confusion of thought; and folly will
appeal to him who has no brains at all; but best of all,
a man will like his own works, as being of a character
thoroughly at one with himself. This is a truth as old
as Epicharmus of fabulous memory—

> Θαυμαστὸν οὐδὲν ἐστί με ταῦθ' οὕτω λέγειν
> Καὶ ἀνδάνειν αὐτοῖσιν αὐτούς, καὶ δοκεῖν
> Καλῶς πεφυκέναι. καὶ γὰρ ὁ κύων κυνί
> Κάλλιστον εἶμεν φαίνεται, κωὶ βοῦς βοΐ
> Ὄνος δ' ὄνῳ κάλλιστόν [ἐστιν], ὗς δ' ὑΐ.

The sense of this passage—for it should not be lost—is that we should not be surprised if people are pleased with themselves, and fancy that they are in good case; for to a dog the best thing in the world is a dog; to an ox, an ox; to an ass, an ass; and to a sow, a sow.

The strongest arm is unavailing to give impetus to a featherweight; for, instead of speeding on its way and hitting its mark with effect, it will soon fall to the ground, having expended what little energy was given to it, and possessing no mass of its own to be the vehicle of momentum. So it is with great and noble thoughts, nay, with the very masterpieces of genius, when there are none but little, weak, and perverse minds to appreciate them,— a fact which has been deplored by a chorus of the wise in all ages. Jesus, the son of Sirach, for instance, declares that *He that telleth a tale to a fool speaketh to one in slumber: when he hath told his tale, he will say, What is the matter?* [26] And Hamlet says, *A knavish speech sleeps in a fool's ear.*[27] And Goethe is of the same opinion, that a dull ear mocks at the wisest word,

> *Das glücklichste Wort es wird verhöhnt,*
> *Wenn der Hörer ein Schiefohr ist:*

and again, that we should not be discouraged if people are stupid, for you can make no rings if you throw your stone into a marsh.

> *Du wirkest nicht, Alles bleibt so stumpf:*
> *Sei guter Dinge!*
> *Der Stein in Sumpf*
> *Macht keine Ringe.*

Lichtenberg asks: *When a head and a book come into collision, and one sounds hollow, is it always the book?* And in another place: *Works like this are as a mirror; if an ass looks in, you cannot expect an apostle to look out.*

[26] Ecclesiasticus, xxii., 8.
[27] Act. iv., Sc. 2.

We should do well to remember old Gellert's fine and touching lament, that the best gifts of all find the fewest admirers, and that most men mistake the bad for the good,—a daily evil that nothing can prevent, like a plague which no remedy can cure. There is but one thing to be done, though how difficult!—the foolish must become wise,—and that they can never be. The value of life they never know; they see with the outer eye but never with the mind and praise the trivial because the good is strange to them:—

> *Nie kennen sie den Werth der Dinge,*
> *Ihr Auge schliesst, nicht ihr Verstand;*
> *Sie loben ewig das Geringe*
> *Weil sei das Gute nie gekannt.*

To the intellectual incapacity which, as Goethe says, fails to recognize and appreciate the good which exists, must be added something which comes into play everywhere, the moral baseness of mankind, here taking the form of envy. The new fame that a man wins raises him afresh over the heads of his fellows, who are thus degraded in proportion. All conspicuous merit is obtained at the cost of those who possess none; or, as Goethe has it in the *Westöstlicher Divan,* another's praise is one's own depreciation—

> *Wenn wir Andern Ehre geben*
> *Müssen wir uns selbst entadeln.*

We see, then, how it is that, whatever be the form which excellence takes, mediocrity, the common lot of by far the greatest number, is leagued against it in a conspiracy to resist, and if possible, to suppress it. The pass-word of this league is *à bas le mérite.* Nay more; those who have done something themselves, and enjoy a certain amount of fame, do not care about the appearance of a new reputation, because its success is apt to throw theirs into the shade. Hence, Goethe declares that if we had to depend for our life upon the favor of others, we should never have lived at all; from their desire to appear important themselves, people gladly ignore our very existence:—

> *Hätte ich gezaudert zu werden,*
> *Bis man mir's Leben geögnnt,*
> *Ich wäre noch nicht auf Erden,*
> *Wie ihr begreifen könnt,*
> *Wenn ihr seht, wie sie sich geberden,*
> *Die, um etwas zu scheinen,*
> *Mich gerne möchten verneinen.*

Honor, on the contrary, generally meets with fair appreciation, and is not exposed to the onslaught of envy; nay, every man is credited with the possession of it until the contrary is proved. But fame has to be won in despite of envy, and the tribunal which awards the laurel is composed of judges biased against the applicant from the very first. Honor is something which we are able and ready to share with everyone; fame suffers encroachment and is rendered more unattainable in proportion as more people come by it. Further, the difficulty of winning fame by any given work stands in reverse ratio to the number of people who are likely to read it; and hence it is so much harder to become famous as the author of a learned work than as a writer who aspires only to amuse. It is hardest of all in the case of philosophical works, because the result at which they aim is rather vague, and, at the same time, useless from a material point of view; they appeal chiefly to readers who are working on the same lines themselves.

It is clear, then, from what I have said as to the difficulty of winning fame, that those who labor, not out of love for their subject, nor from pleasure in pursuing it, but under the stimulus of ambition, rarely or never leave mankind a legacy of immortal works. The man who seeks to do what is good and genuine, must avoid what is bad, and be ready to defy the opinions of the mob, nay, even to despise it and its misleaders. Hence the truth of the remark, (especially insisted upon by Osirius *de Gloria*), that fame shuns those who seek it, and seeks those who shun it; for the one adapt themselves to the taste of their contemporaries, and the others work in defiance of it.

But, difficult though it be to acquire fame, it is an easy thing to keep when once acquired. Here, again, fame is in direct opposition to honor, with which everyone is presumably to be accredited. Honor has not to be won; it must only not be lost. But there lies the difficulty! For by a single unworthy action, it is gone irretrievably. But fame, in the proper sense of the word, can never disappear; for the action or work by which it was acquired can never be undone; and fame attaches to its author, even though he does nothing to deserve it anew. The fame which vanishes, or is outlived, proves itself thereby to be spurious, in other words, unmerited, and due to a momentary overestimate of a man's work; not to speak of the kind of fame which Hegel enjoyed, and which Lichtenberg describes as *trumpeted forth by a clique of admiring undergraduates—the resounding echo of empty heads;—such a fame as will make posterity smile when it lights upon a grotesque architecture of words, a fine nest with the birds long ago flown; it will knock at the door of this decayed structure of conventionalities and find it utterly empty!— not even a trace of thought there to invite the passer-by.*

The truth is that fame means nothing but what a man is in comparison with others. It is essentially relative in character, and therefore only indirectly valuable; for it vanishes the moment other people become what the famous man is. Absolute value can be predicated only of what a man possesses under any and all circumstances,—here, what a man is directly and in himself. It is the possession of a great heart or a great head, and not the mere fame of it, which is worth having, and conducive to happiness. Not fame, but that which deserves to be famous, is what a man should hold in esteem. This is, as it were, the true underlying substance, the fame is only an accident, affecting its subject chiefly as a kind of external symptom, which serves to confirm his own opinion of himself. Light is not visible unless it meets with something to reflect it; and talent is sure of itself only when its fame is noised abroad. But fame is not a certain symptom of merit; because you can have the one without the other; or, as Lessing nicely puts it, *Some people obtain fame, and others deserve it.*

It would be a miserable existence which should make its value or want of value depend upon what other people think; but such would be the life of a hero or a genius if its worth consisted in fame, that is, in the applause of the world. Every man lives and exists on his own account, and, therefore, mainly in and for himself; and what he is and the whole manner of his being concern himself more than anyone else; so if he is not worth much in this respect, he cannot be worth much otherwise. The idea which other people form of his existence is something secondary, derivative, exposed to all the chances of fate, and in the end affecting him but very indirectly. Besides, other people's heads are a wretched place to be the home of a man's true happiness—a fanciful happiness perhaps, but not a real one.

And what a mixed company inhabits the Temple of Universal Fame!—generals, ministers, charlatans, jugglers, dancers, singers, millionaires and Jews! It is a temple in which more sincere recognition, more genuine esteem, is given to the several excellencies of such folk, than to superiority of mind, even of a high order, which obtains from the great majority only a verbal acknowledgment.

From the point of view of human happiness, fame is, surely, nothing but a very rare and delicate morsel for the appetite that feeds on pride and vanity—an appetite which, however carefully concealed, exists to an immoderate degree in every man, and is, perhaps strongest of all in those who set their hearts on becoming famous at any cost. Such people generally have to wait some time in uncertainty as to their own value, before the opportunity comes which will put it to the proof and let other people see what they are made of; but until then, they feel as if they were suffering secret injustice.[28]

But, as I explained at the beginning of this chapter, an unreasonable value is set upon other people's opinion, and one quite disproportionate to its real worth. Hobbes has some strong remarks on this subject; and no doubt he is quite right. *Mental pleasure,* he writes, *and ecstasy of any kind, arise when, on comparing ourselves with others, we come to the conclusion that we may think well of ourselves.* So we can easily understand the great value which is always attached to fame, as worth any sacrifices if there is the slightest hope of attaining it.

> *Fame is the spur that the clear spirit doth raise*
> *(That hath infirmity of noble mind)*
> *To scorn delights and live laborious days.*[29]

And again:

> *How hard it is to climb*
> *The heights where Fame's proud temple shines afar!*

We can thus understand how it is that the vainest people in the world are always talking about *la gloire,* with the most implicit faith in it as a stimulus to great actions and great works. But there can be no doubt that fame is something secondary in its character, a mere echo or reflection—as it were, a shadow or symptom—of merit: and, in any case, what excites admiration must be of more

[28] Our greatest pleasure consists in being admired; but those who admire us, even if they have every reason to do so, are slow to express their sentiments. Hence he is the happiest man who, no matter how, manages sincerely to admire himself—so long as other people leave him alone.

[29] Milton. *Lycidas.*

value than the admiration itself. The truth is that a man
is made happy, not by fame, but by that which brings
him fame, by his merits, or to speak more correctly, by
the disposition and capacity from which his merits proceed, whether they be moral or intellectual. The best side
of a man's nature must of necessity be more important for
him than for anyone else: the reflection of it, the opinion
which exists in the heads of others, is a matter that can
affect him only in a very subordinate degree. He who
deserves fame without getting it possesses by far the more
important element of happiness, which should console him
for the loss of the other. It is not that a man is thought
to be great by masses of incompetent and often infatuated
people, but that he really is great, which should move us
to envy his position; and his happiness lies, not in the
fact that posterity will hear of him, but that he is the
creator of thoughts worthy to be treasured up and studied
for hundreds of years.

Besides, if a man has done this, he possesses something
which cannot be wrested from him; and unlike fame, it
is a possession dependent entirely upon himself. If admiration were his chief aim, there would be nothing in him
to admire. This is just what happens in the case of false,
that is, unmerited fame; for its recipient lives upon it
without actually possessing the solid substratum of which
fame is the outward and visible sign. False fame must
often put its possessor out of conceit with himself; for
the time may come when, in spite of the illusions borne
of self-love, he will feel giddy on the heights which he was
never meant to climb, or look upon himself as spurious
coin; and in the anguish of threatened discovery and well-
merited degradation, he will read the sentence of posterity
on the foreheads of the wise—like a man who owes his
property to a forged will.

The truest fame, the fame that comes after death, is

never heard of by its recipient; and yet he is called a happy man.

His happiness lay both in the possession of those great qualities which won him fame, and in the opportunity that was granted him of developing them—the leisure he had to act as he pleased, to dedicate himself to his favorite pursuits. It is only work done from the heart that ever gains the laurel.

Greatness of soul, or wealth of intellect, is what makes a man happy—intellect, such as, when stamped on its productions, will receive the admiration of centuries to come,—thoughts which make him happy at the time, and will in their turn be a source of study and delight to the noblest minds of the most remote posterity. The value of posthumous fame lies in deserving it; and this is its own reward. Whether works destined to fame attain it in the lifetime of their author is a chance affair, of no very great importance. For the average man has no critical power of his own, and is absolutely incapable of appreciating the difficulty of a great work. People are always swayed by authority; and where fame is widespread, it means that ninety-nine out of a hundred take it on faith alone. If a man is famed far and wide in his own lifetime, he will, if he is wise, not set too much value upon it, because it is no more than the echo of a few voices, which the chance of a day has touched in his favor.

Would a musician feel flattered by the loud applause of an audience if he knew that they were nearly all deaf, and that, to conceal their infirmity, they set to work to clap vigorously as soon as ever they saw one or two persons applauding? And what would he say if he got to know that those one or two persons had often taken bribes to secure the loudest applause for the poorest player?

It is easy to see why contemporary praise so seldom develops into posthumous fame. D'Alembert, in an extremely fine description of the temple of literary fame, remarks that the sanctuary of the temple is inhabited by the great dead, who during their life had no place there, and by a very few living persons, who are nearly all ejected on their death. Let me remark, in passing, that to erect a monument to a man in his lifetime is as much as declaring that posterity is not to be trusted in its judgment of him. If a man does happen to see his own true fame, it can very rarely be before he is old, though there have been artists and musicians who have been exceptions to this rule, but very few philosophers. This is confirmed by the portraits of people celebrated by their works; for most of them are taken only after their subjects have attained celebrity, generally depicting them as old and grey; more especially if philosophy has been the work of their lives. From the eudæmonistic standpoint, this is a very proper arrangement; as fame and youth are too much for a mortal at one and the same time. Life is such a poor business that the strictest economy must be exercised in its good things. Youth has enough and to spare in itself, and must rest content with what it has. But when the delights and joys of life fall away in old age, as the leaves from a tree in autumn, fame buds forth opportunely, like a plant that is green in winter. Fame is, as it were, the fruit that must grow all the summer before it can be enjoyed at Yule. There is no greater consolation in age than the feeling of having put the whole force of one's youth into works which still remain young.

Finally, let us examine a little more closely the kinds of fame which attach to various intellectual pursuits; for it is with fame of this sort that my remarks are more immediately concerned.

I think it may be said broadly that the intellectual superiority it denotes consists in forming theories, that is, new combinations of certain facts. These facts may be of very different kinds; but the better they are known, and the more they come within everyday experience, the greater and wider will be the fame which is to be won by theorizing about them.

For instance, if the facts in question are numbers or lines or special branches of science, such as physics, zoology, botany, anatomy, or corrupt passages in ancient authors, or undecipherable inscriptions, written, it may be, in some unknown alphabet, or obscure points in history; the kind of fame that may be obtained by correctly manipulating such facts will not extend much beyond those who make a study of them—a small number of persons, most of whom live retired lives and are envious of others who become famous in their special branch of knowledge.

But if the facts be such as are known to everyone, for example, the fundamental characteristics of the human mind or the human heart, which are shared by all alike; or the great physical agencies which are constantly in operation before our eyes, or the general course of natural laws; the kind of fame which is to be won by spreading the light of a new and manifestly true theory in regard to them, is such as in time will extend almost all over the civilized world: for if the facts be such as everyone can grasp, the theory also will be generally intelligible. But the extent of the fame will depend upon the difficulties overcome; and the more generally known the facts are, the harder it will be to form a theory that shall be both new and true: because a great many heads will have been occupied with them, and there will be little or no possibility of saying anything that has not been said before.

On the other hand, facts which are not accessible to everybody, and can be got at only after much difficulty and labor, nearly always admit of new combinations and theories; so that, if sound understanding and judgment are brought to bear upon them—qualities which do not involve very high intellectual power—a man may easily be so fortunate as to light upon some new theory in regard to them which shall be also true. But fame won on such paths does not extend much beyond those who possess a knowledge of the facts in question. To solve problems of this sort requires, no doubt, a great deal of study and labor, if only to get at the facts; whilst on the path where the greatest and most widespread fame is to be won, the facts may be grasped without any labor at all. But just in proportion as less labor is necessary, more talent or genius is required; and between such qualities and the drudgery of research no comparison is possible, in respect either of their intrinsic value, or of the estimation in which they are held.

And so people who feel that they possess solid intellectual capacity and a sound judgment, and yet cannot claim the highest mental powers, should not be afraid of laborious study; for by its aid they may work themselves above the great mob of humanity who have the facts constantly before their eyes, and reach those secluded spots which are accessible to learned toil.

For this is a sphere where there are infinitely fewer rivals, and a man of only moderate capacity may soon find an opportunity of proclaiming a theory which shall be both new and true; nay, the merit of his discovery will partly rest upon the difficulty of coming at the facts. But applause from one's fellow-students, who are the only persons with a knowledge of the subject, sounds very faint to the far-off multitude. And if we follow up this sort of fame far enough, we shall at last come to a point where facts very difficult to get at are in themselves sufficient to lay a foundation of fame, without any necessity for forming a theory;—travels, for instance, in remote and little-known countries, which make a man famous by what he has seen, not by what he has thought. The great advantage of this kind of fame is that to relate what one has seen, is much easier than to impart one's thoughts, and people are apt to understand descriptions better than ideas, reading the one more readily than the other: for, as Asmus says,

> *When one goes forth a-voyaging*
> *He has a tale to tell.*

And yet for all that, a personal acquaintance with celebrated travelers often reminds us of a line from Horace—new scenes do not always mean new ideas—

Cœlum non animum mutant qui trans mare currunt.[30]

But if a man finds himself in possession of great mental faculties, such as alone should venture on the solution of the hardest of all problems—those which concern nature as a whole and humanity in its widest range, he will do well to extend his view equally in all directions, without ever straying too far amid the intricacies of various by-paths, or invading regions little known; in other words, without occupying himself with special branches of knowledge, to say nothing of their petty details. There is no necessity for him to seek out subjects difficult of access, in order to escape a crowd of rivals; the common objects of life will give him material for new theories at once serious and true; and the service he renders will be appreciated by all those—and they form a great part of mankind—who know the facts of which he treats. What a vast distinction there is between students of physics, chemistry, anatomy, mineralogy, zoology, philology, history, and the men who deal with the great facts of human life, the poet and the philosopher!

[30] Epist. I, II.

The Art of Literature

ON AUTHORSHIP

THERE are, first of all, two kinds of authors: those who write for the subject's sake, and those who write for writing's sake. While the one have had thoughts or experiences which seem to them worth communicating, the others want money; and so they write, for money. Their thinking is part of the business of writing. They may be recognized by the way in which they spin out their thoughts to the greatest possible length; then, too, by the very nature of their thoughts, which are only half-true, perverse, forced, vacillating; again, by the aversion they generally show to saying anything straight out, so that they may seem other than they are. Hence their writing is deficient in clearness and definiteness, and it is not long before they betray that their only object in writing at all is to cover paper. This sometimes happens with the best authors; now and then, for example, with Lessing in his *Dramaturgie*, and even in many of Jean Paul's romances. As soon as the reader perceives this, let him throw the book away; for time is precious. The truth is that when an author begins to write for the sake of covering paper, he is cheating the reader; because he writes under the pretext that he has something to say.

Writing for money and reservation of copyright are, at bottom, the ruin of literature. No one writes anything that is worth writing, unless he writes entirely for the sake of his subject. What an inestimable boon it would be, if in every branch of literature there were only a few books, but those excellent! This can never happen, as long as money is to be made by writing. It seems as though the

money lay under a curse; for every author degenerates
as soon as he begins to put pen to paper in any way for
the sake of gain. The best works of the greatest men all
come from the time when they had to write for nothing
or for very little. And here, too, that Spanish proverb
holds good, which declares that honor and money are not
to be found in the same purse—*honora y provecho no
caben en un saco.* The reason why Literature is in such
a bad plight nowadays is simply and solely that people
write books to make money. A man who is in want sits
down and writes a book, and the public is stupid enough to
buy it. The secondary effect of this is the ruin of language.

A great many bad writers make their whole living by
that foolish mania of the public for reading nothing but
what has just been printed,—journalists, I mean. Truly,
a most appropriate name. In plain language it is *journey-
men, day-laborers!*

Again, it may be said that there are three kinds of
authors. First come those who write without thinking.
They write from a full memory, from reminiscences; it
may be, even straight out of other people's books. This
class is the most numerous. Then come those who do
their thinking whilst they are writing. They think in
order to write; and there is no lack of them. Last of
all come those authors who think before they begin to
write. They are rare.

Authors of the second class, who put off their thinking
until they come to write, are like a sportsman who goes
forth at random and is not likely to bring very much home.
On the other hand, when an author of the third or rare
class writes, it is like a *battue.* Here the game has been
previously captured and shut up within a very small
space; from which it is afterwards let out, so many at
a time, into another space, also confined. The game cannot possibly escape the sportsman; he has nothing to do

but aim and fire—in other words, write down his thoughts. This is a kind of sport from which a man has something to show.

But even though the number of those who really think seriously before they begin to write is small, extremely few of them think about *the subject itself:* the remainder think only about the books that have been written on the subject, and what has been said by others. In order to think at all, such writers need the more direct and powerful stimulus of having other people's thoughts before them. These become their immediate theme; and the result is that they are always under their influence, and so never, in any real sense of the word, are original. But the former are roused to thought by the subject itself, to which their thinking is thus immediately directed. This is the only class that produces writers of abiding fame.

It must, of course, be understood that I am speaking here of writers who treat of great subjects; not of writers on the art of making brandy.

Unless an author takes the material on which he writes out of his own head, that is to say, from his own observation, he is not worth reading. Book-manufacturers, compilers, the common run of history-writers, and many others of the same class, take their material immediately out of books; and the material goes straight to their finger-tips without even paying freight or undergoing examination as it passes through their heads, to say nothing of elaboration or revision. How very learned many a man would be if he knew everything that was in his own books! The consequence of this is that these writers talk in such a loose and vague manner, that the reader puzzles his brain in vain to understand what it is of which they are really thinking. They are thinking of nothing. It may now and then be the case that the book from which they copy has been composed exactly in the same way: so that writing of this sort is like a plaster cast of a cast; and in the end, the bare outline of the face; and that, too, hardly recognizable, is all that is left to your Antinous. Let compilations be read as seldom as possible. It is difficult to avoid them altogether; since compilations also include those text-books which contain in a small space the accumulated knowledge of centuries.

There is no greater mistake than to suppose that the last work is always the more correct; that what is written later on is in every case an improvement on what was written before; and that change always means progress. Real thinkers, men of right judgment, people who are in earnest with their subject,—these are all exceptions only. Vermin is the rule everywhere in the world: it is always on the alert, taking the mature opinions of the thinkers, and industriously seeking to improve upon them (save the mark!) in its own peculiar way.

If the reader wishes to study any subject, let him beware of rushing to the newest books upon it, and confining his attention to them alone, under the notion that science is always advancing, and that the old books have been drawn upon in the writing of the new. They have been drawn upon, it is true; but how? The writer of the new book often does not understand the old books thoroughly, and yet he is unwilling to take their exact words; so he bungles them, and says in his own bad way that which has been said very much better and more clearly by the old writers, who wrote from their own lively knowledge of the subject. The new writer frequently omits the best things they say, their most striking illustrations, their happiest remarks; because he does not see their value or feel how pregnant they are. The only thing that appeals to him is what is shallow and insipid.

It often happens that an old and excellent book is ousted by new and bad ones, which, written for money,

appear with an air of great pretension and much puffing
on the part of friends. In science a man tries to make
his mark by bringing out something fresh. This often
means nothing more than that he attacks some received
theory which is quite correct, in order to make room for
his own false notions. Sometimes the effort is successful
for a time; and then a return is made to the old and true
theory. These innovators are serious about nothing but
their own precious self: it is this that they want to put
forward, and the quick way of doing so, as they think,
is to start a paradox. Their sterile heads take naturally
to the path of negation; so they begin to deny truths that
have long been admitted—the vital power, for example,
the sympathetic nervous system, *generatio equivoca*, Bi-
chat's distinction between the working of the passions and
the working of intelligence; or else they want us to return
to crass atomism, and the like. Hence it frequently happens that the *course of science is retrogressive.*

To this class of writers belong those translators who
not only translate their author but also correct and revise
him; a proceeding which always seems to me impertinent.
To such writers I say: Write books yourself which are
worth translating, and leave other people's works as they
are!

The reader should study, if he can, the real authors,
the men who have founded and discovered things; or, at
any rate, those who are recognized as the great masters
in every branch of knowledge. Let him buy second-hand
books rather than read their contents in new ones. To
be sure, it is easy to add to any new discovery—*inventis
aliquid addere facile est;* and, therefore, the student, after
well mastering the rudiments of his subject, will have to
make himself acquainted with the more recent additions
to the knowledge of it. And, in general, the following
rule may be laid down here as elsewhere: if a thing is

new, it is seldom good; because if it is good, it is only for a short time new.

What the address is to a letter, the title should be to a book; in other words, its main object should be to bring the book to those amongst the public who will take an interest in its contents. It should, therefore, be expressive; and since by its very nature it must be short, it should be concise, laconic, pregnant, and if possible give the contents in one word. A prolix title is bad; and so is one that says nothing, or is obscure and ambiguous, or even, it may be, false and misleading; this last may possibly involve the book in the same fate as overtakes a wrongly addressed letter. The worst titles of all are those which have been stolen, those, I mean, which have already been borne by other books; for they are in the first place a plagiarism, and secondly the most convincing proof of a total lack of originality in the author. A man who has not enough originality to invent a new title for his book, will be still less able to give it new contents. Akin to these stolen titles are those which have been imitated, that is to say, stolen to the extent of one half; for instance, long after I had produced my treatise *On Will in Nature*, Oersted wrote a book entitled *On Mind in Nature*.

A book can never be anything more than the impress of its author's thoughts; and the value of these will lie either in *the matter about which he has thought*, or in the *form* which his thoughts take, in other words, *what it is that he has thought about it*.

The matter of books is most various; and various also are the several excellences attaching to books on the score of their matter. By matter I mean everything that comes within the domain of actual experience; that is to say, the facts of history and the facts of nature, taken in and by themselves and in their widest sense. Here it is the *thing* treated of, which gives its peculiar character to the book; so that a book can be important, whoever it was that wrote it.

But in regard to the form, the peculiar character of a book depends upon the *person* who wrote it. It may treat of matters which are accessible to everyone and well known; but it is the way in which they are treated, what it is that is thought about them, that gives the book its value; and this comes from its author. If, then, from this point of view a book is excellent and beyond comparison, so is its author. It follows that if a writer is worth reading, his merit rises just in proportion as he owes little to his matter; therefore, the better known and the more hackneyed this is, the greater he will be. The three great tragedians of Greece, for example, all worked at the same subject-matter.

So when a book is celebrated, care should be taken to note whether it is so on account of its matter or its form; and a distinction should be made accordingly.

Books of great importance on account of their matter may proceed from very ordinary and shallow people, by the fact that they alone have had access to this matter; books, for instance, which describe journeys in distant lands, rare natural phenomena, or experiments; or historical occurrences of which the writers were witnesses, or in connection with which they have spent much time and trouble in the research and special study of original documents.

On the other hand, where the matter is accessible to everyone or very well known, everything will depend upon the form; and what it is that is thought about the matter will give the book all the value it possesses. Here only a really distinguished man will be able to produce anything worth reading; for the others will think nothing but what anyone else can think. They will just produce an impress of their own minds; but this is a print of which everyone possesses the original.

However, the public is very much more concerned to have matter than form; and for this very reason it is deficient in any high degree of culture. The public shows its preference in this respect in the most laughable way when it comes to deal with poetry; for there it devotes much trouble to the task of tracking out the actual events or personal circumstances in the life of the poet which served as the occasion of his various works; nay, these events and circumstances come in the end to be of greater importance than the works themselves; and rather than read Goethe himself, people prefer to read what has been written about him, and to study the legend of Faust more industriously than the drama of that name. And when Bürger declared that "people would write learned disquisitions on the question, Who Leonora really was," we find this literally fulfilled in Goethe's case; for we now possess a great many learned disquisitions on Faust and the legend attaching to him. Study of this kind is, and remains, devoted to the material of the drama alone. To give such preference to the matter over the form, is as though a man were to take a fine Etruscan vase, not to admire its shape or coloring, but to make a chemical analysis of the clay and paint of which it is composed.

The attempt to produce an effect by means of the material employed—an attempt which panders to this evil tendency of the public—is most to be condemned in branches of literature where any merit there may be lies expressly in the form; I mean, in poetical work. For all that, it is not rare to find bad dramatists trying to fill the house by means of the matter about which they write. For example, authors of this kind do not shrink from putting on the stage any man who is in any way celebrated, no matter whether his life may have been entirely devoid of dramatic incident; and sometimes, even, they do not wait until the persons immediately connected with him are dead.

The distinction between matter and form to which I am here alluding also holds good of conversation. The chief qualities which enable a man to converse well are intelligence, discernment, wit and vivacity: these supply the form of conversation. But it is not long before attention has to be paid to the matter of which he speaks; in other words, the subjects about which it is possible to converse with him—his knowledge. If this is very small, his conversation will not be worth anything, unless he possesses the above-named formal qualities in a very exceptional degree; for he will have nothing to talk about but those facts of life and nature which everybody knows. It will be just the opposite, however, if a man is deficient in these formal qualities, but has an amount of knowledge which lends value to what he says. This value will then depend entirely upon the matter of his conversation; for, as the Spanish proverb has it, *mas sabe el necio en su casa, que el sabio en la agena*—a fool knows more of his own business than a wise man does of others.

ON STYLE

STYLE is the physiognomy of the mind, and a safer index to character than the face. To imitate another man's style is like wearing a mask, which, be it never so fine, is not long in arousing disgust and abhorrence, because it is lifeless; so that even the ugliest living face is better. Hence those who write in Latin and copy the manner of ancient authors, may be said to speak through a mask; the reader, it is true, hears what they say, but he cannot observe their physiognomy too; he cannot see their *style*. With the Latin works of writers who think for themselves, the case is different, and their style is visible; writers, I mean, who have not condescended to any sort of imitation, such as Scotus Erigena, Petrarch, Bacon, Descartes, Spinoza, and many others. An affectation in style is like making grimaces. Further, the language in which a man writes is the physiognomy of the nation to which he belongs; and here there are many hard and fast differences, beginning from the language of the Greeks, down to that of the Caribbean islanders.

To form a provincial estimate of the value of a writer's productions, it is not directly necessary to know the subject on which he has thought, or what it is that he has said about it; that would imply a perusal of all his works. It will be enough, in the main, to know *how* he has thought. This, which means the essential temper or general quality of his mind, may be precisely determined by his style. A man's style shows the *formal* nature of all his thoughts— the formal nature which can never change, be the subject or the character of his thoughts what it may: it is, as it were, the dough out of which all the contents of his mind are kneaded. When Eulenspiegel was asked how long it would take to walk to the next village, he gave the seemingly incongruous answer: *Walk*. He wanted to find out by the man's pace the distance he would cover in a given time. In the same way, when I have read a few pages of an author, I know fairly well how far he can bring me.

Every mediocre writer tries to mask his own natural style, because in his heart he knows the truth of what I am saying. He is thus forced, at the outset, to give up any attempt at being frank or naïve—a privilege which is thereby reserved for superior minds, conscious of their own worth, and therefore sure of themselves. What I mean is that these everyday writers are absolutely unable to resolve upon writing just as they think; because they have a notion that, were they to do so, their work might possibly look very childish and simple. For all that, it would not be without its value. If they would only go honestly to work, and say, quite simply, the things they have really thought, and just as they have thought them, these writers would be readable and, within their own proper sphere, even instructive.

But instead of that, they try to make the reader believe that their thoughts have gone much further and deeper than is really the case. They say what they have to say in long sentences that wind about in a forced and unnatural way; they coin new words and write prolix periods which go round and round the thought and wrap it up in a sort of disguise. They tremble between the two separate aims of communicating what they want to say and of concealing it. Their object is to dress it up so that it may look learned or deep, in order to give people the impression that there is very much more in it than for the moment meets the eye. They either jot down their thoughts bit by bit, in short, ambiguous, and paradoxical sentences, which apparently mean much more than they say,—of this kind of writing Schelling's treatises on natural philosophy are a splendid instance; or else they hold forth with a deluge of words and the most intolerable diffusiveness, as though no end of fuss were necessary to make the reader understand the deep meaning of their sentences, whereas it is some quite simple if not actually trivial idea,—examples of which may be found in plenty in the popular works of Fichte, and the philosophical manuals of a hundred other miserable dunces not worth mentioning; or, again, they try to write in some particular style which they been pleased to take up and think very grand, a style, for example, *par excellence* profound and scientific, where the reader is tormented to death by the narcotic effect of longspun periods without a single idea in them,—such as are furnished in a special measure by those most impudent of all mortals, the Hegelians [1]; or it may be that it is an intellectual style they have striven after, where it seems as though their object were to go crazy altogether; and so on in many other cases. All these endeavors to put off the *nascetur ridiculus mus*—to avoid showing the funny little creature that is born after such mighty throes—often make it difficult to know what it is that they really mean. And then, too, they write down words, nay, even whole sentences, without attaching any meaning to them themselves, but in the hope that some one else will get sense out of them.

And what is at the bottom of all this? Nothing but the untiring effort to sell words for thoughts; a mode of merchandise that is always trying to make fresh openings for itself, and by means of odd expressions, turns of phrase, and combinations of every sort, whether new or

[1] In their Hegel-gazette, commonly known as *Jahrbücher der wissenschaftlichen Literatur.*

used in a new sense, to produce the appearance of intellect in order to make up for the very painfully felt lack of it.

It is amusing to see how writers with this object in view will attempt first one mannerism and then another, as though they were putting on the mask of intellect! This mask may possibly deceive the inexperienced for a while, until it is seen to be a dead thing, with no life in it at all; it is then laughed at and exchanged for another. Such an author will at one moment write in a dithyrambic vein, as though he were tipsy; at another, nay, on the very next page, he will be pompous, severe, profundly learned and prolix, stumbling on in the most cumbrous way and chopping up everything very small; like the late Christian Wolf, only in a modern dress. Longest of all lasts the mask of unintelligibility; but this is only in Germany, whither it was introduced by Fichte, perfected by Schelling, and carried to its highest pitch in Hegel—always with the best results.

And yet nothing is easier than to write so that no one can understand; just as contrarily, nothing is more difficult than to express deep things in such a way that every one must necessarily grasp them. All the arts and tricks I have been mentioning are rendered superfluous if the author really has any brains; for that allows him to show himself as he is, and confirms to all time Horace's maxim that good sense is the source and origin of good style:

Scribendi recte sapere est et principium et fons.

But those authors I have named are like certain workers in metal, who try a hundred different compounds to take the place of gold—the only metal which can never have any substitute. Rather than do that, there is nothing against which a writer should be more upon his guard than the manifest endeavor to exhibit more intellect than he really has; because this makes the reader suspect that he possesses very little; since it is always the case that if a man affects anything, whatever it may be, it is just there that he is deficient.

That is why it is praise to an author to say that he is *naïve;* it means that he need not shrink from showing himself as he is. Generally speaking, to be naïve is to be attractive; while lack of naturalness is everywhere repulsive. As a matter of fact we find that every really great writer tries to express his thoughts as purely, clearly, definitely and shortly as possible. Simplicity has always been held to be a mark of truth; it is also a mark of genius. Style receives its beauty from the thought it expresses; but with sham-thinkers the thoughts are supposed to be fine because of the style. Style is nothing but the mere silhouette of thought; and an obscure or bad style means a dull or confused brain.

The first rule, then, for ι good style is that *the author should have something to say;* nay, this is in itself almost all that is necessary. Ah, how much it means! The neglect of this rule is a fundamental trait in the philosophical writing, and, in fact, in all the reflective literature, of my country, more especially since Fichte. These writers all let it be seen that they want to appear as though they had something to say; whereas they have nothing to say. Writing of this kind was brought in by the pseudo-philosophers at the Universities, and now it is current everywhere, even among the first literary notabilities of the age. It is the mother of that strained and vague style, where there seem to be two or even more meanings in the sentence; also of that prolix and cumbrous manner of expression, called *le stile empesé;* again, of that mere waste of words which consists in pouring them out like a flood; finally, of that trick of concealing the direst poverty of thought under a farrago of never-ending chatter, which clacks away like a windmill and quite stupefies one—stuff which a man may read for hours together without getting hold of a single clearly expressed and definite idea.[2] However, people are easy-going, and they have formed the habit of reading page upon page of all sorts of such verbiage, without having any particular idea of what the author really means. They fancy it is all as it should be, and fail to discover that he is writing simply for writing's sake.

On the other hand, a good author, fertile in ideas, soon wins his reader's confidence that, when he writes, he has really and truly *something to say;* and this gives the intelligent reader patience to follow him with attention. Such an author, just because he really has something to say, will never fail to express himself in the simplest and most straightforward manner; because his object is to awake the very same thought in the reader that he has in himself, and no other. So he will be able to affirm with Boileau that his thoughts are everywhere open to the light of the day, and that his verse always says something, whether it says it well or ill:

Ma pensée au grand jour partout s'offre et s'expose,
Et mon vers, bien ou mal, dit toujours quelque chose:

while of the writers previously described it may be asserted, in the words of the same poet, that they talk much and never say anything at all—*qui parlant beaucoup ne disent jamais rien.*

Another characteristic of such writers is that they always avoid a positive assertion wherever they can possibly do so, in order to leave a loophole for escape in case of need. Hence they never fail to choose the more *abstract* way of expressing themselves; whereas intelligent people use the more *concrete;* because the latter brings things more within

[2] Select examples of the art of writing in this style are to be found almost *passim* in the *Jahrbücher* published at Halle, afterwards called the *Deutschen Jahrbücher.*

the range of actual demonstration, which is the source of all evidence.

There are many examples proving this preference for abstract expression; and a particularly ridiculous one is afforded by the use of the verb *to condition* in the sense of *to cause* or *to produce*. People say *to condition something* instead of *to cause it*, because being abstract and indefinite it says less; it affirms that *A* cannot happen without *B*, instead of that *A* is caused by *B*. A back door is always left open; and this suits people whose secret knowledge of their own incapacity inspires them with a perpetual terror of all positive assertion; while with other people it is merely the effect of that tendency by which everything that is stupid in literature or bad in life is immediately imitated —a fact proved in either case by the rapid way in which it spreads. The Englishman uses his own judgment in what he writes as well as in what he does; but there is no nation of which this eulogy is less true than of the Germans. The consequence of this state of things is that the word *cause* has of late almost disappeared from the language of literature, and people talk only of *condition*. The fact is worth mentioning because it is so characteristically ridiculous.

The very fact that these commonplace authors are never more than half-conscious when they write, would be enough to account for their dullness of mind and the tedious things they produce. I say they are only half-conscious, because they really do not themselves understand the meaning of the words they use: they take words ready-made and commit them to memory. Hence when they write, it is not so much words as whole phrases that they put together—*phrases banales*. This is the explanation of that palpable lack of clearly-expressed thought in what they say. The fact is that they do not possess the die to give this stamp to their writing; clear thought of their own is just what they have not got. And what do we find in its place?—a vague, enigmatical intermixture of words, current phrases, hackneyed terms, and fashionable expressions. The result is that the foggy stuff they write is like a page printed with very old type.

On the other hand, an intelligent author really speaks to us when he writes, and that is why he is able to rouse our interest and commune with us. It is the intelligent author alone who puts individual words together with a full consciousness of their meaning, and chooses them with deliberate design. Consequently, his discourse stands to that of the writer described above, much as a picture that has been really painted, to one that has been produced by the use of a stencil. In the one case, every word, every touch of the brush, has a special purpose; in the other, all is done mechanically. The same distinction may be observed in music. For just as Lichtenberg says that Garrick's soul seemed to be in every muscle in his body, so it is the omnipresence of intellect that always and everywhere characterizes the work of genius.

I have alluded to the tediousness which marks the works of these writers; and in this connection it is to be observed, generally, that tediousness is of two kinds; objective and subjective. A work is objectively tedious when it contains the defect in question; that is to say, when its author has no perfectly clear thought or knowledge to communicate. For if a man has any clear thought or knowledge in him, his aim will be to communicate it, and he will direct his energies to this end; so that the ideas he furnishes are everywhere clearly expressed. The result is that he is neither diffuse, nor unmeaning, nor confused, and consequently not tedious. In such a case, even though the author is at bottom in error, the error is at any rate clearly worked out and well thought over, so that it is at least formally correct; and thus some value always attaches to the work. But for the same reason a work that is objectively tedious is at all times devoid of any value whatever.

The other kind of tediousness is only relative: a reader may find a work dull because he has no interest in the question treated of in it, and this means that his intellect is restricted. The best work may, therefore, be tedious subjectively, tedious, I mean, to this or that particular person; just as, contrarily, the worst work may be subjectively engrossing to this or that particular person who has an interest in the question treated of, or in the writer of the book.

It would generally serve writers in good stead if they would see that, whilst a man should, if possible, think like a great genius, he should talk the same language as everyone else. Authors should use common words to say uncommon things. But they do just the opposite. We find them trying to wrap up trivial ideas in grand words, and to clothe their very ordinary thoughts in the most extraordinary phrases, the most far-fetched, unnatural, and out-of-the-way expressions. Their sentences perpetually stalk about on stilts. They take so much pleasure in bombast, and write in such a high-flown, bloated, affected, hyperbolical and acrobatic style that their prototype is Ancient Pistol, whom his friend Falstaff once impatiently told to say what he had to say *like a man of this world*.[3]

There is no expression in any other language exactly answering to the French *stile empesé;* but the thing itself exists all the more often. When associated with affectation, it is in literature what assumption of dignity, grand airs and primness are in society; and equally intolerable. Dullness of mind is fond of donning this dress; just as in ordinary life it is stupid people who like being demure and formal.

[3] *King Henry IV.,* Part II. Act. v. Sc. 3.

An author who writes in the prim style resembles a man who dresses himself up in order to avoid being confounded or put on the same level with a mob—a risk never run by the *gentleman,* even in his worst clothes. The plebeian may be known by a certain showiness of attire and a wish to have everything spick and span; and in the same way, the commonplace person is betrayed by his style.

Nevertheless, an author follows a false aim if he tries to write exactly as he speaks. There is no style of writing but should have a certain trace of kinship with the *epigraphic* or *monumental* style, which is, indeed, the ancestor of all styles. For an author to write as he speaks is just as reprehensible as the opposite fault, to speak as he writes; for this gives a pedantic effect to what he says, and at the same time makes him hardly intelligible.

An obscure and vague manner of expression is always and everywhere a very bad sign. In ninety-nine cases out of a hundred it comes from vagueness of thought; and this again almost always means that there is something radically wrong and incongruous about the thought itself—in a word, that it is incorrect. When a right thought springs up in the mind, it strives after expression and is not long in reaching it; for clear thought easily find words to fit it. If a man is capable of thinking anything at all, he is also always able to express it in clear, intelligible, and unambiguous terms. Those writers who construct difficult, obscure, involved, and equivocal sentences, most certainly do not know aright what it is that they want to say: they have only a dull consciousness of it, which is still in the stage of struggle to shape itself as thought. Often, indeed, their desire is to conceal from themselves and others that they really have nothing at all to say. They wish to appear to know what they do not know, to think what they do not think, to say what they do not say. If a man has some real communication to make, which will he choose—

an indistinct or a clear way of expressing himself? Even Quintilian remarks that things which are said by a highly educated man are often easier to understand and much clearer; and that the less educated a man is, the more obscurely he will write—*plerumque accidit ut faciliora sint ad intelligendum et lucidiora multo que a doctissimo quoque dicuntur . . . . Erit ergo etiam obscurior quo quisque deterior.*

An author should avoid enigmatical phrases; he should know whether he wants to say a thing or does not want to say it. It is this indecision of style that makes so many writers insipid. The only case that offers an exception to this rule arises when it is necessary to make a remark that is in some way improper.

As exaggeration generally produces an effect the opposite of that aimed at; so words, it is true, serve to make thought intelligible—but only up to a certain point. If words are heaped up beyond it, the thought becomes more and more obscure again. To find where the point lies is the problem of style, and the business of the critical faculty; for a word too much always defeats its purpose. This is what Voltaire means when he says that *the adjective is the enemy of the substantive.* But, as we have seen, many people try to conceal their poverty of thought under a flood of verbiage.

Accordingly let all redundacy be avoided, all stringing together of remarks which have no meaning and are not worth perusal. A writer must make a sparing use of the reader's time, patience and attention; so as to lead him to believe that his author writes what is worth careful study, and will reward the time spent upon it. It is always better to omit something good than to add that which is not worth saying at all. This is the right application of Hesiod's maxim, πλέον ἥμισυ πάντος[4]—the half is more

[4] *Works and Days,* 40.

than the whole. *Le secret pour être ennuyeux, c'est de tout dire.* Therefore, if possible, the quintessence only! mere leading thoughts! nothing that the reader would think for himself. To use many words to communicate few thoughts is everywhere the unmistakable sign of mediocrity. To gather much thought into few words stamps the man of genius.

Truth is most beautiful undraped; and the impression it makes is deep in proportion as its expression has been simple. This is so, partly because it then takes unobstructed possession of the hearer's whole soul, and leaves him no by-thought to distract him; partly, also, because he feels that here he is not being corrupted or cheated by the arts of rhetoric, but that all the effect of what is said comes from the thing itself. For instance, what declamation on the vanity of human existence could ever be more telling than the words of Job? *Man that is born of a woman hath but a short time to live and is full of misery. He cometh up, and is cut down, like a flower; he fleeth as it were a shadow, and never continueth in one stay.*

For the same reason Goethe's naïve poetry is incomparably greater than Schiller's rhetoric. It is this, again, that makes many popular songs so affecting. As in architecture an excess of decoration is to be avoided, so in the art of literature a writer must guard against all rhetorical finery, all useless amplification, and all superfluity of expression in general; in a word, he must strive after *chastity* of style. Every word that can be spared is hurtful if it remains. The law of simplicity and naïveté holds good of all fine art; for it is quite possible to be at once simple and sublime.

True brevity of expression consists in everywhere saying only what is worth saying, and in avoiding tedious detail about things which everyone can supply for himself. This involves correct discrimination between what is necessary

and what is superfluous. A writer should never be brief
at the expense of being clear, to say nothing of being
grammatical. It shows lamentable want of judgment to
weaken the expression of a thought, or to stunt the meaning of a period for the sake of using a few words less. But
this is the precise endeavor of that false brevity nowadays
so much in vogue, which proceeds by leaving out useful
words and even by sacrificing grammar and logic. It is
not only that such writers spare a word by making a
single verb or adjective to do duty for several different periods, so that the reader, as it were, has to grope his way
through them in the dark; they also practice, in many
other respects, an unseemingly economy of speech, in the
effort to effect what they foolishly take to be brevity of
expression and conciseness of syle. By omitting something
that might have thrown a light over the whole sentence,
they turn it into a conundrum, which the reader tries to
· solve by going over it again and again.[5]

It is wealth and weight of thought, and nothing else,
that gives brevity to style, and makes it concise and pregnant. If a writer's ideas are important, luminous, and
generally worth communicating, they will necessarily fur-
nish matter and substance enough to fill out the periods
which give them expression, and make these in all their
parts both grammatically and verbally complete; and so
much will this be the case that no one will ever find them
hollow, empty or feeble. The diction will everywhere be

[5] *Translator's Note.*—In the original, Schopenhauer here
enters upon a lengthy examination of certain common errors in
the writing and speaking of German. His remarks are addressed to his own countrymen, and would lose all point, even
if they were intelligible, in an English translation. But for
those who practice their German by conversing or corresponding
with Germans, let me recommend what he there says as a useful
corrective to a slipshod style, such as can easily be contracted
if it is assumed that the natives of a country always know their
own language perfectly.

brief and pregnant, and allow the thought to find intelligible and easy expression, and even unfold and move about with grace.

Therefore instead of contracting his words and forms of speech, let a writer enlarge his thoughts. If a man has been thinned by illness and finds his clothes too big, it is not by cutting them down, but by recovering his usual bodily condition, that he ought to make them fit him again.

Let me here mention an error of style, very prevalent nowadays, and, in the degraded state of literature and the neglect of ancient languages, always on the increase; I mean *subjectivity*. A writer commits this error when he thinks it enough if he himself knows what he means and wants to say, and takes no thought for the reader, who is left to get at the bottom of it as best he can. This is as though the author were holding a monologue; whereas, it ought to be a dialogue; and a dialogue, too, in which he must express himself all the more clearly inasmuch as he cannot hear the questions of his interlocutor.

Style should for this very reason never be subjective, but *objective;* and it will not be objective unless the words are so set down that they directly force the reader to think precisely the same thing as the author thought when he wrote them. Nor will this result be obtained unless the author has always been careful to remember that thought so far follows the law of gravity that it travels from head to paper much more easily than from paper to head; so that he must assist the latter passage by every means in his power. If he does this, a writer's words will have a purely objective effect, like that of a finished picture in oils; whilst the subjective style is not much more certain in its working than spots on the wall, which look like figures only to one whose phantasy has been accidentally aroused by them; other people see nothing but spots and blurs. The difference in question applies to literary method as a whole; but it is often established also in particular instances. For example, in a recently published work I found the following sentence: *I have not written in order to increase the number of existing books.* This means just the opposite of what the writer wanted to say, and is nonsense as well.

He who writes carelessly confesses thereby at the very outset that he does not attach much importance to his own thoughts. For it is only where a man is convinced of the truth and importance of his thoughts, that he feels the enthusiasm necessary for an untiring and assiduous effort to find the clearest, finest, and strongest expression for them, —just as for sacred relics or priceless works of art there are provided silvern or golden receptacles. It was this feeling that led ancient authors, whose thoughts, expressed in their own words, have lived thousands of years, and therefore bear the honored title of *classics*, always to write with care. Plato, indeed, is said to have written the introduction to his *Republic* seven times over in different ways.[6]

As neglect of dress betrays want of respect for the company a man meets, so a hasty, careless, bad style shows an outrageous lack of regard for the reader, who then rightly punishes it by refusing to read the book. It is especially amusing to see reviewers criticising the works of others in their own most careless style—the style of a hireling. It is as though a judge were to come into court in dressing-gown and slippers! If I see a man badly and dirtily dressed, I feel some hesitation, at first, in entering into conversation with him: and when, on taking up a book, I am struck at once by the negligence of its style, I put it away.

[6] *Translator's Note.*—It is a fact worth mentioning that the first twelve words of the *Republic* are placed in the exact order which would be natural in English.

Good writing should be governed by the rule that a man can think only one thing clearly at a time; and, therefore, that he should not be expected to think two or even more things in one and the same moment. But this is what is done when a writer breaks up his principal sentence into little pieces, for the purpose of pushing into the gaps thus made two or three other thoughts by way of parenthesis; thereby unnecessarily and wantonly confusing the reader. And here it is again my own countrymen who are chiefly in fault. That German lends itself to this way of writing, makes the thing possible, but does not justify it. No prose reads more easily or pleasantly than French, because, as a rule, it is free from the error in question. The Frenchman strings his thoughts together, as far as he can, in the most logical and natural order, and so lays them before his reader one after the other for convenient deliberation, so that every one of them may receive undivided attention. The German, on the other hand, weaves them together into a sentence which he twists and crosses, and crosses and twists again; because he wants to say six things all at once, instead of advancing them one by one. His aim should be to attract and hold the reader's attention; but, above and beyond neglect of this aim, he demands from the reader that he shall set the above mentioned rule at defiance, and think three or four different thoughts at one and the same time; or since that is impossible, that his thoughts shall succeed each other as quickly as the vibrations of a cord. In this way an author lays the foundation of his *stile empesé*, which is then carried to perfection by the use of high-flown, pompous expressions to communicate the simplest things, and other artifices of the same kind.

In those long sentences rich in involved parenthesis, like a box of boxes one within another, and padded out like roast geese stuffed with apples, it is really the *memory* that is chiefly taxed; while it is the understanding and the judgment which should be called into play, instead of having their activity thereby actually hindered and weakened.[7] This kind of sentence furnishes the reader with mere half-phrases, which he is then called upon to collect carefully and store up in his memory, as though they were the pieces of a torn letter, afterwards to be completed and made sense of by the other halves to which they respectively belong. He is expected to go on reading for a little without exercising any thought, nay, exerting only his memory, in the hope that, when he comes to the end of the sentence, he may see its meaning and so receive something to think about; and he is thus given a great deal to learn by heart before obtaining anything to understand. This is manifestly wrong and an abuse of the reader's patience.

The ordinary writer has an unmistakable preference for this style, because it causes the reader to spend time and trouble in understanding that which he would have understood in a moment without it; and this makes it look as though the writer had more depth and intelligence than the reader. This is, indeed, one of those artifices referred to above, by means of which mediocre authors unconsciously, and as it were by instinct, strive to conceal their poverty of thought and give an appearance of the opposite. Their ingenuity in this respect is really astounding.

It is manifestly against all sound reason to put one thought obliquely on top of another, as though both together formed a wooden cross. But this is what is done where a writer interrupts what he has begun to say, for the purpose of inserting some quite alien matter; thus depositing with the reader a meaningless half-sentence, and bidding him keep it until the completion comes. It is much

[7] *Translator's Note.*—This sentence in the original is obviously meant to illustrate the fault of which it speaks. It does so by the use of a construction very common in German, but happily unknown in English; where, however, the fault itself exists none the less, though in different form.

as though a man were to treat his guests by handing them an empty plate in the hope of something appearing upon it. Commas used for a similar purpose belong to the same family as notes at the foot of the page and parenthesis in the middle of the text; all three differ only in degree. If Demosthenes and Cicero occasionally inserted words by parenthesis, they would have done better to have refrained.

But this style of writing becomes the height of absurdity when the parenthesis are not even fitted into the frame of the sentence, but wedged in so as directly to shatter it. If, for instance, it is an impertinent thing to interrupt another person when he is speaking, it is no less impertinent to interrupt oneself. But all bad, careless, and hasty authors, who scribble with the bread actually before their eyes, use this style of writing six times on a page, and rejoice in it. It consists in—it is advisable to give rule and example together, wherever it is possible—breaking up one phrase in order to glue in another. Nor is it merely out of laziness that they write thus. They do it out of stupidity; they think there is a charming *légèreté* about it; that it gives life to what they say. No doubt there are a few rare cases where such a form of sentence may be pardonable.

Few write in the way in which an architect builds; who, before he sets to work, sketches out his plan and thinks it over down to its smallest details. Nay, most people write only as though they were playing dominoes; and, as in this game, the pieces are arranged half by design, half by chance, so it is with the sequence and connection of their sentences. They only have an idea of what the general shape of their work will be, and of the aim they set before themselves. Many are ignorant even of this, and write as the coral-insects build; period joins to period, and the Lord only knows what the author means.

Life now-a-days goes at a gallop; and the way this affects literature is to make it extremely superficial and slovenly.

ON THE STUDY OF LATIN

THE abolition of Latin as the universal language of learned men, together with the rise of that provincialism which attaches to national literatures, has been a real misfortune for the cause of knowledge in Europe. For it was chiefly through the medium of the Latin language that a learned public existed in Europe at all—a public to which every book as it came out directly appealed. The number of minds in the whole of Europe that are capable of thinking and judging is small, as it is; but when the audience is broken up and severed by differences of language, the good these minds can do is very much weakened. This is a great disadvantage; but a second and worse one will follow, namely, that the ancient languages will cease to be taught at all. The neglect of them is rapidly gaining ground both in France and Germany.

If it should really come to this, then farewell, humanity! farewell, noble taste and high thinking! The age of barbarism will return, in spite of railways, telegraphs and balloons. We shall thus in the end lose one more advantage possessed by all our ancestors. For Latin is not only a key to the knowledge of Roman antiquity; it also directly opens up to us the Middle Age in every country in Europe, and modern times as well, down to about the year 1750. Erigena, for example, in the ninth century, John of Salisbury in the twelfth, Raimond Lully in the thirteenth, with a hundred others, speak straight to us in the very language that they naturally adopted in thinking of learned matters. They thus come quite close to us even at this distance of time: we are in direct contact with them, and really come to know them. How would it have been if every one of them spoke in the language that was peculiar to his time and country? We should not understand even the half of what they said. A real intellectual contact with them would be impossible. We should see them like shadows on the farthest horizon, or, may be, through the translator's telescope.

It was with an eye to the advantage of writing in Latin that Bacon, as he himself expressly states, proceeded to translate his *Essays* into that language, under the title *Sermones fideles;* at which work Hobbes assisted him.[1]

Here let me observe, by way of parenthesis, that when patriotism tries to urge its claims in the domain of knowledge, it commits an offence which should not be tolerated. For in those purely human questions which interest all men alike, where truth, insight, beauty, should be a sole account, what can be more impertinent than to let preference for the nation to which a man's precious self happens to belong, affect the balance of judgment, and thus supply a reason for doing violence to truth and being unjust to the great minds of a foreign country in order to make much of the smaller minds of one's own! Still, there are writers in every nation in Europe, who afford examples of this vulgar feeling. It is this which led Yriarte to caricature them in the thirty-third of his charming *Literary Fables.*[2]

[1] Cf. Thomae Hobbes vita: *Carolopoli apud Eleutherium Anglicum,* 1681, p. 22.

[2] *Translator's Note.*—Tomas de Yriarte (1750-91), a Spanish poet, and keeper of archives in the War Office at Madrid. His two best known works are a didactic poem, entitled *La Musica,* and the *Fables* here quoted, which satirize the peculiar foibles of literary men. They have been translated into many languages; into English by Rockliffe (3rd edition, 1866). The fable in question describes how, at a picnic of the animals, a discussion arose as to which of them carried off the palm for superiority of talent. The praises of the ant, the dog, the bee, and the parrot were sung in turn; but at last the ostrich stood up and declared for the dromedary. Whereupon the dromedary

In learning a language, the chief difficulty consists in making acquaintance with every idea which it expresses, even though it should use words for which there is no exact equivalent in the mother tongue; and this often happens. In learning a new language a man has, as it were, to mark out in his mind the boundaries of quite new spheres of ideas, with the result that spheres of ideas arise where none were before. Thus he not only learns words, he gains ideas too.

This is nowhere so much the case as in learning ancient languages, for the differences they present in their mode of expression as compared with modern languages is greater than can be found amongst modern languages as compared with one another. This is shown by the fact that in translating into Latin, recourse must be had to quite other turns of phrase than are used in the original. The thought that is to be translated has to be melted down and recast; in other words, it must be analyzed and then recomposed. It is just this process which makes the study of the ancient languages contribute so much to the education of the mind.

It follows from this that a man's thought varies according to the language in which he speaks. His ideas undergo a fresh modification, a different shading, as it were, in the study of every new language. Hence an acquaintance with many languages is not only of much indirect advantage, but it is also a direct means of mental culture, in that it corrects and matures ideas by giving prominence to their many-sided nature and their different varieties of meaning, as also that it increases dexterity of thought; for in the

---

stood up and declared for the ostrich. No one could discover the reason for this mutual compliment. Was it because both were such uncouth beasts, or had such long necks, or were neither of them particularly clever or beautiful? or was it because each had a hump? *No!* said the fox, *you are all wrong. Don't you see they are both foreigners?* Cannot the same be said of many men of learning?

process of learning many languages, ideas become more and more independent of words. The ancient languages effect this to a greater degree than the modern, in virtue of the difference to which I have alluded.

From what I have said, it is obvious that to imitate the style of the ancients in their own language, which is so very much superior to ours in point of grammatical perfection, is the best way of preparing for a skillful and finished expression of thought in the mother-tongue. Nay, if a man wants to be a great writer, he must not omit to do this: just as, in the case of sculpture or painting, the student must educate himself by copying the great masterpieces of the past, before proceeding to original work. It is only by learning to write Latin that a man comes to treat diction as an art. The material in this art is language, which must therefore be handled with the greatest care and delicacy.

The result of such study is that a writer will pay keen attention to the meaning and value of words, their order and connection, their grammatical forms. He will learn how to weigh them with precision, and so become an expert in the use of that precious instrument which is meant not only to express valuable thought, but to preserve it as well. Further, he will learn to feel respect for the language in which he writes and thus be saved from any attempt to remodel it by arbitrary and capricious treatment. Without this schooling, a man's writing may easily degenerate into mere chatter.

To be entirely ignorant of the Latin language is like being in a fine country on a misty day. The horizon is extremely limited. Nothing can be seen clearly except that which is quite close; a few steps beyond, everything is buried in obscurity. But the Latinist has a wide view, embracing modern times, the Middle Age and Antiquity;

and his mental horizon is still further enlarged if he studies Greek or even Sanscrit.

If a man knows no Latin, he belongs to the vulgar, even though he be a great virtuoso on the electrical machine and have the base of hydrofluoric acid in his crucible.

There is no better recreation for the mind than the study of the ancient classics. Take any one of them into your hand, be it only for half an hour, and you will feel yourself refreshed, relieved, purified, ennobled, strengthened; just as though you had quenched your thirst at some pure spring. Is this the effect of the old language and its perfect expression, or is it the greatness of the minds whose works remain unharmed and unweakened by the lapse of a thousand years? Perhaps both together. But this I know. If the threatened calamity should ever come, and the ancient languages cease to be taught, a new literature will arise, of such barbarous, shallow and worthless stuff as never was seen before.

ON MEN OF LEARNING

WHEN one sees the number and variety of institutions which exist for the purpose of education, and the vast throng of scholars and masters, one might fancy the human race to be very much concerned about truth and wisdom. But here, too, appearances are deceptive. The masters teach in order to gain money, and strive, not after wisdom, but the outward show and reputation of it; and the scholars learn, not for the sake of knowledge and insight, but to be able to chatter and give themselves airs. Every thirty years a new race comes into the world—a youngster that knows nothing about anything, and after summarily devouring in all haste the results of human knowledge as they have been accumulated for thousands of years, aspires to be thought cleverer than the whole of the past. For this purpose he goes to the University, and takes to reading books—new books, as being of his own age and standing. Everything he reads must be briefly put, must be new! he is new himself. Then he falls to and criticises. And here I am not taking the slightest account of studies pursued for the sole object of making a living.

Students, and learned persons of all sorts and every age, aim as a rule at acquiring *information* rather than insight. They pique themselves upon knowing about everything—stones, plants, battles, experiments, and all the books in existence. It never occurs to them that information is only a means of insight, and in itself of little or no value; that it is his way of *thinking* that makes a man a philosopher. When I hear of these portents of learning and their imposing erudition, I sometimes say to myself: Ah, how little they must have had to think about, to have been able to read so much! And when I actually find it reported of the elder Pliny that he was continually reading or being read to, at table, on a journey, or in his bath, the question forces itself upon my mind, whether the man was so very lacking in thought of his own that he had to have alien thought incessantly instilled into him; as though he were a consumptive patient taking jellies to keep himself alive. And neither his undiscerning credulity nor his inexpressibly repulsive and barely intelligible style—which seems like a man taking notes, and economical of paper—is of a kind to give me high opinion of his power of independent thought.

We have seen that much reading and learning is prejudicial to thinking for oneself; and, in the same way, through much writing and teaching, a man loses the habit of being quite clear, and therefore thorough, in regard to the things he knows and understands; simply because he has left himself no time to acquire clearness or thoroughness. And so, when clear knowledge fails him in his utterances, he is forced to fill out the gaps with words and phrases. It is this, and not the dryness of the subject-matter, that makes most books such tedious reading. There is a saying that a good cook can make a palatable dish even out of an old shoe; and a good writer can make the dryest things interesting.

With by far the largest number of learned men, knowledge is a means, not an end. That is why they will never achieve any great work; because, to do that, he who pursues knowledge must pursue it as an end, and treat everything else, even existence itself, as only a means. For everything which a man fails to pursue for its own sake is but half-pursued; and true excellence, no matter in what sphere, can be attained only where the work has been produced for its own sake alone, and not as a means to further ends.

And so, too, no one will ever succeed in doing anything really great and original in the way of thought, who does not seek to acquire knowledge for himself, and, making this the immediate object of his studies, decline to trouble himself about the knowledge of others. But the average man of learning studies for the purpose of being able to teach and write. His head is like a stomach and intestines which let the food pass through them undigested. That is just why his teaching and writing is of so little use. For it is not upon undigested refuse that people can be nourished, but solely upon the milk which secretes from the very blood itself.

The wig is the appropriate symbol of the man of learning, pure and simple. It adorns the head with a copious quantity of false hair, in lack of one's own: just as erudition means endowing it with a great mass of alien thought. This, to be sure, does not clothe the head so well and naturally, nor is it so generally useful, nor so suited for all purposes, nor so firmly rooted; nor when alien thought is used up, can it be immediately replaced by more from the same source, as is the case with that which springs from soil of one's own. So we find Sterne, in his *Tristram Shandy*, boldly asserting that *an ounce of a man's own wit is worth a ton of other people's.*

And in fact the most profound erudition is no more akin to genius than a collection of dried plants is like Nature, with its constant flow of new life, ever fresh, every young, ever changing. There are no two things more opposed than the childish naïveté of an ancient author and the learning of his commentator.

Dilettanti, dilettanti! This is the slighting way in which those who pursue any branch of art or learning for the love and enjoyment of the thing,—*per il loro diletto,* are spoken of by those who have taken it up for the sake of gain, attracted solely by the prospect of money. This contempt of theirs comes from the base belief that no man will seriously devote himself to a subject, unless he is spurred on to it by want, hunger, or else some form of greed. The public is of the same way of thinking; and hence its general respect for professionals and its distrust of *dilettanti*. But the truth is that the *dilettante* treats his subject as an end, whereas the professional, pure and simple, treats it merely as a means. He alone will be really in earnest about a matter, who has a direct interest therein, takes to it because he likes it, and pursues it *con amore*. It is these, and not hirelings, that have always done the greatest work.

In the republic of letters it is as in other republics; favor is shown to the plain man—he who goes his way in silence and does not set up to be cleverer than others. But the abnormal man is looked upon as threatening danger; people band together against him, and have, oh! such a majority on their side.

The condition of this republic is much like that of a small State in America, where every man is intent only upon his own advantage, and seeks reputation and power for himself, quite heedless of the general weal, which then goes to ruin. So it is in the republic of letters; it is himself, and himself alone, that a man puts forward, because he wants to gain fame. The only thing in which all agree is in trying to keep down a really eminent man, if he should chance to show himself, as one who would be a common peril. From this it is easy to see how it fares with knowledge as a whole.

Between professors and independent men of learning there has always been from of old a certain antagonism, which may perhaps be likened to that existing between dogs and wolves. In virtue of their position, professors enjoy great facilities for becoming known to their contemporaries. Contrarily, independent men of learning enjoy, by their position, great facilities for becoming known to posterity; to which it is necessary that, amongst other and much rarer gifts, a man should have a certain leisure and free-dom. As mankind takes a long time in finding out on whom to bestow its attention, they may both work to-gether side by side.

He who holds a professorship may be said to receive his food in the stall; and this is the best way with ruminant animals. But he who finds his food for himself at the hands of Nature is better off in the open field.

Of human knowledge as a whole and in every branch of it, by far the largest part exists nowhere but on paper, —I mean, in books, that paper memory of mankind. Only a small part of it is at any given period really active in the minds of particular persons. This is due, in the main, to the brevity and uncertainty of life; but it also comes from the fact that men are lazy and bent on pleasure. Every generation attains, on its hasty passage through existence, just so much of human knowledge as it needs, and then soon disappears. Most men of learning are very super-ficial. Then follows a new generation, full of hope, but ignorant, and with everything to learn from the begin-ning. It seizes, in its turn, just so much as it can grasp or find useful on its brief journey and then too goes its way. How badly it would fare with human knowledge if it were not for the art of writing and printing! This it is that makes libraries the only sure and lasting memory of the human race, for its individual members have all of them but a very limited and imperfect one. Hence most men of learning are as loth to have their knowledge examined as merchants to lay bare their books.

Human knowledge extends on all sides farther than the eye can reach; and of that which would be generally worth knowing, no one man can possess even the thou-sandth part.

All branches of learning have thus been so much enlarged that he who would "do something" has to pursue
no more than one subject and disregard all others. In his
own subject he will then, it is true, be superior to the vulgar; but in all else he will belong to it. If we add to this,
neglect of the ancient languages, which is now-a-days on the
increase and doing away with all general education in the
humanities—for a mere smattering of Latin and Greek is of
no use—we shall come to have men of learning who outside
their own subject display an ignorance truly bovine.

An exclusive specialist of this kind stands on a par with
a workman in a factory, whose whole life is spent in making one particular kind of screw, or catch, or handle, for
some particular instrument or machine, in which, indeed,
he attains incredible dexterity. The specialist may also be
likened to a man who lives in his own house and never
leaves it. There he is perfectly familiar with everything,
every little step, corner, or board; much as Quasimodo in
Victor Hugo's *Nôtre Dame* knows the cathedral; but outside it, all is strange and unknown.

For true culture in the humanities it is absolutely necessary that a man should be many-sided and take large
views; and for a man of learning in the higher sense of
the word, an extensive acquaintance with history is needful.
He, however, who wishes to be a complete philosopher,
must gather into his head the remotest ends of human
knowledge: for where else could they ever come together?

It is precisely minds of the first order that will never be
specialists. For their very nature is to make the whole
of existence their problem; and this is a subject upon which
they will in some form provide mankind with a new revelation. For he alone can deserve the name of genius who
takes the All, the Essential, the Universal, for the theme of
his achievements; not he who spends his life in explaining
some special relation of things one to another.

ON THINKING FOR ONESELF

A LIBRARY may be very large; but if it is in disorder, it is not so useful as one that is small but well arranged. In the same way, a man may have a great mass of knowledge, but if he has not worked it up by thinking it over for himself, it has much less value than a far smaller amount which he has thoroughly pondered. For it is only when a man looks at his knowledge from all sides, and combines the things he knows by comparing truth with truth, that he obtains a complete hold over it and gets it into his power. A man cannot turn over anything in his mind unless he knows it; he should, therefore, learn something; but it is only when he has turned it over that he can be said to know it.

Reading and learning are things that anyone can do of his own free will; but not so *thinking*. Thinking must be kindled, like a fire by a draught; it must be sustained by some interest in the matter in hand. This interest may be of purely objective kind, or merely subjective. The latter comes into play only in things that concern us personally Objective interest is confined to heads that think by nature; to whom thinking is as natural as breathing; and they are very rare. This is why most men of learning show so little of it.

It is incredible what a different effect is produced upon the mind by thinking for oneself, as compared with reading. It carries on and intensifies that original difference in the nature of two minds which leads the one to think and the other to read. What I mean is that reading forces alien thoughts upon the mind—thoughts which are as foreign to the drift and temper in which it may be for the moment, as the seal is to the wax on which it stamps its imprint. The mind is thus entirely under compulsion from without; it is driven to think this or that, though for the moment it may not have the slightest impulse or inclination to do so.

But when a man thinks for himself, he follows the impulse of his own mind, which is determined for him at the time, either by his environment or some particular recollection. The visible world of a man's surroundings does not, as reading does, impress a *single* definite thought upon his mind, but merely gives the matter and occasion which lead him to think what is appropriate to his nature and present temper. So it is, that much reading deprives the mind of all elasticity; it is like keeping a spring continually under pressure. The safest way of having no thoughts of one's own is to take up a book every moment one has nothing else to do. It is this practice which explains why erudition makes most men more stupid and silly than they are by nature, and prevents their writings obtaining any measure of success. They remain, in Pope's words:

For ever reading, never to be read![1]

Men of learning are those who have done their reading in the pages of a book. Thinkers and men of genius are those who have gone straight to the book of Nature; it is they who have enlightened the world and carried humanity further on its way.

If a man's thoughts are to have truth and life in them, they must, after all, be his own fundamental thoughts; for these are the only ones that he can fully and wholly understand. To read another's thoughts is like taking the leavings of a meal to which we have not been invited, or putting on the clothes which some unknown visitor has laid

[1] *Dunciad,* iii, 194.

aside. The thought we read is related to the thought which springs up in ourselves, as the fossil-impress of some prehistoric plant to a plant as it buds forth in spring-time.

Reading is nothing more than a substitute for thought of one's own. It means putting the mind into leading-strings. The multitude of books serves only to show how many false paths there are, and how widely astray a man may wander if he follows any of them. But he who is guided by his genius, he who thinks for himself, who thinks spontaneously and exactly, possesses the only compass by which he can steer aright. A man should read only when his own thoughts stagnate at their source, which will happen often enough even with the best of minds. On the other hand, to take up a book for the purpose of scaring away one's own original thoughts is sin against the Holy Spirit. It is like running away from Nature to look at a museum of dried plants or gaze at a landscape in copperplate.

A man may have discovered some portion of truth or wisdom, after spending a great deal of time and trouble in thinking it over for himself and adding thought to thought; and it may sometimes happen that he could have found it all ready to hand in a book and spared himself the trouble. But even so, it is a hundred times more valuable if he has acquired it by thinking it out for himself. For it is only when we gain our knowledge in this way that it enters as an integral part, a living member, into the whole system of our thought; that it stands in complete and firm relation with what we know; that it is understood with all that underlies it and follows from it; that it wears the color, the precise shade, the distinguishing mark, of our own way of thinking; that it comes exactly at the right time, just as we felt the necessity for it; that it stands fast and cannot be forgotten. This is the perfect application, nay, the interpretation, of Goethe's advice to earn our inheritance for ourselves so that we may really possess it:

Was due ererbt von deinen Vätern hast,
Erwirb es, um es zu besitzen.[2]

The man who thinks for himself, forms his own opinions and learns the authorities for them only later on, when they serve but to strengthen his belief in them and in himself. But the book-philosopher starts from the authorities. He reads other people's books, collects their opinions, and so forms a whole for himself, which resembles an automaton made up of anything but flesh and blood. Contrarily, he who thinks for himself creates a work like a living man as made by Nature. For the work comes into being as a man does; the thinking mind is impregnated from without, and it then forms and bears its child.

Truth that has been merely learned is like an artificial limb, a false tooth, a waxen nose; at best, like a nose made out of another's flesh; it adheres to us only because it is put on. But truth acquired by thinking of our own is like a natural limb; it alone really belongs to us. This is the fundamental difference between the thinker and the mere man of learning. The intellectual attainments of a man who thinks for himself resemble a fine painting, where the light and shade are correct, the tone sustained, the color perfectly harmonized; it is true to life. On the other hand, the intellectual attainments of the mere man of learning are like a large palette, full of all sorts of colors, which at most are systematically arranged, but devoid of harmony, connection and meaning.

Reading is thinking with some one else's head instead of one's own. To think with one's own head is always to aim at developing a coherent whole—a system, even though it be not a strictly complete one; and nothing hinders this so much as too strong a current of others' thoughts, such as comes of continual reading. These thoughts, springing every one of them from different minds, belonging to

[2] *Faust*, I. 329.

different systems, and tinged with different colors, never of themselves flow together into an intellectual whole; they never form a unity of knowledge, or insight, or conviction; but, rather, fill the head with a Babylonian confusion of tongues. The mind that is over-loaded with alien thought is thus deprived of all clear insight, and is well-nigh disorganized. This is a state of things observable in many men of learning; and it makes them inferior in sound sense, correct judgment and practical tact, to many illiterate persons who, after obtaining a little knowledge from without, by means of experience, intercourse with others, and a small amount of reading, have always subordinated it to, and embodied it with, their own thought.

The really scientific *thinker* does the same thing as these illiterate persons, but on a larger scale. Although he has need of much knowledge, and so must read a great deal, his mind is nevertheless strong enough to master it all, to assimilate and incorporate it with the system of his thoughts, and so to make it fit in with the organic unity of his insight, which, though vast, is always growing. And in the process, his own thought, like the bass in an organ, always dominates everything and is never drowned by other tones, as happens with minds which are full of mere antiquarian lore; where shreds of music, as it were, in every key, mingle confusedly, and no fundamental note is heard.

Those who have spent their lives in reading, and taken their wisdom from books, are like people who have obtained precise information about a country from the descriptions of many travellers. Such people can tell a great deal about it; but, after all, they have no connected, clear, and profound knowledge of its real condition. But those who have spent their lives in thinking, resemble the travellers themselves; they alone really know what they are talking about; they are acquainted with the actual state of affairs, and are quite at home in the subject.

The thinker stands in the same relation to the ordinary book-philosopher as an eye-witness does to the historian; he speaks from direct knowledge of his own. That is why all those who think for themselves come, at bottom, to much the same conclusion. The differences they present are due to their different points of view; and when these do not affect the matter, they all speak alike. They merely express the result of their own objective perception of things. There are many passages in my works which I have given to the public only after some hesitation, because of their paradoxical nature; and afterwards I have experienced a pleasant surprise in finding the same opinion recorded in the works of great men who lived long ago.

The book-philosopher merely reports what one person has said and another meant, or the objections raised by a third, and so on. He compares different opinions, ponders, criticises, and tries to get at the truth of the matter; herein on a par with the critical historian. For instance, he will set out to inquire whether Leibnitz was not for some time a follower of Spinoza, and questions of a like nature. The curious student of such matters may find conspicuous examples of what I mean in Herbart's *Analytical Elucidation of Morality and Natural Right,* and in the same author's *Letters on Freedom.* Surprise may be felt that a man of the kind should put himself to so much trouble; for, on the face of it, if he would only examine the matter for himself, he would speedily attain his object by the exercise of a little thought. But there is a small difficulty in the way. It does not depend upon his own will. A man can always sit down and read, but not—think. It is with thoughts as with men; they cannot always be summoned at pleasure; we must wait for them to come. Thought about a subject must appear of itself by a happy and harmonious combination of external stimulus with mental temper and attention; and it is just that which never seems to come to these people.

This truth may be illustrated by what happens in the case of matters affecting our own personal interest. When it is necessary to come to some resolution in a matter of that kind, we cannot well sit down at any given moment and think over the merits of the case and make up our mind; for, if we try to do so, we often find ourselves unable, at that particular moment, to keep our mind fixed upon the subject; it wanders off to other things. Aversion to the matter in question is sometimes to blame for this. In such a case we should not use force, but wait for the proper frame of mind to come of itself. It often comes unexpectedly and returns again and again; and the variety of temper in which we approach it at different moments puts the matter always in a fresh light. It is this long process which is understood by the term *a ripe resolution.* For the work of coming to a resolution must be distributed; and in the process much that is overlooked at one moment occurs to us at another; and the repugnance vanishes when we find, as we usually do, on a closer inspection, that things are not so bad as they seemed.

This rule applies to the life of the intellect as well as to matters of practice. A man must wait for the right moment. Not even the greatest mind is capable of thinking for itself at all times. Hence a great mind does well to spend its leisure in reading, which, as I have said, is a substitute for thought; it brings stuff to the mind by letting another person do the thinking; although that is always done in a manner not our own. Therefore, a man should not read too much, in order that his mind may not become accustomed to the substitute and thereby forget the reality; that it may not form the habit of walking in well-worn paths; nor by following an alien course of thought grow a stranger to its own. Least of all should a man quite withdraw his gaze from the real world for the mere sake of reading; as the impulse and the temper which prompt to thought of one's own come far oftener from the world of reality than from the world of books. The real life that a man sees before him is the natural subject of thought; and in its strength as the primary element of existence, it can more easily than anything else rouse and influence the thinking mind.

After these considerations, it will not be matter for surprise that a man who thinks for himself can easily be distinguished from the book-philosopher by the very way in which he talks, by his marked earnestness, and the originality, directness, and personal conviction that stamp all his thoughts and expressions. The book-philosopher, on the other hand, lets it be seen that everything he has is second-hand; that his ideas are like the number and trash of an old furniture-shop, collected together from all quarters. Mentally, he is dull and pointless—a copy of a copy. His literary style is made up of conventional, nay, vulgar phrases, and terms that happen to be current; in this respect much like a small State where all the money that circulates is foreign, because it has no coinage of its own.

Mere experience can as little as reading supply the place of thought. It stands to thinking in the same relation in which eating stands to digestion and assimilation. When experience boasts that to its discoveries alone is due the advancement of the human race, it is as though the mouth were to claim the whole credit of maintaining the body in health.

The works of all truly capable minds are distinguished by a character of *decision* and *definiteness*, which means they are clear and free from obscurity. A truly capable mind always knows definitely and clearly what is it that it wants to express, whether its medium is prose, verse, or music. Other minds are not decisive and not definite; and by this they may be known for what they are.

The characteristic sign of a mind of the highest order is that it always judges at first hand. Everything it ad-

vances is the result of thinking for itself; and this is everywhere evident by the way in which it gives its thoughts
utterance. Such a mind is like a Prince. In the realm of
intellect its authority is imperial, whereas the authority of
minds of a lower order is delegated only; as may be seen
in their style, which has no independent stamp of its own.

Every one who really thinks for himself is so far like a
monarch. His position is undelegated and supreme. His
judgments, like royal decrees, spring from his own sovereign power and proceed directly from himself. He ac-
knowledges authority as little as a monarch admits a
command; he subscribes to nothing but what he has himself authorized. The multitude of common minds, laboring
under all sorts of current opinions, authorities, prejudices,
is like the people, which silently obeys the law and accepts
orders from above.

Those who are so zealous and eager to settle debated
questions by citing authorities, are really glad when they
are able to put the understanding and the insight of others
into the field in place of their own, which are wanting.
Their number is legion. For, as Seneca says, there is no
man but prefers belief to the exercise of judgment—*unus-
quisque mavult credere quam judicare.* In their contro-
versies such people make a promiscuous use of the weapon
of authority, and strike out at one another with it. If
any one chances to become involved in such a contest, he
will do well not to try reason and argument as a mode of
defence; for against a weapon of that kind these people
are like Siegfrieds, with a skin of horn, and dipped in
the flood of incapacity for thinking and judging. They
will meet his attack by bringing up their authorities as a
way of abashing him—*argumentum ad verecundiam,* and
then cry out that they have won the battle.

In the real world, be it never so fair, favorable and
pleasant, we always live subject to the law of gravity

which we have to be constantly overcoming. But in the world of intellect we are disembodied spirits, held in bondage to no such law, and free from penury and distress. Thus it is that there exists no happiness on earth like that which, at the auspicious moment, a fine and fruitful mind finds in itself.

The presence of a thought is like the presence of a woman we love. We fancy we shall never forget the thought nor become indifferent to the dear one. But out of sight, out of mind! The finest thought runs the risk of being irrevocably forgotten if we do not write it down, and the darling of being deserted if we do not marry her.

There are plenty of thoughts which are valuable to the man who thinks them; but only few which have enough strength to produce repercussive or reflect action—I mean, to win the reader's sympathy after they have been put on paper.

But still it must not be forgotten that a true value attaches only to what a man has thought in the first instance *for his own case.* Thinkers may be classed according as they think chiefly for their own case or for that of others. The former are the genuine independent thinkers; they really think and are really independent; they are the true *philosophers;* they alone are in earnest. The pleasure and the happiness of their existence consists in thinking. The others are the *sophists;* they want to seem that which they are not, and seek their happiness in what they hope to get from the world. They are in earnest about nothing else. To which of these two classes a man belongs may be seen by his whole style and manner. Lichtenberg is an example for the former class; Herder, there can be no doubt, belongs to the second.

When one considers how vast and how close to us is *the problem of existence*—this equivocal, tortured, fleeting, dream-like existence of ours—so vast and so close that a man no sooner discovers it than it overshadows and ob-

scures all other problems and aims; and when one sees how
all men, with few and rare exceptions, have no clear consciousness of the problem, nay, seem to be quite unaware
of its presence, but busy themselves with everything rather
than with this, and live on, taking no thought but for the
passing day and the hardly longer span of their own personal future, either expressly discarding the problem or
else over-ready to come to terms with it by adopting some
system of popular metaphysics and letting it satisfy them;
when, I say, one takes all this to heart, one may come to
the opinion that man may be said to be *a thinking being*
only in a very remote sense, and henceforth feel no special
surprise at any trait of human thoughtlessness or folly;
but know, rather, that the normal man's intellectual range
of vision does indeed extend beyond that of the brute,
whose whole existence is, as it were, a continual present,
with no consciousness of the past or the future, but not
such an immeasurable distance as is generally supposed.

This is, in fact, corroborated by the way in which most
men converse; where their thoughts are found to be
chopped up fine, like chaff, so that for them to spin out
a discourse of any length is impossible.

If this world were peopled by really thinking beings, it
could not be that noise of every kind would be allowed
such generous limits, as is the case with the most horrible
and at the same time aimless form of it.[3] If Nature had
meant man to think, she would not have given him ears;
or, at any rate, she would have furnished them with air-
tight flaps, such as are the enviable possession of the bat.
But man is a poor animal like the rest, and his powers are
meant only to maintain him in the struggle for existence;
so he must need keep his ears always open, to announce of
themselves, by night as by day, the approach of the pursuer.

[3] *Translator's Note.*—Schopenhauer refers to the cracking of
whips. See the Essay *On Noise* in *Studies in Pessimism.*

ON SOME FORMS OF LITERATURE

IN THE DRAMA, which is the most perfect reflection of human existence, there are three stages in the presentation of the subject, with a corresponding variety in the design and scope of the piece.

At the first, which is also the most common, stage, the drama is never anything more than merely *interesting*. The persons gain our attention by following their own aims, which resemble ours; the action advances by means of intrigue and the play of character and incident; while wit and raillery season the whole.

At the second stage, the drama becomes *sentimental*. Sympathy is roused with the hero and, indirectly, with ourselves. The action takes a pathetic turn; but the end is peaceful and satisfactory.

The climax is reached with the third stage, which is the most difficult. There the drama aims at being *tragic*. We are brought face to face with great suffering and the storm and stress of existence; and the outcome of it is to show the vanity of all human effort. Deeply moved, we are either directly prompted to disengage our will from the struggle of life, or else a chord is struck in us which echoes a similar feeling.

The beginning, it is said, is always difficult. In the drama it is just the contrary; for these the difficulty always lies in the end. This is proved by countless plays which promise very well for the first act or two, and then become muddled, stick or falter—notoriously so in the fourth act— and finally conclude in a way that is either forced or un- satisfactory or else long foreseen by every one. Sometimes, too, the end is positively revolting, as in Lessing's *Emilia Galotti*, which sends the spectators home in a temper.

This difficulty in regard to the end of a play arises partly because it is everywhere easier to get things into a tangle than to get them out again; partly also because at the beginning we give the author *carte blanche* to do as he likes, but, at the end, make certain definite demands upon him. Thus we ask for a conclusion that shall be either quite happy or else quite tragic; whereas human affairs do not easily take so decided a turn; and then we expect that it shall be natural, fit and proper, unlabored, and at the same time foreseen by no one.

These remarks are also applicable to an epic and to a novel; but the more compact nature of the drama makes the difficulty plainer by increasing it.

E nihilo nihil fit. That nothing can come from nothing is a maxim true in fine art as elsewhere. In composing an historical picture, a good artist will use living men as a model, and take the groundwork of the faces from life; and then proceed to idealize them in point of beauty or expression. A similar method, I fancy, is adopted by good novelists. In drawing a character they take a general outline of it from some real person of their acquaintance, and then idealize and complete it to suit their purpose.

A NOVEL will be of a high and noble order, the more it represents of inner, and the less it represents of outer, life; and the ratio between the two will supply a means of judging any novel, of whatever kind, from *Tristram Shandy* down to the crudest and most sensational tale of knight or robber. *Tristram Shandy* has, indeed, as good as no action at all; and there is not much in *La Nouvelle Heloise* and *Wilhelm Meister*. Even *Don Quixote* has relatively little; and what there is, very unimportant, and introduced merely for the sake of fun. And these four are the best of all existing novels.

Consider, further, the wonderful romances of Jean Paul, and how much inner life is shown on the narrowest basis of actual event. Even in Walter Scott's novels there is a great preponderance of inner over outer life, and incident is never brought in except for the purpose of giving play to thought and emotion; whereas, in bad novels, incident is there on its own account. Skill consists in setting the inner life in motion with the smallest possible array of circumstance; for it is this inner life that really excites our interest.

The business of the novelist is not to relate great events, but to make small ones interesting.

HISTORY, which I like to think of as the contrary of poetry (ἱστορούμενον—πεποιημένον), is for time what geography is for space; and it is no more to be called a science, in any strict sense of the word, than is geography, because it does not deal with universal truths, but only with particular details. History has always been the favorite study of those who wish to learn something, without having to face the effort demanded by any branch of real knowledge, which taxes the intelligence. In our time history is a favorite pursuit; as witness the numerous books upon the subject which appear every year.

If the reader cannot help thinking, with me, that history is merely the constant recurrence of similar things, just as in a kaleidoscope the same bits of glass are represented, but in different combinations, he will not be able to share all this lively interest; nor, however, will he censure it. But there is a ridiculous and absurd claim, made by many people, to regard history as a part of philosophy, nay, as philosophy itself; they imagine that history can take its place.

The preference shown for history by the greater public in all ages may be illustrated by the kind of conversation which is so much in vogue everywhere in society. It generally consists in one person relating something and then another person relating something else; so that in this way everyone is sure of receiving attention. Both here and in the case of history it is plain that the mind is occupied with particular details. But as in science, so also in every worthy conversation, the mind rises to the consideration of some general truth.

This objection does not, however, deprive history of its value. Human life is short and fleeting, and many millions of individuals share in it, who are swallowed by that monster of oblivion which is waiting for them with ever-open jaws. It is thus a very thankworthy task to try to rescue something—the memory of interesting and important events, or the leading features and personages of some epoch—from the general shipwreck of the world.

From another point of view, we might look upon history as the sequel to zoology; for while with all other animals it is enough to observe the species, with man individuals, and therefore individual events have to be studied; because every man possesses a character as an individual. And since individuals and events are without number or end, an essential imperfection attaches to history. In the study of it, all that a man learns never contributes to lessen that which he has still to learn. With any real science, a perfection of knowledge is, at any rate, conceivable.

When we gain access to the histories of China and of India, the endlessness of the subject-matter will reveal to us the defects in the study, and force our historians to see that the object of science is to recognize the many in the one, to perceive the rules in any given example, and to apply to the life of nations a knowledge of mankind; not to go on counting up facts *ad infinitum*.

There are two kinds of history; the history of politics and the history of literature and art. The one is the history of the will; the other, that of the intellect. The first is a tale of woe, even of terror: it is a record of agony, struggle, fraud, and horrible murder *en masse.* The second is everywhere pleasing and serene, like the intellect when left to itself, even though its path be one of error. Its chief branch is the history of philosophy. This is, in fact, its fundamental bass, and the notes of it are heard even in the other kind of history. These deep tones guide the formation of opinion, and opinion rules the world. Hence philosophy, rightly understood, is a material force of the most powerful kind, though very slow in its working. The philosophy of a period is thus the fundamental bass of its history.

The NEWSPAPER is the second-hand in the clock of history; and it is not only made of baser metal than those which point to the minute and the hour, but it seldom goes right. The so-called leading article is the chorus to the drama of passing events.

Exaggeration of every kind is as essential to journalism as it is to the dramatic art; for the object of journalism is to make events go as far as possible. Thus it is that all journalists are, in the very nature of their calling, alarmists; and this is their way of giving interest to what they write. Herein they are like little dogs; if anything stirs, they immediately set up a shrill bark.

Therefore, let us carefully regulate the attention to be paid to this trumpet of danger, so that it may not disturb our digestion. Let us recognize that a newspaper is at best but a magnifying-glass, and very often merely a shadow on the wall.

The *pen* is to thought what the stick is to walking; but you walk most easily when you have no stick, and you think with the greatest perfection when you have no pen in your hand. It is only when a man begins to be old that he likes to use a stick and is glad to take up his pen.

When an *hypothesis* has once come to birth in the mind,

or gained a footing there, it leads a life so far comparable with the life of an organism, as that it assimilates matter from the outer world only when it is like in kind with it and beneficial; and when, contrarily, such matter is not like in kind but hurtful, the hypothesis, equally with the organism, throws it off, or, if forced to take it, gets rid of it again entire.

To gain *immortality* an author must possess so many excellences that while it will not be easy to find anyone to understand and appreciate them all, there will be men in every age who are able to recognize and value some of them. In this way the credit of his book will be maintained throughout the long course of centuries, in spite of the fact that human interests are always changing.

An author like this, who has a claim to the continuance of his life even with posterity, can only be a man who, over the wide earth, will seek his like in vain, and offer a palpable contrast with everyone else in virtue of his unmistakable distinction. Nay, more: were he, like the wandering Jew, to live through several generations, he would still remain in the same superior position. If this were not so, it would be difficult to see why his thoughts should not perish like those of other men.

Metaphors and *similes* are of great value, in so far as they explain an unknown relation by a known one. Even the more detailed simile which grows into a parable or an allegory, is nothing more than the exhibition of some relation in its simplest, most visible and palpable form. The growth of ideas rests, at bottom, upon similes; because ideas arise by a process of combining the similarities and neglecting the differences between things. Further, intelligence, in the strict sense of the word, ultimately consists in a seizing of relations; and a clear and pure grasp of relations is all the more often attained when the comparison is made between cases that lie wide apart from one another, and between things of quite different nature. As long as a relation is known to me as existing only in a single case, I have but an *individual* idea of it—in other words, only an intuitive knowledge of it; but as soon as I see the same relation in two different cases, I have a *general* idea of its whole nature, and this is a deeper and more perfect knowledge.

Since, then, similes and metaphors are such a powerful engine of knowledge, it is a sign of great intelligence in a writer if his similes are unusual and, at the same time, to the point. Aristotle also observes that by far the most important thing to a writer is to have this power of metaphor; for it is a gift which cannot be acquired, and it is a mark of genius.

As regards *reading*, to require that a man shall retain everything he has ever read, is like asking him to carry about with him all he has ever eaten. The one kind of food has given him bodily, and the other mental, nourishment; and it is through these two means that he has grown to be what he is. The body assimilates only that which is like it; and so a man retains in his mind only that which interests him, in other words, that which suits his system of thought or his purposes in life.

If a man wants to read good books, he must make a point of avoiding bad ones; for life is short, and time and energy limited.

Repetitio est mater studiorum. Any book that is at all important ought to be at once read through twice; partly because, on a second reading, the connection of the different portions of the book will be better understood, and the beginning comprehended only when the end is known; and partly because we are not in the same temper and disposition on both readings. On the second perusal we get a new view of every passage and a different impression of the whole book, which then appears in another light.

A man's works are the quintessence of his mind, and even though he may possess very great capacity, they will always be incomparably more valuable than his conversation. Nay, in all essential matters his works will not only make up for the lack of personal intercourse with him, but they will far surpass it in solid advantages. The writings even of a man of moderate genius may be edifying, worth reading and instructive, because they are his quintessence—the result and fruit of all his thought and study; whilst conversation with him may be unsatisfactory.

So it is that we can read books by men in whose company we find nothing to please, and that a high degree of culture leads us to seek entertainment almost wholly from books and not from men.

ON CRITICISM

THE following brief remarks on the critical faculty are chiefly intended to show that, for the most part, there is no such thing. It is a *rara avis;* almost as rare, indeed, as the phœnix, which appears only once in five hundred years.

When we speak of *taste*—an expression not chosen with any regard for it—we mean the discovery, or, it may be only the recognition, of what is *right æsthetically,* apart from the guidance of any rule; and this, either because no rule has as yet been extended to the matter in question, or else because, if existing, it is unknown to the artist, or the critic, as the case may be. Instead of *taste,* we might use the expression *æsthetic sense,* if this were not tautological.

The perceptive critical taste is, so to speak, the female analogue to the male quality of productive talent or genius. Not capable of *begetting* great work itself, it consists in a capacity of *reception,* that is to say, of recognizing as such what is right, fit, beautiful, or the reverse; in other words, of discriminating the good from the bad, of discovering and appreciating the one and condemning the other.

In appreciating a genius, criticism should not deal with the errors in his productions or with the poorer of his works, and then proceed to rate him low; it should attend only to the qualities in which he most excels. For in the sphere of intellect, as in other spheres, weakness and perversity cleave so firmly to human nature that even the most brilliant mind is not wholly and at all times free from them. Hence the great errors to be found even in the works of the greatest men; or as Horace puts it, *quandoque bonus dormitat Homerus.*

That which distinguishes genius, and should be the standard for judging it, is the height to which it is able to soar when it is in the proper mood and finds a fitting occasion—a height always out of the reach of ordinary talent. And, in like manner, it is a very dangerous thing to compare two great men of the same class; for instance, two great poets, or musicians, or philosophers, or artists; because injustice to the one or the other, at least for the moment, can hardly be avoided. For in making a comparison of the kind the critic looks to some particular merit of the one and at once discovers that it is absent in the other, who is thereby disparaged. And then if the process is reversed, and the critic begins with the latter and discovers his peculiar merit, which is quite of a different order from that presented by the former, with whom it may be looked for in vain, the result is that both of them suffer undue depreciation.

There are critics who severally think that it rests with each one of them what shall be accounted good, and what bad. They all mistake their own toy-trumpets for the trombones of fame.

A drug does not effect its purpose if the dose is too large; and it is the same with censure and adverse criticism when it exceeds the measure of justice.

The disastrous thing for intellectual merit is that it must wait for those to praise the good who have themselves produced nothing but what is bad; nay, it is a primary misfortune that it has to receive its crown at the hands of the critical power of mankind—a quality of which most men possess only the weak and impotent semblance, so that the reality may be numbered amongst the rarest gifts of nature. Hence La Bruyère's remark is, unhappily, as true as it is neat. *Après l'esprit de discernement,* he says, *ce qu'il y a*

au monde de plus rare, ce sont les diamans et les perles.
The spirit of discernment! the critical faculty! it is these
that are lacking. Men do not know how to distinguish the
genuine from the false, the corn from the chaff, gold from
copper; or to perceive the wide gulf that separates a genius
from an ordinary man. Thus we have that bad state of
things described in an old-fashioned verse, which gives it
as the lot of the great ones here on earth to be recognized
only when they are gone:

> *Es ist nun das Geschick der Grossen hier auf Erden,*
> *Erst wann sie nicht mehr sind, von uns erkannt zu werden.*

When any genuine and excellent work makes its appearance, the chief difficulty in its way is the amount of bad
work it finds already in possession of the field, and accepted
as though it were good. And then if, after a long time,
the newcomer really succeeds, by a hard struggle, in vindi-
cating his place for himself and winning reputation, he will
soon encounter fresh difficulty from some affected, dull,
awkward imitator, whom people drag in, with the object of
calmly setting him up on the altar beside the genius; not
seeing the difference and really thinking that here they
have to do with another great man. This is what Yriarte
means by the first lines of his twenty-eighth Fable, where
he declares that the ignorant rabble always sets equal
value on the good and the bad:

> *Siempre acostumbra hacer el vulgo necio*
> *De lo bueno y lo malo igual aprecio.*

So even Shakespeare's dramas had, immediately after his
death, to give place to those of Ben Jonson, Massinger,
Beaumont and Fletcher, and to yield the supremacy for a
hundred years. So Kant's serious philosophy was crowded
out by the nonsense of Fichte, Schelling, Jacobi, Hegel. And
even in a sphere accessible to all, we have seen unworthy
imitators quickly diverting public attention from the in-

comparable Walter Scott. For, say what you will, the public has no sense for excellence, and therefore no notion how very rare it is to find men really capable of doing anything great in poetry, philosophy, or art, or that their works are alone worthy of exclusive attention. The dabblers, whether in verse or in any other high sphere, should be every day unsparingly reminded that neither gods, nor men, nor booksellers have pardoned their mediocrity:

mediocribus esse poetis
Non homines, non Di, non concessere columnæ.[1]

Are they not the weeds that prevent the corn coming up, so that they may cover all the ground themselves? And then there happens that which has been well and freshly described by the lamented Feuchtersleben,[2] who died so young: how people cry out in their haste that nothing is being done, while all the while great work is quietly growing to maturity; and then, when it appears, it is not seen or heard in the clamor, but goes its way silently, in modest grief:

"Ist doch,"—rufen sie vermessen—
"Nichts im Werke, nichts gethan!"
Und das Grosse, reift indessen
Still heran.

Es ersheint nun: niemand sieht es,
Niemand hört es im Geschrei
Mit bescheid'ner Trauer zieht es
Still vorbei.

This lamentable death of the critical faculty is not less obvious in the case of science, as is shown by the tenacious life of false and disproved theories. If they are once ac-

[1] Horace, *Ars Poetica*, 372.
[2] *Translator's Note.*—Ernst Freiherr von Feuchtersleben (1806-49), an Austrian physician, philosopher, and poet, and a specialist in medical psychology. The best known of his songs is that beginning *"Es ist bestimmt in Gottes Rath,"* to which Mendelssohn composed one of his finest melodies.

cepted, they may go on bidding defiance to truth for fifty or even a hundred years and more, as stable as an iron pier in the midst of the waves. The Ptolemaic system was still held a century after Copernicus had promulgated his theory. Bacon, Descartes and Locke made their way extremely slowly and only after a long time; as the reader may see by d'Alembert's celebrated Preface to the *Encyclopedia*. Newton was not more successful; and this is sufficiently proved by the bitterness and contempt with which Leibnitz attacked his theory of gravitation in the controversy with Clarke.[3] Although Newton lived for almost forty years after the appearance of the *Principia,* his teaching was, when he died, only to some extent accepted in his own country, whilst outside England he counted scarcely twenty adherents; if we may believe the introductory note to Voltaire's exposition of his theory. It was, indeed, chiefly owing to this treatise of Voltaire's that the system became known in France nearly twenty years after Newton's death. Until then a firm, resolute, and patriotic stand was made by the Cartesian *Vortices;* whilst only forty years previously, this same Cartesian philosophy had been forbidden in the French schools; and now in turn d'Agnesseau, the Chancellor, refused Voltaire the *Imprimatur* for his treatise on the Newtonian doctrine. On the other hand, in our day Newton's absurd theory of color still completely holds the field, forty years after the publication of Goethe's. Hume, too, was disregarded up to his fiftieth year, though he began very early and wrote in a thoroughly popular style. And Kant, in spite of having written and talked all his life long, did not become a famous man until he was sixty.

Artists and poets have, to be sure, more chance than thinkers, because their public is at least a hundred times as large. Still, what was thought of Beethoven and Mozart

[3] See especially §§ 35, 113, 118, 120, 122, 128.

during their lives? what of Dante? what even of Shakespeare? If the latter's contemporaries had in any way
recognized his worth, at least one good and accredited
portrait of him would have come down to us from an age
when the art of painting flourished; whereas we possess
only some very doubtful pictures, a bad copperplate, and
a still worse bust on his tomb.[4] And in like manner, if
he had been duly honored, specimens of his handwriting
would have been preserved to us by the hundred, instead of
being confined, as is the case, to the signatures to a few
legal documents. The Portuguese are still proud of their
only poet Camoëns. He lived, however, on alms collected
every evening in the street by a black slave whom he had
brought with him from the Indies. In time, no doubt,
justice will be done everyone; *tempo è galant' uomo;* but
it is as late and slow in arriving as in a court of law, and
the secret condition of it is that the recipient shall be
no longer alive. The precept of Jesus the son of Sirach is
faithfully followed: *Judge none blessed before his death.*[5]
He, then, who has produced immortal works, must find
comfort by applying to them the words of the Indian myth,
that the minutes of life amongst the immortals seem like
years of earthly existence; and so, too, that years upon
earth are only as the minutes of the immortals.

This lack of critical insight is also shown by the fact
that, while in every century the excellent work of earlier
time is held in honor, that of its own is misunderstood,
and the attention which is its due is given to bad work,
such as every decade carries with it only to be the sport
of the next. That men are slow to recognize genuine merit
when it appears in their own age, also proves that they do
not understand or enjoy or really value the long-acknowl-

[4] A. Wivell: *An Inquiry into the History, Authenticity, and
Characteristics of Shakespeare's Portraits;* with 21 engravings.
London, 1836.

[5] *Ecclesiasticus,* xi. 28.

edged works of genius, which they honor only on the score of authority. The crucial test is the fact that bad work— Fichte's philosophy, for example—if it wins any reputation, also maintains it for one or two generations; and only when its public is very large does its fall follow sooner.

Now, just as the sun cannot shed its light but to the eye that sees it, nor music sound but to the hearing ear, so the value of all masterly work in art and science is conditioned by the kinship and capacity of the mind to which it speaks. It is only such a mind as this that possesses the magic word to stir and call forth the spirits that lie hidden in great work. To the ordinary mind a masterpiece is a sealed cabinet of mystery,—an unfamiliar musical instrument from which the player, however much he may flatter himself, can draw none but confused tones. How different a painting looks when seen in a good light, as compared with some dark corner! Just in the same way, the impression made by a masterpiece varies with the capacity of the mind to understand it.

A fine work, then, requires a mind sensitive to its beauty; a thoughtful work, a mind that can really think, if it is to exist and live at all. But alas! it may happen only too often that he who gives a fine work to the world afterwards feels like a maker of fireworks, who displays with enthusiasm the wonders that have taken him so much time and trouble to prepare, and then learns that he has come to the wrong place, and that the fancied spectators were one and all inmates of an asylum for the blind. Still even that is better than if his public had consisted entirely of men who made fireworks themselves; as in this case, if his display had been extraordinary good, it might possibly have cost him his head.

The source of all pleasure and delight is the feeling of kinship. Even with the sense of beauty it is unquestionably our own species in the animal world, and then again our own race, that appears to us the fairest. So, too, in intercourse with others, every man shows a decided preference for those who resemble him; and a blockhead will find the society of another blockhead incomparably more pleasant than that of any number of great minds put together. Every man must necessarily take his chief pleasure in his own work, because it is the mirror of his own mind, the echo of his own thought; and next in order will come the work of people like him; that is to say, a dull, shallow and perverse man, a dealer in mere words, will give his sincere and hearty applause only to that which is dull, shallow, perverse or merely verbose. On the other hand, he will allow merit to the work of great minds only on the score of authority, in other words, because he is ashamed to speak his opinion; for in reality they give him no pleasure at all. They do not appeal to him; nay, they repel him; and he will not confess this even to himself. The works of genius cannot be fully enjoyed except by those who are themselves of the privileged order. The first recognition of them, however, when they exist without authority to support them, demands considerable superiority of mind.

When the reader takes all this into consideration, he should be surprised, not that great work is so late in winning reputation, but that it wins it at all. And as a matter of fact, fame comes only by a slow and complex process. The stupid person is by degrees forced, and as it were, tamed, into recognizing the superiority of one who stands immediately above him; this one in his turn bows before some one else; and so it goes on until the weight of the votes gradually prevail over their number; and this is just the condition of all genuine, in other words, deserved fame. But until then, the greatest genius, even after he has passed his time of trial, stands like a king amidst a crowd of his own subjects, who do not know him by sight and therefore will not do his behests; unless, indeed, his chief ministers of state are in his train. For no subordinate official·can be the direct recipient of the royal commands, as he knows only the signature of his immediate superior; and this is repeated all the way up into the highest ranks, where the under-secretary attests the minister's signature, and the minister that of the king. There are analogous stages to be passed before a genius can attain widespread fame. This is why his reputation most easily comes to a standstill at the very outset; because the highest authorities, of whom there can be but few, are most frequently not to be found; but the further down he goes in the scale the more numerous are those who take the word from above, so that his fame is no more arrested.

We must console ourselves for this state of things by reflecting that it is really fortunate that the greater number of men do not form a judgment on their own responsibility, but merely take it on authority. For what sort of criticism should we have on Plato and Kant, Homer, Shakespeare and Goethe, if every man were to form his opinion by what he really has and enjoys of these writers, instead of being forced by authority to speak of them in a fit and proper way, however little he may really feel what he says? Unless something of this kind took place, it would be impossible for true merit, in any high sphere, to attain fame at all. At the same time it is also fortunate that every man has just so much critical power of his own as is necessary for recognizing the superiority of those who are placed immediately over him, and for following their lead. This means that the many come in the end to submit to the authority of the few; and there results that hierarchy of critical judgments on which is based the possibility of a steady, and eventually wide-reaching, fame.

The lowest class in the community is quite impervious to the merits of a great genius; and for these people there is nothing left but the monument raised to him, which, by

the impression it produces on their senses, awakes in them
a dim idea of the man's greatness.

Literary journals should be a dam against the uncon-
scionable scribbling of the age, and the ever-increasing
deluge of bad and useless books. Their judgments should
be uncorrupted, just and rigorous; and every piece of bad
work done by an incapable person; every device by which
the empty head tries to come to the assistance of the empty
purse, that is to say, about nine-tenths of all existing books,
should be mercilessly scourged. Literary journals would
then perform their duty, which is to keep down the craving for writing and put a check upon the deception of the
public, instead of furthering these evils by a miserable
toleration, which plays into the hands of author and pub-
lisher, and robs the reader of his time and his money.

If there were such a paper as I mean, every bad writer,
every brainless compiler, every plagiarist from other's
books, every hollow and incapable place-hunter, every
sham-philosopher, every vain and languishing poetaster,
would shudder at the prospect of the pillory in which his
bad work would inevitably have to stand soon after publication. This would paralyze his twitching fingers, to the
true welfare of literature, in which what is bad is not
only useless but positively pernicious. Now, most books
are bad and ought to have remained unwritten. Consequently praise should be as rare as is now the case with
blame, which is withheld under the influence of personal
considerations, coupled with the maxim *accedas socius,
laudes lauderis ut absens.*

It is quite wrong to try to introduce into literature the
same toleration as must necessarily prevail in society towards those stupid, brainless people who everywhere swarm
in it. In literature such people are impudent intruders;
and to disparage the bad is here duty towards the good;
for he who thinks nothing bad will think nothing good

either. Politeness, which has its source in social relations, is in literature an alien, and often injurious, element; because it exacts that bad work shall be called good. In this way the very aim of science and art is directly frustrated.

The ideal journal could, to be sure, be written only by people who joined incorruptible honesty with rare knowledge and still rarer power of judgment; so that perhaps there could, at the very most, be one, and even hardly one, in the whole country; but there it would stand, like a just Aeropagus, every member of which would have to be elected by all the others. Under the system that prevails at present, literary journals are carried on by a clique, and secretly perhaps also by booksellers for the good of the trade; and they are often nothing but coalitions of bad heads to prevent the good ones succeeding. As Goethe once remarked to me, nowhere is there so much dishonesty as in literature.

But, above all, anonymity, that shield of all literary rascality, would have to disappear. It was introduced under the pretext of protecting the honest critic, who warned the public, against the resentment of the author and his friends. But where there is one case of this sort, there will be a hundred where it merely serves to take all responsibility from the man who cannot stand by what he has said, or possibly to conceal the shame of one who has been cowardly and base enough to recommend a book to the public for the purpose of putting money into his own pocket. Often enough it is only a cloak for covering the obscurity, incompetence and insignificance of the critic. It is incredible what impudence these fellows will show, and what literary trickery they will venture to commit, as soon as they know they are safe under the shadow of anonymity. Let me recommend a general *Anti-criticism*, a universal medicine or panacea, to put a stop to all anonymous reviewing, whether it praises the bad or blames the good: *Rascal! your name!* For a man to wrap himself up and draw his hat over his face, and then fall upon people who are walking about without any disguise—this is not the part of a gentleman, it is the part of a scoundrel and a knave.

An anonymous review has no more authority than an anonymous letter; and one should be received with the same mistrust as the other. Or shall we take the name of the man who consents to preside over what is, in the strict sense of the word, *une société anonyme* as a guarantee for the veracity of his colleagues?

Even Rousseau, in the preface to the *Nouvelle Heloïse,* declares *tout honnête homme doit avouer les livres qu'il publie;* which in plain language means that every honorable man ought to sign his articles, and that no one is honorable who does not do so. How much truer this is of polemical writing, which is the general character of reviews! Riemer was quite right in the opinion he gives in his *Reminiscences of Goethe:*[6] *An overt enemy,* he says, *an enemy who meets you face to face, is an honorable man, who will treat you fairly, and with whom you can come to terms and be reconciled: but an enemy who conceals himself* is a base, cowardly scoundrel, *who has not courage enough to avow his own judgment; it is not his opinion that he cares about, but only the secret pleasures of wreaking his anger without being found out or punished.* This will also have been Goethe's opinion, as he was generally the source from which Riemer drew his observations. And, indeed, Rousseau's maxim applies to every line that is printed. Would a man in a mask ever be allowed to harangue a mob, or speak in any assembly; and that, too, when he was going to attack others and overwhelm them with abuse?

Anonymity is the refuge for all literary and journalistic

[6] Preface, p. xxix.

rascality. It is a practice which must be completely stopped. Every article, even in a newspaper, should be accompanied by the name of its author; and the editor should be made strictly responsible for the accuracy of the signature. The freedom of the press should be thus far restricted; so that when a man publicly proclaims through the far-sounding trumpet of the newspaper, he should be answerable for it, at any rate with his honor, if he has any; and if he has none, let his name neutralize the effect of his words. And since even the most insignificant person is known in his own circle, the result of such a measure would be to put an end to two-thirds of the newspaper lies, and to restrain the audacity of many a poisonous tongue.

ON REPUTATION

WRITERS may be classified as meteors, planets and fixed stars. A meteor makes a striking effect for a moment. You look up and cry *There!* and it is gone for ever. Planets and wandering stars last a much longer time. They often outshine the fixed stars and are confounded with them by the inexperienced; but this only because they are near. It is not long before they must yield their place; nay, the light they give is reflected only, and the sphere of their influence is confined to their own orbit—their contemporaries. Their path is one of change and movement, and with the circuit of a few years their tale is told. Fixed stars are the only ones that are constant; their position in the firmament is secure; they shine with a light of their own; their effect to-day is the same as it was yesterday, because, having no parallax, their appearance does not alter with a difference in our standpoint. They belong not to *one* system, *one* nation only, but to the universe. And just because they are so very far away, it is usually many years before their light is visible to the inhabitants of this earth.

We have seen in the previous chapter that where a man's merits are of a high order, it is difficult for him to win reputation, because the public is uncritical and lacks discernment. But another and no less serious hindrance to fame comes from the envy it has to encounter. For even in the lowest kinds of work, envy balks even the beginnings of a reputation, and never ceases to cleave to it up to the last. How great a part is played by envy in the wicked ways of the world! Ariosto is right in saying that the dark side of our mortal life predominates, so full it is of this evil:

> *questa assai più oscura che serena*
> *Vita mortal, tutta d'invidia piena.*

For envy is the moving spirit of that secret and informal,

though flourishing, alliance everywhere made by mediocrity against individual eminence, no matter of what kind. In his own sphere of work no one will allow another to be distinguished: he is an intruder who cannot be tolerated. *Si quelq'un excelle parmi nous, qu'il aille exceller ailleurs!* this is the universal password of the second-rate. In addition, then, to the rarity of true merit and the difficulty it has in being understood and recognized, there is the envy of thousands to be reckoned with, all of them bent on suppressing, nay, on smothering it altogether. No one is taken for what he is, but for what others make of him; and this is the handle used by mediocrity to keep down distinction, by not letting it come up as long as that can possibly be prevented.

There are two ways of behaving in regard to merit: either to have some of one's own, or to refuse any to others. The latter method is more convenient, and so it is generally adopted. As envy is a mere sign of deficiency, so to envy merit argues the lack of it. My excellent Balthazar Gracian has given a very fine account of this relation between envy and merit in a lengthy fable, which may be found in his *Discreto* under the heading *Hombre de ostentacion*. He describes all the birds as meeting together and conspiring against the peacock, because of his magnificent feathers. *If*, said the magpie, *we could only manage to put a stop to the cursed parading of his tail, there would soon be an end of his beauty; for what is not seen is as good as what does not exist.*

This explains how modesty came to be a virtue. It was invented only as a protection against envy. That there have always been rascals to urge this virtue, and to rejoice heartily over the bashfulness of a man of merit, has been shown at length in my chief work.[1] In Lichtenberg's *Miscellaneous Writings* I find this sentence quoted: *Modesty should*

[1] *Welt als Wille*, Vol. II. c. 37.

be the virtue of those who possess no other. Goethe has a
well-known saying, which offends many people: *It is only
knaves who are modest!—Nur die Lumpen sind bescheiden!*
but it has its prototype in Cervantes, who includes in his
Journey up Parnassus certain rules of conduct for poets,
and amongst them the following: *Everyone whose verse
shows him to be a poet should have a high opinion of himself, relying on the proverb that he is a knave who thinks
himself one.* And Shakespeare, in many of his Sonnets,
which gave him the only opportunity he had of speaking
of himself, declares, with a confidence equal to his ingenu-
ousness, that what he writes is immortal.[2]

A method of underrating good work often used by envy
—in reality, however, only the obverse side of it—consists
in the dishonorable and unscrupulous laudation of the bad;
for no sooner does bad work gain currency than it draws
attention from the good. But however effective this method
may be for a while, especially if it is applied on a large
scale, the day of reckoning comes at last, and the fleeting
credit given to bad work is paid off by the lasting discredit
which overtakes those who abjectly praised it. Hence these
critics prefer to remain anonymous.

A like fate threatens, though more remotely those who
depreciate and censure good work; and consequently many
are too prudent to attempt it. But there is another way;
and when a man of eminent merit appears, the first effect
he produces it often only to pique all his rivals, just as the

[2] Collier, one of his critical editors, in his Introduction to the
Sonettes, remarks upon this point: "In many of them are to
be found most remarkable indications of self-confidence and of
assurance in the immortality of his verses, and in this respect
the author's opinion was constant and uniform. He never
scruples to express it, . . . and perhaps there is no writer of
ancient or modern times who, for the quantity of such writings
left behind him, has so frequently or so strongly declared that
what he had produced in this department of poetry 'the world
would not willingly let die.'"

peacock's tail offended the birds. This reduces them to a deep silence; and their silence is so unanimous that it savors of preconcertion. Their tongues are all paralyzed. It is the *silentium livoris* described by Seneca. This malicious silence, which is technically known as *ignoring*, may for a long time interfere with the growth of reputation; if, as happens in the higher walks of learning, where a man's immediate audience is wholly composed of rival workers and professed students, who then form the channel of his fame, the greater public is obliged to use its suffrage without being able to examine the matter for itself. And if, in the end, that malicious silence is broken in upon by the voice of praise, it will be but seldom that this happens entirely apart from some ulterior aim, pursued by those who thus manipulate justice. For, as Goethe says in the *Westöstlicher Divan*, a man can get no recognition, either from many persons or from only one, unless it is to publish abroad the critic's own discernment:

> *Denn es ist kein Anerkenen,*
> *Weder Vieler, noch des Einen,*
> *Wenn es nicht am Tage fördert,*
> *Wo man selbst was möchte scheinen.*

The credit you allow to another man engaged in work similar to your own or akin to it, must at bottom be withdrawn from yourself; and you can praise him only at the expense of your own claims.

Accordingly, mankind is in itself not at all inclined to award praise and reputation; it is more disposed to blame and find fault, whereby it indirectly praises itself. If, notwithstanding this, praise is won from mankind, some extraneous motive must prevail. I am not here referring to the disgraceful way in which mutual friends will puff one another into a reputation; outside of that, an effectual motive is supplied by the feeling that next to the merit of doing something oneself, comes that of correctly appreciating and recognizing what others have done. This accords with the threefold division of heads drawn up by Hesiod,[3] and afterwards by Machiavelli.[4] *There are*, says the latter, *in the capacities of mankind, three varieties: one man will understand a thing by himself; another so far as it is explained to him; a third, neither of himself nor when it is put clearly before him.* He, then, who abandons hope of making good his claims to the first class, will be glad to seize the opportunity of taking a place in the second. It is almost wholly owing to this state of things that merit may rest assured of ultimately meeting with recognition.

To this also is due the fact that when the value of a work has once been recognized and may no longer be concealed or denied, all men vie in praising and honoring it; simply because they are conscious of thereby doing themselves an honor. They act in the spirit of Xenophon's remark: *he must be a wise man who knows what is wise.* So when they see that the prize of original merit is for ever out of their reach, they hasten to possess themselves of that which comes second best—the correct appreciation of it. Here it happens as with an army which has been forced to yield; when, just as previously every man wanted to be foremost in the fight, so now every man tries to be foremost in running away. They all hurry forward to offer their applause to one who is now recognized to be worthy of praise, in virtue of a recognition, as a rule unconscious, of that law of homogeneity which I mentioned in the last chapter; so that it may seem as though their way of thinking and looking at things were homogeneous with that of the celebrated man, and that they may at least save the honor of their literary taste, since nothing else is left them.

From this it is plain that, whereas it is very difficult to win fame, it is not hard to keep it when once attained; and also that a reputation which comes quickly does not last very long; for here too, *quod cito fit, cito perit.* It is

---

[3] *Works and Days*, 293.   [4] *The Prince*, ch. 22.

obvious that if the ordinary average man can easily recognize, and the rival workers willingly acknowledge, the value of any performance, it will not stand very much above the capacity of either of them to achieve it for themselves. *Tantum quisque laudate, quantum se posse sperat imitari* —a man will praise a thing only so far as he hopes to be able to imitate it himself. Further, it is a suspicious sign if a reputation comes quickly; for an application of the laws of homogeneity will show that such a reputation is nothing but the direct applause of the multitude. What this means may be seen by a remark once made by Phocion, when he was interrupted in a speech by the loud cheers of the mob. Turning to his friends, standing close by, he asked: *have I made a mistake and said something stupid?* [5]

Contrarily, a reputation that is to last a long time must be slow in maturing, and the centuries of its duration have generally to be bought at the cost of contemporary praise. For that which is to keep its position so long, must be of a perfection difficult to attain; and even to recognize this perfection requires men who are not always to be found, and never in numbers sufficiently great to make themselves heard; whereas envy is always on the watch and doing its best to smother their voice. But with moderate talent, which soon meets with recognition, there is the danger that those who possess it will outlive both it and themselves; so that a youth of fame may be followed by an old age of obscurity. In the case of great merit, on the other hand, a man may remain unknown for many years, but make up for it later on by attaining a brilliant reputation. And if it should be that this comes only after he is no more, well! he is to be reckoned amongst those of whom Jean Paul says that extreme unction is their baptism. He may console himself by thinking of the Saints, who also are canonized only after they are dead.

[5] Plutarch, *Apophthegms.*

Thus what Mahlmann [6] has said so well in *Herodes* holds good; in this world truly great work never pleases at once, and the god set up by the multitude keeps his place on the altar but a short time:

> *Ich denke, das wahre Grosse in der Welt*
> *Ist immer nur Das was nicht gleich gefällt*
> *Und wen der Pöbel zum Gotte weiht,*
> *Der steht auf dem Altar nur kurze Zeit.*

It is worth mention that this rule is most directly confirmed in the case of pictures, where, as connoisseurs well know, the greatest masterpieces are not the first to attract attention. If they make a deep impression, it is not after one, but only after repeated, inspection; but then they excite more and more admiration every time they are seen.

Moreover, the chances that any given work will be quickly and rightly appreciated, depend upon two conditions: firstly, the character of the work, whether high or low, in other words, easy or difficult to understand; and, secondly, the kind of public it attracts, whether large or small. This latter condition is, no doubt, in most instances a corollary of the former; but it also partly depends upon whether the work in question admits, like books and musical compositions, of being produced in great numbers. By the compound action of these two conditions, achievements which serve no materially useful end—and these alone are under consideration here—will vary in regard to the chances they have of meeting with timely recognition and due appreciation; and the order of precedence, beginning with those who have the greatest chance, will be somewhat as follows: acrobats, circus riders, ballet-dancers, jugglers, actors, singers, musicians, composers, poets (both the last on account of the multiplication of their works), architects, painters, sculptors, philosophers.

[6] *Translator's Note.*—August Mahlmann (1771–1826), journalist, poet and story-writer. His *Herodes vor Bethlehem* is a parody of Kotzebue's *Hussiten vor Naumburg*.

The last place of all is unquestionably taken by philosophers because their works are meant not for entertainment, but for instruction, and because they presume some knowledge on the part of the reader, and require him to make an effort of his own to understand them. This makes their public extremely small, and causes their fame to be more remarkable for its length than for its breadth. And, in general, it may be said that the possibility of a man's fame lasting a long time, stands in almost inverse ratio with the chance that it will be early in making its appearance; so that, as regards length of fame, the above order of precedence may be reversed. But, then, the poet and the composer will come in the end to stand on the same level as the philosopher; since, when once a work is committed to writing, it is possible to preserve it to all time. However, the first place still belongs by right to the philosopher, because of the much greater scarcity of good work in this sphere, and the high importance of it; and also because of the possibility it offers of an almost perfect translation into any language. Sometimes, indeed, it happens that a philosopher's fame outlives even his works themselves; as has happened with Thales, Empedocles, Heraclitus, Democritus, Parmenides, Epicurus and many others.

My remarks are, as I have said, confined to achievements that are not of any material use. Work that serves some practical end, or ministers directly to some pleasure of the senses, will never have any difficulty in being appreciated. No first-rate pastry-cook could long remain obscure in any town, to say nothing of having to appeal to posterity.

Under fame of rapid growth is also to be reckoned fame of a false and artificial kind; where, for instance, a book is worked into a reputation by means of unjust praise, the help of friends, corrupt criticism, prompting from above and collusion from below. All this tells upon the multitude, which is rightly presumed to have no power of judging for itself. This sort of fame is like a swimming bladder, by its aid a heavy body may keep afloat. It bears up for a certain time, long or short according as the bladder is well sewed up and blown; but still the air comes out gradually, and the body sinks. This is the inevitable fate of all works which are famous by reason of something outside of themselves. False praise dies away; collusion comes to an end; critics declare the reputation ungrounded; it vanishes, and is replaced by so much the greater contempt. Contrarily, a genuine work, which, having the source of its fame in itself, can kindle admiration afresh in every age, resembles a body of low specific gravity, which always keeps up of its own accord, and so goes floating down the stream of time.

Men of great genius, whether their work be in poetry, philosophy or art, stand in all ages like isolated heroes, keeping up single-handed a desperate struggling against the onslaught of an army of opponents.[7] Is not this characteristic of the miserable nature of mankind? The dullness, grossness, perversity, silliness and brutality of by far the greater part of the race, are always an obstacle to the efforts of the genius, whatever be the method of his art; they so form that hostile army to which at last he has to succumb. Let the isolated champion achieve what he may: it is slow to be acknowledged; it is late in being appreciated, and then only on the score of authority; it may easily fall into neglect again, at any rate for a while. Ever afresh it finds itself opposed by false, shallow, and insipid ideas, which are better suited to that large majority, that so generally hold the field. Though the critic may step forth and say, like Hamlet when he held up the two

[7] *Translator's Note.*—At this point Schopenhauer interrupts the thread of his discourse to speak at length upon an example of false fame. Those who are at all acquainted with the philosopher's views will not be surprised to find that the writer thus held up to scorn is Hegel; and readers of the other volumes in this series will, with the translator, have had by now quite enough of the subject. The passage is therefore omitted.

portraits to his wretched mother, *Have you eyes? Have you eyes?* alas! they have none. When I watch the behavior of a crowd of people in the presence of some great master's work, and mark the manner of their applause, they often remind me of trained monkeys in a show. The monkey's gestures are, no doubt, much like those of men; but now and again they betray that the real inward spirit of these gestures is not in them. Their irrational nature peeps out.

It is often said of a man that *he is in advance of his age;* and it follows from the above remarks that this must be taken to mean that he is in advance of humanity in general. Just because of this fact, a genius makes no direct appeal except to those who are too rare to allow of their ever forming a numerous body at any one period. If he is in this respect not particularly favored by fortune, he will be *misunderstood by his own age;* in other words, he will remain unaccepted until time gradually brings together the voices of those few persons who are capable of judging a work of such high character. Then posterity will say: *This man was in advance of his age,* instead of *in advance of humanity;* because humanity will be glad to lay the burden of its own faults upon a single epoch.

Hence, if a man has been superior to his own age, he would also have been superior to any other; provided that, in that age, by some rare and happy chance, a few just men, capable of judging in the sphere of his achievements, had been born at the same time with him; just as when, according to a beautiful Indian myth, Vishnu becomes incarnate as a hero, so, too, Brahma at the same time appears as the singer of his deeds; and hence Valmiki, Vyasa and Kalidasa are incarnations of Brahma.

In this sense, then, it may be said that every immortal work puts its age to the proof, whether or no it will be able to recognize the merit of it. As a rule, the men of any age stand such a test no better than the neighbors of Philemon and Baucis, who expelled the deities they failed to recognize. Accordingly, the right standard for judging the intellectual worth of any generation is supplied, not by the great minds that make their appearance in it—for their capacities are the work of Nature, and the possibility of cultivating them a matter of chance circumstance—but by the way in which contemporaries receive their works; whether, I mean, they give their applause soon and with a will, or late and in niggardly fashion, or leave it to be bestowed altogether by posterity.

This last fate will be especially reserved for works of a high character. For the happy chance mentioned above will be all the more certain not to come, in proportion as there are few to appreciate the kind of work done by great minds. Herein lies the immeasurable advantage possessed by poets in respect of reputation; because their work is accessible to almost everyone. If it had been possible for Sir Walter Scott to be read and criticised by only some hundred persons, perhaps in his life-time any common scribbler would have been preferred to him; and afterwards, when he had taken his proper place, it would also have been said in his honor that he was *in advance of his age*. But if envy, dishonesty and the pursuit of personal aims are added to the incapacity of those hundred persons who, in the name of their generation, are called upon to pass judgment on a work, then indeed it meets with the same sad fate as attends a suitor who pleads before a tribunal of judges one and all corrupt.

In corroboration of this, we find that the history of literature generally shows all those who made knowledge and insight their goal to have remained unrecognized and neglected, whilst those who paraded with the vain show of it received the admiration of their contemporaries, together with the emoluments.

The effectiveness of an author turns chiefly upon his getting the reputation that he should be read. But by practicing various arts, by the operation of chance, and by certain natural affinities, this reputation is quickly won by a hundred worthless people: while a worthy writer may come by it very slowly and tardily. The former possess friends to help them; for the rabble is always a numerous body which holds well together. The latter has nothing but enemies; because intellectual superiority is everywhere and under all circumstances the most hateful thing in the world, and especially to bunglers in the same line of work, who want to pass for something themselves.[8]

This being so, it is a prime condition for doing any great work—any work which is to outlive its own age, that a man pay no heed to his contemporaries, their views and opinions, and the praise or blame which they bestow. This condition is, however, fulfilled of itself when a man really does anything great, and it is fortunate that it is so. For if, in producing such a work, he were to look to the general opinion or the judgment of his colleagues, they would lead him astray at every step. Hence, if a man wants to go down to posterity, he must withdraw from the influence of his own age. This will, of course, generally mean that he must also renounce any influence upon it, and be ready to buy centuries of fame by foregoing the applause of his contemporaries.

For when any new and wide-reaching truth comes into the world—and if it is new, it must be paradoxical—an obstinate stand will be made against it as long as possible; nay, people will continue to deny it even after they slacken their opposition and are almost convinced of its truth. Meanwhile it goes on quietly working its way, and, like

[8] If the professors of philosophy should chance to think that I am here hinting at them and the tactics they have for more than thirty years pursued toward my works, they have hit the nail upon the head.

an acid, undermining everything around it. From time to time a crash is heard; the old error comes tottering to the ground, and suddenly the new fabric of thought stands revealed, as though it were a monument just uncovered. Everyone recognizes and admires it. To be sure, this all comes to pass for the most part very slowly. As a rule, people discover a man to be worth listening to only after he is gone; their *hear, hear,* resounds when the orator has left the platform.

Works of the ordinary type meet with a better fate. Arising as they do in the course of, and in connection with, the general advance in contemporary culture, they are in close alliance with the spirit of their age—in other words, just those opinions which happen to be prevalent at the time. They aim at suiting the needs of the moment. If they have any merit, it is soon recognized; and they gain currency as books which reflect the latest ideas. Justice, nay, more than justice, is done to them. They afford little scope for envy; since, as was said above, a man will praise a thing only so far as he hopes to be able to imitate it himself.

But those rare works which are destined to become the property of all mankind and to live for centuries are, at their origin, too far in advance of the point at which culture happens to stand, and on that very account foreign to it and the spirit of their own time. They neither belong to it nor are they in any connection with it, and hence they excite no interest in those who are dominated by it. They belong to another, a higher stage of culture, and a time that is still far off. Their course is related to that of ordinary works as the orbit of Uranus to the orbit of Mercury. For the moment they get no justice done to them. People are at a loss how to treat them; so they leave them alone, and go their own snail's pace for themselves. Does the worm see the eagle as it soars aloft?

Of the number of books written in any language about one in 100,000 forms a part of its real and permanent literature. What a fate this one book has to endure before it outstrips those 100,000 and gains its due place of honor! Such a book is the work of an extraordinary and eminent mind, and therefore it is specifically different from the others; a fact which sooner or later becomes manifest.

Let no one fancy that things will ever improve in this respect. No! the miserable constitution of humanity never changes, though it may, to be sure, take somewhat varying forms with every generation. A distinguished mind seldom has its full effect in the life-time of its possessor; because, at bottom, it is completely and properly understood only by minds already akin to it.

As it is a rare thing for even one man out of many millions to tread the path that leads to immortality, he must of necessity be very lonely. The journey to posterity lies through a horribly dreary region, like the Lybian desert, of which, as is well known, no one has any idea who has not seen it for himself. Meanwhile let me before all things recommend the traveler to take light baggage with him; otherwise he will have to throw away too much on the road. Let him never forget the words of Balthazar Gracian: *lo bueno si breve, dos vezes bueno*—good work is doubly good if it is short. This advice is specially applicable to my own countrymen.

Compared with the short span of time they live, men of great intellect are like huge buildings, standing on a small plot of ground. The size of the building cannot be seen by anyone, just in front of it; nor, for an analogous reason, can the greatness of a genius be estimated while he lives. But when a century has passed, the world recognizes it and wishes him back again.

If the perishable son of time has produced an imperishable work, how short his own life seems compared with

that of his child! He is like Semela or Maia—a mortal
mother who gave birth to an immortal son; or, contrarily,
he is like Achilles in regard to Thetis. What a contrast
there is between what is fleeting and what is permanent!
The short span of a man's life, his necessitous, afflicted,
unstable existence, will seldom allow of his seeing even the
beginning of his immortal child's brilliant career; nor will
the father himself be taken for that which he really is. It
may be said, indeed, that a man whose fame comes after
him is the reverse of a nobleman, who is preceded by it.

However, the only difference that it ultimately makes
to a man to receive his fame at the hands of contemporaries
rather than from posterity is that, in the former case, his
admirers are separated from him by space, and in the
latter by time. For even in the case of contemporary
fame, a man does not, as a rule, see his admirers actually
before him. Reverence cannot endure close proximity;
it almost always dwells at some distance from its object;
and in the presence of the person revered it melts like
butter in the sun. Accordingly, if a man is celebrated
with his contemporaries, nine-tenths of those amongst
whom he lives will let their esteem be guided by his rank
and fortune; and the remaining tenth may perhaps have
a dull consciousness of his high qualities, because they have
heard about him from remote quarters. There is a fine
Latin letter of Petrarch's on this incompatibility between
reverence and the presence of the person, and between
fame and life. It comes second in his *Epistolæ familiares,*[9]
and it is addressed to Thomas Messanensis. He there
observes, amongst other things, that the learned men of
his age all made it a rule to think little of a man's writings
if they had even once seen him.

Since distance, then, is essential if a famous man is to
be recognized and revered, it does not matter whether it

[9] In the Venetian edition of 1492.

is distance of space or of time. It is true that he may sometimes hear of his fame in the one case, but never in the other; but still, genuine and great merit may make up for this by confidently anticipating its posthumous fame. Nay, he who produces some really great thought is conscious of his connection with coming generations at the very moment he conceives it; so that he feels the extension of his existence through centuries and thus lives *with* posterity as well as *for* it. And when, after enjoying a great man's work, we are seized with admiration for him, and wish him back, so that we might see and speak with him, and have him in our possession, this desire of ours is not unrequited; for he, too, has had his longing for that posterity which will grant the recognition, honor, gratitude and love denied by envious contemporaries.

If intellectual works of the highest order are not allowed their due until they come before the tribunal of posterity, a contrary fate is prepared for certain brilliant errors which proceed from men of talent, and appear with an air of being well grounded. These errors are defended with so much acumen and learning that they actually become famous with their own age, and maintain their position at least during their author's lifetime. Of this sort are many false theories and wrong criticisms; also poems and works of art, which exhibit some false taste or mannerism favored by contemporary prejudice. They gain reputation and currency simply because no one is yet forthcoming who knows how to refute them or otherwise prove their falsity; and when he appears, as he usually does, in the next generation, the glory of these works is brought to an end. Posthumous judges, be their decision favorable to the appellant or not, form the proper court for quashing the verdict of contemporaries. That is why it is difficult and rare to be victorious in both tribunals.

The unfailing tendency of time to correct knowledge

and judgment should always be kept in view as a means of allaying anxiety, whenever any grievous error appears, whether in art, or science, or practical life, and gains ground; or when some false and thoroughly perverse policy of movement is undertaken and receives applause at the hands of men. No one should be angry, or still less, despondent; but simply imagine that the world has already abandoned the error in question, and now only requires time and experience to recognize of its own accord that which a clear vision detected at the first glance.

When the facts themselves are eloquent of a truth, there is no need to rush to its aid with words: for time will give it a thousand tongues. How long it may be before they speak, will of course depend upon the difficulty of the subject and the plausibility of the error; but come they will, and often it would be of no avail to try to anticipate them. In the worst cases it will happen with theories as it happens with affairs in practical life; where sham and deception, emboldened by success, advance to greater and greater lengths, until discovery is made almost inevitable. It is just so with theories; through the blind confidence of the blockheads who broach them, their absurdity reaches such a pitch that at last it is obvious even to the dullest eye. We may thus say to such people: *the wilder your statements, the better.*

There is also some comfort to be found in reflecting upon all the whims and crotchets which had their day and have now utterly vanished. In style, in grammar, in spelling, there are false notions of this sort which last only three or four years. But when the errors are on a large scale, while we lament the brevity of human life, we shall, in any case, do well to lag behind our own age when we see it on a downward path. For there are two ways of not keeping on a level with the times. A man may be below it; or he may be above it.

ON GENIUS

No difference of rank, position, or birth, is so great as the gulf that separates the countless millions who use their head only in the service of their belly, in other words, look upon it as an instrument of the will, and those very few and rare persons who have the courage to say: No! it is too good for that; my head shall be active only in its own service; it shall try to comprehend the wondrous and varied spectacle of this world, and then reproduce it in some form, whether as art or as literature, that may answer to my character as an individual. These are the truly noble, the real *noblesse* of the world. The others are serfs and go with the soil—*blebæ adscripti*. Of course, I am here referring to those who have not only the courage, but also the call, and therefore the right, to order the head to quit the service of the will; with a result that proves the sacrifice to have been worth the making. In the case of those to whom all this can only partially apply, the gulf is not so wide; but even though their talent be small, so long as it is real, there will always be a sharp line of demarcation between them and the millions.[1]

The works of fine art, poetry and philosophy produced by a nation are the outcome of the superfluous intellect existing in it.

[1] The correct scale for adjusting the hierarchy of intelligences is furnished by the degree in which the mind takes merely individual or approaches universal views of things. The brute recognizes only the individual as such: its comprehension does not extend beyond the limits of the individual. But man reduces the individual to the general; herein lies the exercise of his reason; and the higher his intelligence reaches, the nearer do his general ideas approach the point at which they become universal.

For him who can understand aright—*cum grano salis*—
the relation between the genius and the normal man may,
perhaps, be best expressed as follows: A genius has a
double intellect, one for himself and the service of his
will; the other for the world, of which he becomes the
mirror, in virtue of his purely objective attitude towards
it. The work of art or poetry or philosophy produced by
the genius is simply the result, or quintessence, of this con-
templative attitude, elaborated according to certain technical rules.

The normal man, on the other hand, has only a single
intellect, which may be called *subjective* by contrast with
the *objective* intellect of genius. However acute this subjective intellect may be—and it exists in very various
degrees of perfection—it is never on the same level with
the double intellect of genius; just as the open chest notes
of the human voice, however high, are essentially different
from the falsetto notes. These, like the two upper octaves
of the flute and the harmonics of the violin, are produced
by the column of air dividing itself into two vibrating
halves, with a node between them; when the open chest
notes of the human voice and the lower octave of the flute
are produced by the undivided column of air vibrating as
a whole. This illustration may help the reader to understand that specific peculiarity of genius which is unmis-
takably stamped on the works, and even on the physiognomy, of him who is gifted with it. At the same time
it is obvious that a double intellect like this must, as a
rule, obstruct the service of the will; and this explains the
poor capacity often shown by genius in the conduct of
life. And what specially characterizes genius is that it
has none of that sobriety of temper which is always to
be found in the ordinary simple intellect, be it acute
or dull.

The brain may be likened to a parasite which is nour-

ished as a part of the human frame without contributing
directly to its inner economy; it is securely housed in
the topmost story, and there leads a self-sufficient and
independent life. In the same way it may be said that
a man endowed with great mental gifts leads, apart from
the individual life common to all, a second life, purely of
the intellect. He devotes himself to the constant increase,
rectification and extension, not of mere learning, but of
real systematic knowledge and insight; and remains un-
touched by the fate that overtakes him personally, so long
as it does not disturb him in his work. It is thus a life
which raises a man and sets him above fate and its changes.
Always thinking, learning, experimenting, practicing his
knowledge, the man soon comes to look upon this second
life as the chief mode of existence, and his merely personal
life as something subordinate, serving only to advance ends
higher than itself.

An example of this independent, separate existence is
furnished by Goethe. During the war in the Champagne,
and amid all the bustle of the camp, he made observations
for his theory of color; and as soon as the numberless
calamities of that war allowed of his retiring for a short
time to the fortress of Luxembourg, he took up the manu-
script of his *Farbenlehre*. This is an example which we,
the salt of the earth, should endeavor to follow by never
letting anything disturb us in the pursuit of our intellectual life, however much the storm of the world may
invade and agitate our personal environment; always remembering that we are the sons, not of the bondwoman,
but of the free. As our emblem and coat of arms, I pro-
pose a tree mightily shaken by the wind, but still bearing
its ruddy fruit on every branch; with the motto *Dum con-
vellor mitescunt*, or *Conquassata sed ferax*.

That purely intellectual life of the individual has its
counterpart in humanity as a whole. For there, too, the

real life is the life of the *will*, both in the empirical and
in the transcendental meaning of the word. The purely
intellectual life of humanity lies in its effort to increase
knowledge by means of the sciences, and its desire to perfect the arts. Both science and art thus advance slowly
from one generation to another, and grow with the centuries, every race as it hurries by furnishing its contribu-
tion. This intellectual life, like some gift from heaven,
hovers over the stir and movement of the world; or it is,
as it were, a sweet-scented air developed out of the ferment
itself—the real life of mankind, dominated by will; and
side by side with the history of nations, the history of
philosophy, science and art takes its innocent and blood-
less way.

The difference between the genius and the ordinary man
is, no doubt, a *quantitative* one, in so far as it is a difference of degree; but I am tempted to regard it also as
qualitative, in view of the fact that ordinary minds, notwithstanding individual variation, have a certain tendency
to think alike. Thus on similar occasions their thoughts
at once all take a similar direction, and run on the same
lines; and this explains why their judgments constantly
agree—not, however, because they are based on truth. To
such lengths does this go that certain fundamental views
obtain amongst mankind at all times, and are always being
repeated and brought forward anew, whilst the great minds
of all ages are in open or secret opposition to them.

A genius is a man in whose mind the world is presented
as an object is presented in a mirror, but with a degree
more of clearness and a greater distinction of outline than
is attained by ordinary people. It is from him that humanity may look for most instruction; for the deepest
insight into the most important matters is to be acquired,
not by an observant attention to detail, but by a close
study of things as a whole. And if his mind reaches matu-

rity, the instruction he gives will be conveyed now in one form, now in another. Thus genius may be defined as an eminently clear consciousness of things in general, and therefore, also of that which is opposed to them, namely, one's own self.

The world looks up to a man thus endowed, and expects to learn something about life and its real nature. But several highly favorable circumstances must combine to produce genius, and this is a very rare event. It happens only now and then, let us say once in a century, that a man is born whose intellect so perceptibly surpasses the normal measure as to amount to that second faculty which seems to be accidental, as it is out of all relation to the will. He may remain a long time without being recognized or appreciated, stupidity preventing the one and envy the other. But should this once come to pass, mankind will crowd round him and his works, in the hope that he may be able to enlighten some of the darkness of their existence or inform them about it. His message is, to some extent, a revelation, and he himself a higher being, even though he may be but little above the ordinary standard.

Like the ordinary man, the genius is what he is chiefly for himself. This is essential to his nature: a fact which can neither be avoided nor altered. What he may be for others remains a matter of chance and of secondary importance. In no case can people receive from his mind more than a reflection, and then only when he joins with them in the attempt to get his thought into their heads; where, however, it is never anything but an exotic plant, stunted and frail.

In order to have original, uncommon, and perhaps even immortal thoughts, it is enough to estrange oneself so fully from the world of things for a few moments, that the most ordinary objects and events appear quite new and unfamiliar. In this way their true nature is disclosed. What is here demanded cannot, perhaps, be said to be difficult; it is not in our power at all, but is just the province of genius.

By itself, genius can produce original thoughts just as little as a woman by herself can bear children. Outward circumstances must come to fructify genius, and be, as it were, a father to its progeny.

The mind of genius is among other minds what the carbuncle is among precious stones: it sends forth light of its own, while the others reflect only that which they have received. The relation of the genius to the ordinary mind may also be described as that of an idio-electrical body to one which merely is a conductor of electricity.

The mere man of learning, who spends his life in teaching what he has learned, is not strictly to be called a man of genius; just as idio-electrical bodies are not conductors. Nay, genius stands to mere learning as the words to the music in a song. A man of learning is a man who has learned a great deal; a man of genius, one from whom we learn something which the genius has learned from nobody. Great minds, of which there is scarcely one in a hundred millions, are thus the lighthouses of humanity; and without them mankind would lose itself in the boundless sea of monstrous error and bewilderment.

And so the simple man of learning, in the strict sense of the word—the ordinary professor, for instance—looks upon the genius much as we look upon a hare, which is good to eat after it has been killed and dressed up. So long as it is alive, it is only good to shoot at.

He who wishes to experience gratitude from his contemporaries, must adjust his pace to theirs. But great things are never produced in this way. And he who wants to do great things must direct his gaze to posterity, and in firm confidence elaborate his work for coming generations.

No doubt, the result may be that he will remain quite unknown to his contemporaries, and comparable to a man who, compelled to spend his life upon a lonely island, with great effort sets up a monument there, to transmit to future sea-farers the knowledge of his existence. If he thinks it a hard fate, let him console himself with the reflection that the ordinary man who lives for practical aims only, often suffers a like fate, without having any compensation to hope for; inasmuch as he may, under favorable conditions, spend a life of material production, earning, buying, building, fertilizing, laying out, founding, establishing, beautifying with daily effort and unflagging zeal, and all the time think that he is working for himself; and yet in the end it is his descendants who reap the benefit of it all, and sometimes not even his descendants. It is the same with the man of genius; he, too, hopes for his reward and for honor at least; and at last finds that he has worked for posterity alone. Both, to be sure, have inherited a great deal from their ancestors.

The compensation I have mentioned as the privilege of genius lies, not in what it is to others, but in what it is to itself. What man has in any real sense lived more than he whose moments of thought make their echoes heard through the tumult of centuries? Perhaps, after all, it would be the best thing for a genius to attain undisturbed possession of himself, by spending his life in enjoying the pleasure of his own thoughts, his own works, and by admitting the world only as the heir of his ample existence. Then the world would find the mark of his existence only after his death, as it finds that of the Ichnolith.[2]

It is not only in the activity of his highest powers that

[2] *Translator's Note.*—For an illustration of this feeling in poetry, Schopenhauer refers the reader to Byron's *Prophecy of Dante:* introd. to C. 4.

the genius surpasses ordinary people. A man who is unusually well-knit, supple and agile, will perform all his
movements with exceptional ease, even with comfort, because he takes a direct pleasure in an activity for which
he is particularly well-equipped, and therefore often exercises it without any object. Further, if he is an acrobat
or a dancer, not only does he take leaps which other
people cannot execute, but he also betrays rare elasticity
and agility in those easier steps which others can also
perform, and even in ordinary walking. In the same way
a man of superior mind will not only produce thoughts
and works which could never have come from another;
it will not be here alone that he will show his greatness;
but as knowledge and thought form a mode of activity
natural and easy to him, he will also delight himself in
them at all times, and so apprehend small matters which
are within the range of other minds, more easily, quickly
and correctly than they. Thus he will take a direct and
lively pleasure in every increase of knowledge, every problem solved, every witty thought, whether of his own or
another's; and so his mind will have no further aim than
to be constantly active. This will be an inexhaustible
spring of delight; and boredom, that spectre which haunts
the ordinary man, can never come near him.

Then, too, the masterpieces of past and contemporary
men of genius exist in their fullness for him alone. If a
great product of genius is recommended to the ordinary,
simple mind, it will take as much pleasure in it as the
victim of gout receives in being invited to a ball. The
one goes for the sake of formality, and the other reads
the book so as not to be in arrear. For La Bruyère was
quite right when he said: *All the wit in the world is lost
upon him who has none.* The whole range of thought of
a man of talent, or of a genius, compared with the thoughts
of the common man, is, even when directed to objects es-

sentially the same, like a brilliant oil-painting, full of life, compared with a mere outline or a weak sketch in water-color.

All this is part of the reward of genius, and compensates him for a lonely existence in a world with which he has nothing in common and no sympathies. But since size is relative, it comes to the same thing whether I say, Caius was a great man, or Caius has to live amongst wretchedly small people: for Brobdingnag and Lilliput vary only in the point from which they start. However great, then, however admirable or instructive, a long posterity may think the author of immortal works, during his lifetime he will appear to his contemporaries small, wretched, and insipid in proportion. This is what I mean by saying that as there are three hundred degrees from the base of a tower to the summit, so there are exactly three hundred from the summit to the base. Great minds thus owe little ones some indulgence; for it is only in virtue of these little minds that they themselves are great.

Let us, then, not be surprised if we find men of genius generally unsociable and repellent. It is not their want of sociability that is to blame. Their path through the world is like that of a man who goes for a walk on a bright summer morning. He gazes with delight on the beauty and freshness of nature, but he has to rely wholly on that for entertainment; for he can find no society but the peasants as they bend over the earth and cultivate the soil. It is often the case that a great mind prefers soliloquy to the dialogue he may have in this world. If he condescends to it now and then, the hollowness of it may possibly drive him back to his soliloquy; for in forgetfulness of his interlocutor, or caring little whether he understands or not, he talks to him as a child talks to a doll.

Modesty in a great mind would, no doubt, be pleasing

to the world; but, unluckily, it is an *contradicto in adjecto*. It would compel a genius to give the thoughts and opinions, nay, even the method and style, of the million preference over his own; to set a higher value upon them; and, wide apart as they are, to bring his views into harmony with theirs, or even suppress them altogether, so as to let the others hold the field. In that case, however, he would either produce nothing at all, or else his achievements would be just upon a level with theirs. Great, genuine and extraordinary work can be done only in so far as its author disregards the method, the thoughts, the opinions of his contemporaries, and quietly works on, in spite of their criticism, on his side despising what they praise. No one becomes great without arrogance of this sort. Should his life and work fall upon a time which cannot recognize and appreciate him, he is at any rate true to himself; like some noble traveler forced to pass the night in a miserable inn; when morning comes, he contentedly goes his way.

A poet or philosopher should have no fault to find with his age if it only permits him to do his work undisturbed in his own corner; nor with his fate if the corner granted him allows of his following his vocation without having to think about other people.

For the brain to be a mere laborer in the service of the belly, is indeed the common lot of almost all those who do not live on the work of their hands; and they are far from being discontented with their lot. But it strikes despair into a man of great mind, whose brain-power goes beyond the measure necessary for the service of the will; and he prefers, if need be, to live in the narrowest circumstances, so long as they afford him the free use of his time for the development and application of his faculties; in other words, if they give him the leisure which is invaluable to him.

It is otherwise with ordinary people: for them leisure has no value in itself, nor is it, indeed, without its dangers, as these people seem to know. The technical work of our time, which is done to an unprecedented perfection, has, by increasing and multiplying objects of luxury, given the favorites of fortune a choice between more leisure and culture upon the one side, and additional luxury and good living, but with increased activity, upon the other; and, true to their character, they choose the latter, and prefer champagne to freedom. And they are consistent in their choice; for, to them, every exertion of the mind which does not serve the aims of the will is folly. Intellectual effort for its own sake, they call eccentricity. Therefore, persistence in the aims of the will and the belly will be concentricity; and, to be sure, the will is the centre, the kernel of the world.

But in general it is very seldom that any such alternative is presented. For as with money, most men have no superfluity, but only just enough for their needs, so with intelligence; they possess just what will suffice for the service of the will, that is, for the carrying on of their business. Having made their fortune, they are content to gape or to indulge in sensual pleasures or childish amusements, cards or dice; or they will talk in the dullest way, or dress up and make obeisance to one another. And how few are those who have even a little superfluity of intellectual power! Like the others they too make themselves a pleasure; but it is a pleasure of the intellect. Either they will pursue some liberal study which brings them in nothing, or they will practice some art; and in general, they will be capable of taking an objective interest in things, so that it will be possible to converse with them. But with the others it is better not to enter into any relations at all; for, except when they tell the results of their own experience or give an account of their special vocation, or at any rate impart what they have learned from some one else, their conversation will not be worth listening to; and if anything is said to them, they will rarely grasp or understand it aright, and it will in most cases be opposed to their own opinions. Balthazar Gracian describes them very strikingly as men who are not men— *hombres che non lo son*. And Giordano Bruno says the same thing: *What a difference there is in having to do with men compared with those who are only made in their image and likeness!*[3] And how wonderfully this passage agrees with that remark in the Kurral: *The common people look like men but I have never seen anything quite like them.* If the reader will consider the extent to which these ideas agree in thought and even in expression, and in the wide difference between them in point of date and nationality, he cannot doubt but that they are at one with the facts of life. It was certainly not under the influence of those passages that, about twenty years ago, I tried to get a snuff-box made, the lid of which should have two fine chestnuts represented upon it, if possible in mosaic; together with a leaf which was to show that they were horse-chestnuts. This symbol was meant to keep the thought constantly before my mind. If anyone wishes for entertainment, such as will prevent him feeling solitary even when he is alone, let me recommend the company of dogs, whose moral and intellectual qualities may almost afford delight and gratification.

Still, we should always be careful to avoid being unjust. I am often surprised by the cleverness, and now and again by the stupidity of my dog; and I have similar experiences with mankind. Countless times, in indignation at their incapacity, their total lack of discernment, their bestiality, I have been forced to echo the old complaint that folly is the mother and the nurse of the human race:

[3] Opera: ed. Wagner, I. 224.

*Humani generis mater nutrixque profecto
Stultitia est.*

But at other times I have been astounded that from such a race there could have gone forth so many arts and sciences, abounding in so much use and beauty, even though it has always been the few that produce them. Yet these arts and sciences have struck root, established and perfected themselves: and the race has with persistent fidelity preserved Homer, Plato, Horace and others for thousands of years, by copying and treasuring their writings, thus saving them from oblivion, in spite of all the evils and atrocities that have happened in the world. Thus the race has proved that it appreciates the value of these things, and at the same time it can form a correct view of special achievements or estimate signs of judgment and intelligence. When this takes place amongst those who belong to the great multitude, it is by a kind of inspiration. Sometimes a correct opinion will be formed by the multitude itself; but this is only when the chorus of praise has grown full and complete. It is then like the sound of untrained voices; where there are enough of them, it is always harmonious.

Those who emerge from the multitude, those who are called men of genius, are merely the *lucida intervalla* of the whole human race. They achieve that which others could not possibly achieve. Their originality is so great that not only is their divergence from others obvious, but their individuality is expressed with such force, that all the men of genius who have ever existed show, every one of them, peculiarities of character and mind; so that the gift of his works is one which he alone of all men could ever have presented to the world. This is what makes that simile of Aristo's so true and so justly celebrated: *Natura lo fece e poi ruppe lo stampo.* After Nature stamps a man of genius, she breaks the die.

But there is always a limit to human capacity; and no one can be a great genius without having some decidedly weak side, it may even be, some intellectual narrowness. In other words, there will be some faculty in which he is now and then inferior to men of moderate endowments. It will be a faculty which, if strong, might have been an obstacle to the exercise of the qualities in which he excels. What this weak point is, it will always be hard to define with any accuracy even in a given case. It may be better expressed indirectly; thus Plato's weak point is exactly that in which Aristotle is strong, and *vice versa;* and so, too, Kant is deficient just where Goethe is great.

Now, mankind is fond of venerating something; but its veneration is generally directed to the wrong object, and it remains so directed until posterity comes to set it right. But the educated public is no sooner set right in this, than the honor which is due to genius degenerates; just as the honor which the faithful pay to their saints easily passes into a frivolous worship of relics. Thousands of Christians adore the relics of a saint whose life and doctrine are unknown to them; and the religion of thousands of Buddhists lies more in veneration of the Holy Tooth or some such object, or the vessel that contains it, or the Holy Bowl, or the fossil footstep, or the Holy Tree which Buddha planted, than in the thorough knowledge and faithful practice of his high teaching. Petrarch's house in Arqua; Tasso's supposed prison in Ferrara; Shakespeare's house in Stratford, with his chair; Goethe's house in Weimar, with its furniture; Kant's old hat; the autographs of great men; these things are gaped at with interest and awe by many who have never read their works. They cannot do anything more than just gape.

The intelligent amongst them are moved by the wish to see the objects which the great man habitually had before his eyes; and by a strange illusion, these produce the mistaken notion that with the objects they are bringing back the man himself, or that something of him must cling to them. Akin to such people are those who earnestly strive to acquaint themselves with the subject-matter of a poet's works, or to unravel the personal circumstances and events in his life which have suggested particular passages. This is as though the audience in a theatre were to admire a fine scene and then rush upon the stage to look at the scaffolding that supports it. There are in our day enough instances of these critical investigators, and they prove the truth of the saying that mankind is interested, not in the *form* of a work, that is, in its manner of treatment, but in its actual matter. All it cares for is the theme. To read a philosopher's biography, instead of studying his thoughts, is like neglecting a picture and attending only to the style of its frame, debating whether it is carved well or ill, and how much it cost to gild it.

This is all very well. However, there is another class of persons whose interest is also directed to material and personal considerations, but they go much further and carry it to a point where it becomes absolutely futile. Because a great man has opened up to them the treasures of his inmost being, and, by a supreme effort of his faculties, produced works which not only redound to their elevation and enlightenment, but will also benefit their posterity to the tenth and twentieth generation; because he has presented mankind with a matchless gift, these varlets think themselves justified in sitting in judgment upon his personal morality, and trying if they cannot discover here or there some spot in him which will soothe the pain they feel at the sight of so great a mind, compared with the overwhelming feeling of their own nothingness.

This is the real source of all those prolix discussions, carried on in countless books and reviews, on the moral

aspect of Goethe's life, and whether he ought not to have
married one or other of the girls with whom he fell in love
in his young days; whether, again, instead of honestly
devoting himself to the service of his master, he should
not have been a man of the people, a German patriot,
worthy of a seat in the *Paulskirche*, and so on.   Such
crying ingratitude and malicious detraction prove that
these self-constituted judges are as great knaves morally
as they are intellectually, which is saying a great deal.

A man of talent will strive for money and reputation;
but the spring that moves genius to the production of its
works is not as easy to name.   Wealth is seldom its
reward.   Nor is it reputation or glory; only a Frenchman
could mean that.   Glory is such an uncertain thing, and,
if you look at it closely, of so little value.   Besides it never
corresponds to the effort you have made:

Responsura tuo nunquam est par fama labori.

Nor, again, is it exactly the pleasure it gives you; for this
is almost outweighed by the greatness of the effort.   It
is rather a peculiar kind of instinct, which drives the man
of genius to give permanent form to what he sees and
feels, without being conscious of any further motive.   It
works, in the main, by a necessity similar to that which
makes a tree bear its fruit; and no external condition is
needed but the ground upon which it is to thrive.

On a closer examination, it seems as though, in the case
of a genius, the will to live, which is the spirit of the
human species, were conscious of having, by some rare
chance, and for a brief period, attained a greater clearness
of vision, and were now trying to secure it, or at least
the outcome of it, for the whole species, to which the
individual genius in his inmost being belongs; so that the
light which he sheds about him may pierce the darkness

and dullness of ordinary human consciousness and there produce some good effect.

Arising in some such way, this instinct drives the genius to carry his work to completion, without thinking of reward or applause or sympathy; to leave all care for his own personal welfare; to make his life one of industrious solitude, and to strain his faculties to the utmost. He thus comes to think more about posterity than about contemporaries; because, while the latter can only lead him astray, posterity forms the majority of the species, and time will gradually bring the discerning few who can appreciate him. Meanwhile it is with him as with the artist described by Goethe; he has no princely patron to prize his talents, no friend to rejoice with him:

> *Ein Fürst der die Talente schätzt,*
> *Ein Freund, der sich mit mir ergötzt,*
> *Die haben leider mir gefehlt.*

His work is, as it were, a sacred object and the true fruit of his life, and his aim in storing it away for a more discerning posterity will be to make it the property of mankind. An aim like this far surpasses all others, and for it he wears the crown of thorns which is one day to bloom into a wreath of laurel. All his powers are concentrated in the effort to complete and secure his work; just as the insect, in the last stage of its development, uses its whole strength on behalf of a brood it will never live to see; it puts its eggs in some place of safety, where as it well knows, the young will one day find life and nourishment, and then dies in confidence.

Studies in Pessimism

ON THE SUFFERINGS OF THE WORLD

UNLESS *suffering* is the direct and immediate object of life, our existence must entirely fail of its aim. It is absurd to look upon the enormous amount of pain that abounds everywhere in the world, and originates in needs and necessities inseparable from life itself, as serving no purpose at all and the result of mere chance. Each separate misfortune, as it comes, seems, no doubt, to be something exceptional; but misfortune in general is the rule.

I know of no greater absurdity than that propounded by most systems of philosophy in declaring evil to be negative in its character. Evil is just what is positive; it makes its own existence felt. Leibnitz is particularly concerned to defend this absurdity; and he seeks to strengthen his position by using a palpable and paltry sophism.[1] It is the good which is negative; in other words, happiness and satisfaction always imply some desire fulfilled, some state of pain brought to an end.

This explains the fact that we generally find pleasure to be not nearly so pleasant as we expected, and pain very much more painful.

[1] *Translator's Note*, cf. *Théod*, § 153.—Leibnitz argued that evil is a negative quality—*i.e.*, the absence of good; and that its active and seemingly positive character is an incidental and not an essential part of its nature. Coïd, he said, is only the absence of the power of heat, and the active power of expansion in freezing water is an incidental and not an essential part of the nature of cold. The fact is, that the power of expansion in freezing water is really an increase of repulsion amongst its molecules; and Schopenhauer is quite right in calling the whole argument a sophism.

The pleasure in this world, it has been said, outweighs the pain; or, at any rate, there is an even balance between the two. If the reader wishes to see shortly whether this statement is true, let him compare the respective feelings of two animals, one of which is engaged in eating the other.

The best consolation in misfortune or affliction of any kind will be the thought of other people who are in a still worse plight than yourself; and this is a form of consolation open to every one. But what an awful fate this means for mankind as a whole!

We are like lambs in a field, disporting themselves under the eye of the butcher, who chooses out first one and then another for his prey. So it is that in our good days we are all unconscious of the evil Fate may have presently in store for us—sickness, poverty, mutilation, loss of sight or reason.

No little part of the torment of existence lies in this, that Time is continually pressing upon us, never letting us take breath, but always coming after us, like a taskmaster with a whip. If at any moment Time stays his hand, it is only when we are delivered over to the misery of boredom.

But misfortune has its uses; for, as our bodily frame would burst asunder if the pressure of the atmosphere was removed, so, if the lives of men were relieved of all need, hardship and adversity; if everything they took in hand were successful, they would be so swollen with arrogance that, though they might not burst, they would present the spectacle of unbridled folly—nay they would go mad. And I may say, further, that a certain amount of care or pain or trouble is necessary for every man at all times. A ship without ballast is unstable and will not go straight.

Certain it is that *work, worry, labor* and *trouble,* form the lot of almost all men their whole life long. But if all wishes were fulfilled as soon as they arose, how would men occupy their lives? what would they do with their time? If the world were a paradise of luxury and ease, a land flowing with milk and honey, where every Jack obtained his Jill at once and without any difficulty, men would either die of boredom or hang themselves; or there would be wars, massacres, and murders; so that in the end mankind would inflict more suffering on itself than it has now to accept at the hands of Nature.

In early youth, as we contemplate our coming life, we are like children in a theatre before the curtain is raised, sitting there in high spirits and eagerly waiting for the play to begin. It is a blessing that we do not know what is really going to happen. Could we foresee it, there are times when children might seem like innocent prisoners, condemned, not to death, but to life, and as yet all unconscious of what their sentence means. Nevertheless, every man desires to reach old age; in other words, a state of life of which it may be said: "It is bad to-day, and it will be worse to-morrow; and so on till the worst of all."

If you try to imagine, as nearly as you can, what an amount of misery, pain and suffering of every kind the sun shines upon in its course, you will admit that it would be much better if, on the earth as little as on the moon, the sun were able to call forth the phenomena of life; and if, here as there, the surface were still in a crystalline state.

Again, you may look upon life as an unprofitable episode, disturbing the blessed calm of non-existence. And, in any case, even though things have gone with you tolerably well, the longer you live the more clearly you will feel that, on the whole, life is *a disappointment, nay, a cheat.*

If two men who were friends in their youth meet again when they are old, after being separated for a life-time, the chief feeling they will have at the sight of each other will be one of complete disappointment at life as a whole;

because their thoughts will be carried back to that earlier time when life seemed so fair as it lay spread out before them in the rosy light of dawn, promised so much—and then performed so little. This feeling will so completely predominate over every other that they will not even consider it necessary to give it words; but on either side it will be silently assumed, and form the ground-work of all they have to talk about.

He who lives to see two or three generations is like a man who sits some time in the conjurer's booth at a fair, and witnesses the performance twice or thrice in succession. The tricks were meant to be seen only once; and when they are no longer a novelty and cease to deceive, their effect is gone.

While no man is much to be envied for his lot, there are countless numbers whose fate is to be deplored.

Life is a task to be done. It is a fine thing to say *defunctus est;* it means that the man has done his task.

If children were brought into the world by an act of pure reason alone, would the human race continue to exist? Would not a man rather have so much sympathy with the coming generation as to spare it the burden of existence? or at any rate not take it upon himself to impose that burden upon it in cold blood?

I shall be told, I suppose, that my philosophy is comfortless—because I speak the truth; and people prefer to be assured that everything the Lord has made is good. Go to the priests, then, and leave philosophers in peace! At any rate, do not ask us to accommodate our doctrines to the lessons you have been taught. That is what those rascals of sham philosophers will do for you. Ask them for any doctrine you please, and you will get it. Your University professors are bound to preach optimism; and it is an easy and agreeable task to upset their theories.

I have reminded the reader that every state of welfare,

every feeling of satisfaction, is negative in its character; that is to say, it consists in freedom from pain, which is the positive element of existence. It follows, therefore, that the happiness of any given life is to be measured, not by its joys and pleasures, but by the extent to which it has been free from suffering—from positive evil. If this is the true standpoint, the lower animals appear to enjoy a happier destiny than man. Let us examine the matter a little more closely.

However varied the forms that human happiness and misery may take, leading a man to seek the one and shun the other, the material basis of it all is bodily pleasure or bodily pain. This basis is very restricted: it is simply health, food, protection from wet and cold, the satisfaction of the sexual instinct; or else the absence of these things. Consequently, as far as real physical pleasure is concerned, the man is not better off than the brute, except in so far as the higher possibilities of his nervous system make him more sensitive to every kind of pleasure, but also, it must be remembered, to every kind of pain. But then compared with the brute, how much stronger are the passions aroused in him! what an immeasurable difference there is in the depth and vehemence of his emotions!— yet, in the one case as in the other, all to produce the same result in the end: namely, health, food, clothing, and so on.

The chief source of all this passion is that thought for what is absent and future, which, with man, exercises such a powerful influence upon all he does. It is this that is the real origin of his cares, his hopes, his fears—emotions which affect him much more deeply than could ever be the case with those present joys and sufferings to which the brute is confined. In his powers of reflection, memory and foresight, man possesses, as it were, a machine for condensing and storing up his pleasures and his sorrows. But the brute has nothing of the kind; whenever it is in pain, it is as though it were suffering for the first time, even though the same thing should have previously happened to it time out of number. It has no power of summing up its feelings. Hence its careless and placid temper: how much it is to be envied! But in man reflection comes in, with all the emotions to which it gives rise; and taking up the same elements of pleasure and pain which are common to him and the brute, it develops his susceptibility to happiness and misery to such a degree that, at one moment the man is brought in an instant to a state of delight that may even prove fatal, at another to the depths of despair and suicide.

If we carry our analysis a step farther, we shall find that, in order to increase his pleasures, man has intentionally added to the number and pressure of his needs, which in their original state were not much more difficult to satisfy than those of the brute. Hence luxury in all its forms; delicate food, the use of tobacco and opium, spirituous liquors, fine clothes, and the thousand and one things that he considers necessary to his existence.

And above and beyond all this, there is a separate and peculiar source of pleasure, and consequently of pain, which man has established for himself, also as the result of using his powers of reflection; and this occupies him out of all proportion to its value, nay, almost more than all his other interests put together—I mean ambition and the feeling of honor and shame; in plain words, what he thinks about the opinion other people have of him. Taking a thousand forms, often very strange ones, this becomes the goal of almost all the efforts he makes that are not rooted in physical pleasure or pain. It is true that besides the sources of pleasure which he has in common with the brute, man has the pleasures of the mind as well. These admit of many gradations, from the most innocent trifling or the merest talk up to the highest intellectual achievements; but there is the accompanying boredom to be set against them on the side of suffering. Boredom is a form of suffering unknown to brutes, at any rate in their natural state; it is only the very cleverest of them who show faint traces of it when they are domesticated; whereas in the case of man it has become a downright scourge. The crowd of miserable wretches whose one aim in life is to fill their purses but never to put anything into their heads, offers a singular instance of this torment of boredom. Their wealth becomes a punishment by delivering them up to the misery of having nothing to do; for, to escape it, they will rush about in all directions, traveling here, there and everywhere. No sooner do they arrive in a place than they are anxious to know what amusements it affords; just as though they were beggars asking where they could receive a dole! Of a truth, need and boredom are the two poles of human life. Finally, I may mention that as regards the sexual relation, a man is committed to a peculiar arrangement which drives him obstinately to choose one person. This feeling grows, now and then, into a more or less passionate love,[2] which is the source of little pleasure and much suffering.

It is, however, a wonderful thing that the mere addition of thought should serve to raise such a vast and lofty structure of human happiness and misery; resting, too, on the same narrow basis of joy and sorrow as man holds in common with the brute, and exposing him to such violent emotions, to so many storms of passion, so much convulsion of feeling, that what he has suffered stands written and may be read in the lines on his face. And yet, when all is told, he has been struggling ultimately for the very same things as the brute has attained, and with an incomparably smaller expenditure of passion and pain.

[2] I have treated this subject at length in a special chapter of the second volume of my chief work.

But all this contributes to increase the measures of suffering in human life out of all proportion to its pleasures; and the pains of life are made much worse for man by the fact that death is something very real to him. The brute flies from death instinctively without really knowing what it is, and therefore without ever contemplating it in the way natural to a man, who has this prospect always before his eyes. So that even if only a few brutes die a natural death, and most of them live only just long enough to transmit their species, and then, if not earlier, become the prey of some other animal,—whilst man, on the other hand, manages to make so-called natural death the rule, to which, however, there are a good many exceptions,—the advantage is on the side of the brute, for the reason stated above. But the fact is that man attains the natural term of years just as seldom as the brute; because the unnatural way in which he lives, and the strain of work and emotion, lead to a degeneration of the race; and so his goal is not often reached.

The brute is much more content with mere existence than man; the plant is wholly so; and man finds satisfaction in it just in proportion as he is dull and obtuse. Accordingly, the life of the brute carries less of sorrow with it, but also less of joy, when compared with the life of man; and while this may be traced, on the one side, to freedom from the torment of *care* and *anxiety*, it is also due to the fact that *hope*, in any real sense, is unknown to the brute. It is thus deprived of any share in that which gives us the most and best of our joys and pleasures, the mental anticipation of a happy future, and the inspiriting play of phantasy, both of which we owe to our power of imagination. If the brute is free from care, it is also, in this sense, without hope; in either case, because its consciousness is limited to the present moment, to what it can actually see before it. The brute is an embodiment of present impulses, and hence what elements of fear and hope exist in its nature—and they do not go very far—arise only in relation to objects that lie before it and within reach of those impulses: whereas a man's range of vision embraces the whole of his life, and extends far into the past and future.

Following upon this, there is one respect in which brutes show real wisdom when compared with us—I mean, their quiet, placid enjoyment of the present moment. The tranquillity of mind which this seems to give them often puts us to shame for the many times we allow our thoughts and our cares to make us restless and discontented. And, in fact, those pleasures of hope and anticipation which I have been mentioning are not to be had for nothing. The delight which a man has in hoping for and looking forward to some special satisfaction is a part of the real pleasure attaching to it enjoyed in advance. This is afterwards deducted; for the more we look forward to anything, the less satisfaction we find in it when it comes. But the brute's enjoyment is not anticipated, and therefore, suffers no deduction; so that the actual pleasure of the moment comes to it whole and unimpaired. In the same way, too, evil presses upon the brute only with its own intrinsic weight; whereas with us the fear of its coming often makes its burden ten times more grievous.

It is just this characteristic way in which the brute gives itself up entirely to the present moment that contributes so much to the delight we take in our domestic pets. They are the present moment personified, and in some respects they make us feel the value of every hour that is free from trouble and annoyance, which we, with our thoughts and preoccupations, mostly disregard. But man, that selfish and heartless creature, misuses this quality of the brute to be more content than we are with mere existence, and often works it to such an extent that he allows the brute absolutely nothing more than mere, bare life. The bird which was made so that it might rove over half of the world, he shuts up into the space of a cubic foot, there to die a slow death in longing and crying for freedom; for in a cage it does not sing for the pleasure of it. And when I see how man misuses the dog, his best friend; how he ties up this intelligent animal with a chain, I feel the deepest sympathy with the brute and burning indignation against its master.

We shall see later that by taking a very high standpoint it is possible to justify the sufferings of mankind. But this justification cannot apply to animals, whose sufferings, while in a great measure brought about by men, are often considerable even apart from their agency.[3] And so we are forced to ask, Why and for what purpose does all this torment and agony exist? There is nothing here to give the will pause; it is not free to deny itself and so obtain redemption. There is only one consideration that may serve to explain the sufferings of animals. It is this: that the will to live, which underlies the world of phenomena, must, in their case satisfy its cravings by feeding upon itself. This it does by forming a gradation of phenomena, every one of which exists at the expense of another. I have shown, however, that the capacity for suffering is less in animals than in man. Any further explanation that may be given of their fate will be in the nature of hypothesis, if not actually mythical in character; and I may leave the reader to speculate upon the matter for himself.

Brahma is said to have produced the world by a kind of fall or mistake; and in order to atone for his folly, he is bound to remain in it himself until he works out his redemption. As an account of the origin of things, that is admirable! According to the doctrines of *Buddhism*, the world came into being as the result of some inexplicable

[3] Cf. *Welt als Wille und Vorstellung,* vol. ii. p. 404.

disturbance in the heavenly calm of Nirvana, that blessed state obtained by expiation, which had endured so long a time—the change taking place by a kind of fatality. This explanation must be understood as having at bottom some moral bearing; although it is illustrated by an exactly parallel theory in the domain of physical science, which places the origin of the sun in a primitive streak of mist, formed one knows not how. Subsequently, by a series of moral errors, the world became gradually worse and worse— true of the physical orders as well—until it assumed the dismal aspect it wears to-day. Excellent! The *Greeks* looked upon the world and the gods as the work of an inscrutable necessity. A passable explanation: we may be content with it until we can get a better. Again, *Ormuzd* and *Ahriman* are rival powers, continually at war. That is not bad. But that a God like Jehovah should have created this world of misery and woe, out of pure caprice, and because he enjoyed doing it, and should then have clapped his hands in praise of his own work, and declared everything to be very good—that will not do at all! In its explanation of the origin of the world, Judaism is inferior to any other form of religious doctrine professed by a civilized nation; and it is quite in keeping with this that it is the only one which presents no trace whatever of any belief in the immortality of the soul.[4]

Even though Leibnitz' contention, that this is the best of all possible worlds, were correct, that would not justify God in having created it. For he is the Creator not of the world only, but of possibility itself; and, therefore, he ought to have so ordered possibility as that it would admit of something better.

There are two things which make it impossible to believe that this world is the successful work of an all-wise, all-good, and, at the same time, all-powerful Being; firstly,

[4] See *Parerga*, vol. i. pp. 139 *et seq.*

the misery which abounds in it everywhere; and secondly, the obvious imperfection of its highest product, man, who is a burlesque of what he should be. These things cannot be reconciled with any such belief. On the contrary, they are just the facts which support what I have been saying; they are our authority for viewing the world as the outcome of our own misdeeds, and therefore, as something that had better not have been. Whilst, under the former hypothesis, they amount to a bitter accusation against the Creator, and supply material for sarcasm; under the latter they form an indictment against our own nature, our own will, and teach us a lesson of humility. They lead us to see that, like the children of a libertine, we come into the world with the burden of sin upon us; and that it is only through having continually to atone for this sin that our existence is so miserable, and that its end is death.

There is nothing more certain than the general truth that it is the grievous *sin of the world* which has produced the grievous *suffering of the world*. I am not referring here to the physical connection between these two things lying in the realm of experience; my meaning is metaphysical. Accordingly, the sole thing that reconciles me to the Old Testament is the story of the Fall. In my eyes, it is the only metaphysical truth in that book, even though it appears in the form of an allegory. There seems to me no better explanation of our existence than that it is the result of some false step, some sin of which we are paying the penalty. I cannot refrain from recommending the thoughtful reader a popular, but at the same time, profound treatise on this subject by Claudius[5] which ex-

[5] *Translator's Note.*—Matthias Claudius (1740–1815), a popular poet, and friend of Klopstock, Herder and Lessing. He edited the *Wandsbecker Bote,* in the fourth part of which appeared the treatise mentioned above. He generally wrote under the pseudonym of *Asmus,* and Schopenhauer often refers to him by this name.

hibits the essentially pessimistic spirit of Christianity. It is entitled: *Cursed is the ground for thy sake.*

Between the ethics of the Greeks and the ethics of the Hindoos, there is a glaring contrast. In the one case (with the exception, it must be confessed, of Plato), the object of ethics is to enable a man to lead a happy life; in the other, to free and redeem him from life altogether—as is directly stated in the very first words of the *Sankhya Karika.*

Allied with this is the contrast between the Greek and the Christian idea of death. It is strikingly presented in a visible form on a fine antique sarcophagus in the gallery of Florence, which exhibits, in relief, the whole series of ceremonies attending a wedding in ancient times, from the formal offer to the evening when Hymen's torch lights the happy couple home. Compare with that the Christian coffin, draped in mournful black and surmounted with a crucifix! How much significance there is in these two ways of finding comfort in death. They are opposed to each other, but each is right. The one points to the *affirmation* of the will to live, which remains sure of life for all time, however rapidly its forms may change. The other, in the symbol of suffering and death, points to the *denial* of the will to live, to redemption from this world, the domain of death and devil. And in the question between the affirmation and the denial of the will to live, Christianity is in the last resort right.

The contrast which the New Testament presents when compared with the Old, according to the ecclesiastical view of the matter, is just that existing between my ethical system and the moral philosophy of Europe. The Old Testament represents man as under the dominion of Law, in which, however, there is no redemption. The New Testament declares Law to have failed, frees man from its dominion,[6] and in its stead preaches the kingdom of grace,

[6] Cf. Romans vii; Galatians ii, iii.

to be won by faith, love of neighbor and entire sacrifice of
self. This is the path of redemption from the evil of the
world. The spirit of the New Testament is undoubtedly
asceticism, however your protestants and rationalists may
twist it to suit their purpose. Asceticism is the denial of
the will to live; and the transition from the Old Testament to the New, from the dominion of Law to that of
Faith, from justification by works to redemption through
the Mediator, from the domain of sin and death to eternal
life in Christ, means, when taken in its real sense, the
transition from the merely moral virtues to the denial of
the will to live. My philosophy shows the metaphysical
foundation of justice and the love of mankind, and points
to the goal to which these virtues necessarily lead, if they
are practised in perfection. At the same time it is candid
in confessing that a man must turn his back upon the
world, and that the denial of the will to live is the way of
redemption. It is therefore really at one with the spirit
of the New Testament, whilst all other systems are couched
in the spirit of the Old; that is to say, theoretically as
well as practically, their result is Judaism—mere despotic
theism. In this sense, then, my doctrine might be called
the only true Christian philosophy—however paradoxical
a statement this may seem to people who take superficial
views instead of penetrating to the heart of the matter.

If you want a safe compass to guide you through life,
and to banish all doubt as to the right way of looking at
it, you cannot do better than accustom yourself to regard
this world as a penitentiary, a sort of a penal colony, or
ἐργαστήριον, as the earliest philosopher called it.[7] Amongst
the Christian Fathers, Origen, with praiseworthy courage,
took this view,[8] which is further justified by certain objective theories of life. I refer, not to my own philosophy

[7] Cf. Clem. Alex. Strom. L. iii., c. 3, p. 399.
[8] Augustine de civitate Dei., L. xi. c. 23.

alone, but to the wisdom of all ages, as expressed in Brahmanism and Buddhism, and in the sayings of Greek philosophers like Empedocles and Pythagoras; as also by Cicero, in his remark that the wise men of old used to teach that we come into this world to pay the penalty of crime committed in another state of existence—a doctrine which formed part of the initiation into the mysteries.[9] And Vanini—whom his contemporaries burned, finding that an easier task than to confute him—puts the same thing in a very forcible way. *Man,* he says, *is so full of every kind of misery that, were it not repugnant to the Christian religion, I should venture to affirm that if evil spirits exist at all, they have passed into human form and are now atoning for their crimes.*[10] And true Christianity—using the word in its right sense—also regards our existence as the consequence of sin and error.

If you accustom yourself to this view of life you will regulate your expectations accordingly, and cease to look upon all its disagreeable incidents, great and small, its sufferings, its worries, its misery, as anything unusual or irregular; nay, you will find that everything is as it should be, in a world where each of us pays the penalty of existence in his own peculiar way. Amongst the evils of a penal colony is the society of those who form it; and if the reader is worthy of better company, he will need no words from me to remind him of what he has to put up with at present. If he has a soul above the common, or if he is a man of genius, he will occasionally feel like some noble prisoner of state, condemned to work in the galleys with common criminals; and he will follow his example and try to isolate himself.

In general, however, it should be said that this view of life will enable us to contemplate the so-called imperfec-

[9] Cf. *Fragmenta de philosophia.*
[10] *De admirandis naturæ arcanis;* dial L. p. 35.

tions of the great majority of men, their moral and intellectual deficiencies and the resulting base type of countenance,
without any surprise, to say nothing of indignation; for we
shall never cease to reflect where we are, and that the men
about us are beings conceived and born in sin, and living to.
atone for it. That is what Christianity means in speaking
of the sinful nature of man.

Pardon's the word to all! [11] Whatever folly men commit, be their shortcomings or their vices what they may,
let us exercise forbearance; remembering that when these
faults appear in others, it is our follies and vices that we
behold. They are the shortcomings of humanity, to which
we belong; whose faults, one and all, we share; yes, even
those very faults at which we now wax so indignant, merely
because they have not yet appeared in ourselves. They
are faults that do not lie on the surface. But they exist
down there in the depths of our nature; and should anything call them forth, they will come and show themselves,
just as we now see them in others. One man, it is true,
may have faults that are absent in his fellow; and it is
undeniable that the sum total of bad qualities is in some
cases very large; for the difference of individuality between man and man passes all measure.

In fact, the conviction that the world and man is something that had better not have been, is of a kind to fill
us with indulgence towards one another. Nay, from this
point of view, we might well consider the proper form of
address to be, not *Monsieur, Sir, mein Herr*, but *my fellow-
sufferer, Socî malorum, compagnon de miseres!* This may
perhaps sound strange, but it is in keeping with the facts;
it puts others in a right light; and it reminds us of that
which is the most necessary thing in life—the tolerance,
patience, regard, and love of neighbor, of which everyone
stands in need, and which every man owes to his fellow.

[11] "Cymbeline," Act v. Sc. 5.

THE VANITY OF EXISTENCE

THIS vanity finds expression in the whole way in which things exist; in the infinite nature of Time and Space, as opposed to the finite nature of the individual in both; in the ever-passing present moment as the only mode of actual existence; in the interdependence and relativity of all things; in continual Becoming without ever Being; in constant wishing and never being satisfied; in the long battle which forms the history of life, where every effort is checked by difficulties, and stopped until they are overcome. Time is that in which all things pass away; it is merely the form under which the will to live—the thing-in-itself and therefore imperishable—has revealed to it that its efforts are in vain; it is that agent by which at every moment all things in our hands become as nothing, and lose any real value they possess.

That which *has been* exists no more; it exists as little as that which has *never been*. But of everything that exists you must say, in the next moment, that it has been. Hence something of great importance now past is inferior to something of little importance now present, in that the latter is a *reality*, and related to the former as something to nothing.

A man finds himself, to his great astonishment, suddenly existing, after thousands and thousands of years of non-existence: he lives for a little while; and then, again, comes an equally long period when he must exist no more. The heart rebels against this, and feels that it cannot be true. The crudest intellect cannot speculate on such a subject without having a presentiment that Time is something

231

ideal in its nature. This ideality of Time and Space is the key to every true system of metaphysics; because it provides for quite another order of things than is to be met with in the domain of nature. This is why Kant is so great.

Of every event in our life we can say only for one moment that it *is;* for ever after, that it *was.* Every evening we are poorer by a day. It might, perhaps, make us mad to see how rapidly our short span of time ebbs away; if it were not that in the furthest depths of our being we are secretly conscious of our share in the exhaustible spring of eternity, so that we can always hope to find life in it again.

Consideration of the kind, touched on above, might, indeed, lead us to embrace the belief that the greatest *wisdom* is to make the enjoyment of the present the supreme object of life; because that is the only reality, all else being merely the play of thought. On the other hand, such a course might just as well be called the greatest *folly:* for that which in the next moment exists no more, and vanishes utterly, like a dream, can never be worth a serious effort.

The whole foundation on which our existence rests is the present—the ever-fleeting present. It lies, then, in the very nature of our existence to take the form of constant motion, and to offer no possibility of our ever attaining the rest for which we are always striving. We are like a man running downhill, who cannot keep on his legs unless he runs on, and will inevitably fall if he stops; or, again, like a pole balanced on the tip of one's finger; or like a planet, which would fall into its sun the moment it ceased to hurry forward on its way. Unrest is the mark of existence.

In a world where all is unstable, and nought can endure, but is swept onwards at once in the hurrying whirlpool of change; where a man, if he is to keep erect at all, must always be advancing and moving, like an acrobat on a rope—in such a world, happiness is inconceivable. How can it dwell where, as Plato says, *continual Becoming and never Being* is the sole form of existence? In the first place, a man never is happy, but spends his whole life in striving after something which he thinks will make him so; he seldom attains his goal, and when he does, it is only to be disappointed; he is mostly shipwrecked in the end, and comes into harbor with masts and rigging gone. And then, it is all one whether he has been happy or miserable; for his life was never anything more than a present moment always vanishing; and now it is over.

At the same time it is a wonderful thing that, in the world of human beings as in that of animals in general, this manifold restless motion is produced and kept up by the agency of two simple impulses—hunger and the sexual instinct; aided a little, perhaps, by the influence of boredom, but by nothing else; and that, in the theatre of life, these suffice to form the *primum mobile* of how complicated a machinery, setting in motion how strange and varied a scene!

On looking a little closer, we find that inorganic matter presents a constant conflict between chemical forces, which eventually works dissolution; and on the other hand, that organic life is impossible without continual change of matter, and cannot exist if it does not receive perpetual help from without. This is the realm of *finality;* and its opposite would be *an infinite existence,* exposed to no attack from without, and needing nothing to support it; ἀεὶ ὡσαύτως ὄν, the realm of eternal peace; οὔτε γιγνόμενον οὔτε ἀπλλύμενον some timeless, changeless state, one and undiversified; the negative knowledge of which forms the dominant note of the Platonic philosophy. It is to some such state as this that the denial of the will to live opens up the way.

The scenes of our life are like pictures done in rough mosaic. Looked at close, they produce no effect. There is nothing beautiful to be found in them, unless you stand some distance off. So, to gain anything we have longed for is only to discover how vain and empty it is; and even though we are always living in expectation of better things, at the same time we often repent and long to have the past back again. We look upon the present as something to be put up with while it lasts, and serving only as the way towards our goal. Hence most people, if they glance back when they come to the end of life, will find that all along they have been living *ad interim:* they will be surprised to find that the very thing they disregarded and let slip by unenjoyed, was just the life in the expectation of which they passed all their time. Of how many a man may it not be said that hope made a fool of him until he danced into the arms of death!

Then again, how insatiable a creature is man! Every satisfaction he attains lays the seeds of some new desire, so that there is no end to the wishes of each individual will. And why is this? The real reason is simply that, taken in itself, Will is the lord of all worlds: everything belongs to it, and therefore no one single thing can ever give it satisfaction, but only the whole, which is endless. For all that, it must rouse our sympathy to think how very little the Will, this lord of the world, really gets when it takes the form of an individual; usually only just enough to keep the body together. This is why man is so very miserable.

Life presents itself chiefly as a task—the task, I mean, of subsisting at all, *gagner sa vie*. If this is accomplished, life is a burden, and then there comes the second task of doing something with that which has been won—of warding off boredom, which, like a bird of prey, hovers over us, ready to fall wherever it sees a life secure from need. The first task is to win something; the second, to banish the feeling that it has been won; otherwise it is a burden.

Human life must be some kind of mistake. The truth of this will be sufficiently obvious if we only remember that man is a compound of needs and necessities hard to satisfy; and that even when they are satisfied, all he obtains is a state of painlessness, where nothing remains to him but abandonment to boredom. This is direct proof that existence has no real value in itself; for what is boredom but the feeling of the emptiness of life? If life—the craving for which is the very essence of our being—were possessed of any positive intrinsic value, there would be no such thing as boredom at all: mere existence would satisfy us in itself, and we should want for nothing. But as it is, we take no delight in existence except when we are struggling for something; and then distance and difficulties to be overcome make our goal look as though it would satisfy us—an illusion which vanishes when we reach it; or else when we are occupied with some purely intellectual interest—when in reality we have stepped forth from life to look upon it from the outside, much after the manner of spectators at a play. And even sensual pleasure itself means nothing but a struggle and aspiration, ceasing the moment its aim is attained. Whenever we are not occupied in one of these ways, but cast upon existence itself, its vain and worthless nature is brought home to us; and this is what we mean by boredom. The hankering after what is strange and uncommon—an innate and ineradicable tendency of human nature—shows how glad we are at any interruption of that natural course of affairs which is so very tedious.

That this most perfect manifestation of the will to live, the human organism, with the cunning and complex working of its machinery, must fall to dust and yield up itself and all its strivings to extinction—this is the naïve way in which Nature, who is always so true and sincere in what she says, proclaims the whole struggle of this will as in its very essence barren and unprofitable. Were it of any value in itself, anything unconditioned and absolute, it could not thus end in mere nothing.

If we turn from contemplating the world as a whole, and, in particular, the generations of men as they live their little hour of mock-existence and then are swept away in rapid succession; if we turn from this, and look at life in its small details, as presented, say, in a comedy, how ridiculous it all seems! It is like a drop of water seen through a microscope, a single drop teeming with *infusoria;* or a speck of cheese full of mites invisible to the naked eye. How we laugh as they bustle about so eagerly, and struggle with one another in so tiny a space! And whether here, or in the little span of human life, this terrible activity produces a comic effect.

It is only in the microscope that our life looks so big. It is an indivisible point, drawn out and magnified by the powerful lenses of Time and Space.

ON SUICIDE

As far as I know, none but the votaries of monotheistic, that is to say, Jewish religions, look upon suicide as a crime. This is all the more striking, inasmuch as neither in the Old nor in the New Testament is there to be found any prohibition or positive disapproval of it; so that religious teachers are forced to base their condemnation of suicide on philosophical grounds of their own invention. These are so very bad that writers of this kind endeavor to make up for the weakness of their arguments by the strong terms in which they express their abhorrence of the practice; in other words, they declaim against it. They tell us that suicide is the greatest piece of cowardice; that only a madman could be guilty of it; and other insipidities of the same kind; or else they make the nonsensical remark that suicide is *wrong;* when it is quite obvious that there is nothing in the world to which every man has a more unassailable title than to his own life and person.

Suicide, as I have said, is actually accounted a crime; and a crime which, especially under the vulgar bigotry that prevails in England, is followed by an ignominious burial and the seizure of the man's property; and for that reason, in a case of suicide, the jury almost always brings in a verdict of insanity. Now let the reader's own moral feelings decide as to whether or not suicide is a criminal act. Think of the impression that would be made upon you by the news that some one you know had committed the crime, say, of murder or theft, or been guilty of some act of cruelty or deception; and compare it with your feelings when you hear that he has met a voluntary death. While in the one case a lively sense of indignation and

extreme resentment will be aroused, and you will call loudly
for punishment or revenge, in the other you will be moved
to grief and sympathy; and mingled with your thoughts
will be admiration for his courage, rather than the moral
disapproval which follows upon a wicked action. Who has
not had acquaintances, friends, relations, who of their own
free will have left this world; and are these to be thought
of with horror as criminals? Most emphatically, No! I
am rather of opinion that the clergy should be challenged
to explain what right they have to go into the pulpit, or
take up their pens, and stamp as a crime an action which
many men whom we hold in affection and honor have
committed; and to refuse an honorable burial to those
who relinquish this world voluntarily. They have no
Biblical authority to boast of, as justifying their condemnation of suicide; nay, not even any philosophical arguments that will hold water; and it must be understood
that it is arguments we want, and that we will not be
put off with mere phrases or words of abuse. If the criminal law forbids suicide, that is not an argument valid in
the Church; and besides, the prohibition is ridiculous; for
what penalty can frighten a man who is not afraid of
death itself? If the law punishes people for trying to commit suicide, it is punishing the want of skill that makes
the attempt a failure.

The ancients, moreover, were very far from regarding
the matter in that light. Pliny says: *Life is not so desirable
a thing as to be protracted at any cost. Whoever you are,
you are sure to die, even though your life has been full of
abomination and crime. The chief of all remedies for a
troubled mind is the feeling that among the blessings which
Nature gives to man, there is none greater than an op-
portune death; and the best of it is that every one can
avail himself of it.*[1] And elsewhere the same writer de-

[1] Hist. Nat. Lib. xxviii., 1.

clares: *Not even to God are all things possible; for he could not compass his own death, if he willed to die, and yet in all the miseries of our earthly life, this is the best of his gifts to man.*[2] Nay, in Massilia and on the isle of Ceos, the man who could give valid reasons for relinquishing his life, was handed the cup of hemlock by the magistrate; and that, too, in public.[3] And in ancient times, how many heroes and wise men died a voluntary death. Aristotle,[4] it is true, declared suicide to be an offence against the State, although not against the person; but in Stobæus' exposition of the Peripatetic philosophy there is the following remark: *The good man should flee life when his misfortunes become too great; the bad man, also, when he is too prosperous.* And similarly: *So he will marry and beget children and take part in the affairs of the State, and, generally, practice virtue and continue to live; and then, again, if need be, and at any time necessity compels him, he will depart to his place of refuge in the tomb.*[5] And we find that the Stoics actually praised suicide as a noble and heroic action, as hundreds of passages show; above all in the works of Seneca, who expresses the strongest approval of it. As is well known, the Hindoos look upon suicide as a religious act, especially when it takes the form of self-immolation by widows; but also when it consists in casting oneself under the wheels of the chariot of the god at Juggernaut, or being eaten by crocodiles in the Ganges, or being drowned in the holy tanks in the temples, and so on. The same thing occurs on the stage— that mirror of life. For example, in *L'Orphelin de la Chine,*[6] a celebrated Chinese play, almost all the noble

[2] Loc. cit. Lib. ii. c. 7.

[3] Valerium Maximus; hist. Lib. ii., c. 6, § 7 et 8. Heraclides Ponticus; fragmenta de rebus publicis, ix. Aeliani variæ historiæ, iii., 37. Strabo; Lib. x., c. 5, 6.

[4] *Eth. Nichom.,* v. 15.

[5] Stobæus. *Ecl. Eth.* ii., c. 7, pp. 286, 312.

[6] Traduit par St. Julien, 1834.

characters end by suicide; without the slightest hint anywhere, or any impression being produced on the spectator, that they are committing a crime. And in our own theatre it is much the same—Palmira, for instance, in *Mahomet*, or Mortimer in *Maria Stuart*, Othello, Countess Terzky.[7] Is Hamlet's monologue the meditation of a criminal? He merely declares that if we had any certainty of being annihilated by it, death would be infinitely preferable to the world as it is. But *there lies the rub!*

The reasons advanced against suicide by the clergy of monotheistic, that is to say, Jewish religions, and by those philosophers who adapt themselves thereto, are weak sophisms which can easily be refuted.[8] The most thoroughgoing refutation of them is given by Hume in his *Essay on Suicide*. This did not appeal until after his death, when it was immediately suppressed, owing to the scandalous bigotry and outrageous ecclesiastical tyranny that prevailed in England; and hence only a very few copies of it were sold under cover of secrecy and at a high price. This and another treatise by that great man have come to us from Basle, and we may be thankful for the reprint.[9] It is a great disgrace to the English nation that a purely philosophical treatise, which, proceeding from one of the first thinkers and writers in England, aimed at refuting the current arguments against suicide by the light of cold reason, should be forced to sneak about in that country, as though it were some rascally production, until at last it found refuge on the Continent. At the same time it shows what a good conscience the Church has in such matters.

[7] *Translator's Note.*—Palmira: a female slave in Goethe's play of *Mahomet*. Mortimer: a would-be lover and rescuer of Mary in Schiller's *Maria Stuart*. Countess Terzky: a leading character in Schiller's *Wallenstein's Tod*.

[8] See my treatise on the *Foundation of Morals*, § 5.

[9] *Essays on Suicide* and the *Immortality of the Soul*, by the late David Hume, Basle, 1799, sold by James Decker.

In my chief work I have explained the only valid reason existing against suicide on the score of mortality. It is this: that suicide thwarts the attainment of the highest moral aim by the fact that, for a real release from this world of misery, it substitutes one that is merely apparent. But from a *mistake* to a *crime* is a far cry; and it is as a crime that the clergy of Christendom wish us to regard suicide.

The inmost kernel of Christianity is the truth that suffering—*the Cross*—is the real end and object of life. Hence Christianity condemns suicide as thwarting this end; whilst the ancient world, taking a lower point of view, held it in approval, nay, in honor.[10] But if that is to be accounted a valid reason against suicide, it involves the recognition of asceticism; that is to say, it is valid only from a much higher ethical standpoint than has ever been adopted by moral philosophers in Europe. If we abandon that high standpoint, there is no tenable reason left, on the score of morality, for condemning suicide. The extraordinary energy and zeal with which the clergy of monotheistic religions attack suicide is not supported either by any passages in the Bible or by any considerations of weight; so that it looks as though they must have some secret reason for their contention. May it not be this—that the voluntary surrender of life is a bad compliment

[10] *Translator's Note.*—Schopenhauer refers to *Die Welt als Wille und Vorstellung,* vol. i., § 69, where the reader may find the same argument stated at somewhat greater length. According to Schopenhauer, moral freedom—the highest ethical aim—is to be obtained only by a denial of the will to live. Far from being a denial, suicide is an emphatic assertion of this will. For it is in fleeing from the pleasures, not from the sufferings of life, that this denial consists. When a man destroys his existence as an individual, he is not by any means destroying his will to live. On the contrary, he would like to live if he could do so with satisfaction to himself; if he could assert his will against the power of circumstance; but circumstance is too strong for him.

for him who said that *all things were very good?* If this
is so, it offers another instance of the crass optimism of
these religions,—denouncing suicide to escape being de-
nounced by it.

It will generally be found that, as soon as the terrors
of life reach the point at which they outweigh the terrors of death, a man will put an end to his life. But the
terrors of death offer considerable resistance; they stand
like a sentinel at the gate leading out of this world. Perhaps there is no man alive who would not have already
put an end to his life, if this end had been of a purely
negative character, a sudden stoppage of existence. There
is something positive about it; it is the destruction of the
body; and a man shrinks from that, because his body is
the manifestation of the will to live.

However, the struggle with that sentinel is, as a rule,
not so hard as it may seem from a long way off, mainly
in consequence of the antagonism between the ills of the
body and the ills of the mind. If we are in great bodily
pain, or the pain lasts a long time, we become indifferent
to other troubles; all we think about is to get well. In
the same way great mental suffering makes us insensible
to bodily pain; we despise it; nay, if it should outweigh
the other, it distracts our thoughts, and we welcome it
as a pause in mental suffering. It is this feeling that makes
suicide easy; for the bodily pain that accompanies it loses
all significance in the eyes of one who is tortured by an
excess of mental suffering. This is especially evident in
the case of those who are driven to suicide by some purely
morbid and exaggerated ill-humor. No special effort to
overcome their feelings is necessary, nor do such people
require to be worked up in order to take the step; but
as soon as the keeper into whose charge they are given
leaves them for a couple of minutes, they quickly bring
their life to an end.

When, in some dreadful and ghastly dream, we reach the moment of greatest horror, it awakes us; thereby banishing all the hideous shapes that were born of the night. And life is a dream: when the moment of greatest horror compels us to break it off, the same thing happens.

Suicide may also be regarded as an experiment—a question which man puts to Nature, trying to force her to an answer. The question is this: What change will death produce in a man's existence and in his insight into the nature of things? It is a clumsy experiment to make; for it involves the destruction of the very consciousness which puts the question and awaits the answer.

IMMORTALITY:[1] A DIALOGUE

THRASYMACHOS—PHILALETHES

Thrasymachos. Tell me now, in one word, what shall I
be after my death? And mind you be clear and precise.

Philalethes. All and nothing!

Thrasymachos. I thought so! I gave you a problem,
and you solve it by a contradiction. That's a very stale
trick.

Philalethes. Yes, but you raise transcendental questions, and you expect me to answer them in language that
is only made for immanent knowledge. It's no wonder that
a contradiction ensues.

Thrasymachos. What do you mean by transcendental
questions and immanent knowledge? I've heard these
expressions before, of course; they are not new to me. The
Professor was fond of using them, but only as predicates
of the Deity, and he never talked of anything else; which
was all quite right and proper. He argued thus: if the
Deity was in the world itself, he was immanent; if he was
somewhere outside it, he was transcendent. Nothing could
be clearer and more obvious! You knew where you were.

---

[1] *Translator's Note.*—The word immortality—*Unsterblichkeit*—
does not occur in the original; nor would it, in its usual application, find a place in Schopenhauer's vocabulary. The word he
uses is *Unzerstörbarkeit—indestructibility.* But I have preferred *immortality,* because that word is commonly associated
with the subject touched upon in this little debate. If any
critic doubts the wisdom of this preference, let me ask him to
try his hand at a short, concise, and, at the same time, popu-
larly intelligible rendering of the German original, which runs
thus: *Zur Lehre von der Unzerstörbarkeit unseres wahren
Wesens durch den Tod: kleine dialogische Schlussbelustigung.*

But this Kantian rigmarole won't do any more: it's antiquated and no longer applicable to modern ideas. Why,
we've had a whole row of eminent men in the metropolis
of German learning—

Philalethes. (Aside.) German humbug, he means.

Thrasymachos. The mighty Schleiermacher, for instance,
and that gigantic intellect, Hegel; and at this time of
day we've abandoned that nonsense. I should rather say
we're so far beyond it that we can't put up with it any
more. What's the use of it then? What does it all mean?

Philalethes. Transcendental knowledge is knowledge
which passes beyond the bounds of possible experience,
and strives to determine the nature of things as they are
in themselves. Immanent knowledge, on the other hand,
is knowledge which confines itself entirely with those
bounds; so that it cannot apply to anything but actual
phenomena. As far as you are an individual, death will
be the end of you. But your individuality is not your
true and inmost being: it is only the outward manifestation of it. It is not the *thing-in-itself,* but only the phe-
nomenon presented in the form of time; and therefore
with a beginning and an end. But your real being knows
neither time, nor beginning, nor end, nor yet the limits of
any given individual. It is everywhere present in every
individual; and no individual can exist apart from it. So
when death comes, on the one hand you are annihilated
as an individual; on the other, you are and remain everything. That is what I meant when I said that after your
death you would be all and nothing. It is difficult to find
a more precise answer to your question and at the same
time be brief. The answer is contradictory, I admit; but
it is so simply because your life is in time, and the immortal part of you in eternity. You may put the matter thus: Your immortal part is something that does not
last in time and yet is indestructible; but there you have

another contradiction! You see what happens by trying to bring the transcendental within the limits of immanent knowledge. It is in some sort doing violence to the latter by misusing it for ends it was never meant to serve.

Thrasymachos. Look here, I shan't give two-pence for your immortality unless I'm to remain an individual.

Philalethes. Well, perhaps I may be able to satisfy you on this point. Suppose I guarantee that after death you shall remain an individual, but only on condition that you first spend three months of complete unconsciousness.

Thrasymachos. I shall have no objection to that.

Philalethes. But remember, if people are completely unconscious, they take no account of time. So, when you are dead, it's all the same to you whether three months pass in the world of consciousness, or ten thousand years. In the one case as in the other, it is simply a matter of believing what is told you when you awake. So far, then, you can afford to be indifferent whether it is three months or ten thousand years that pass before you recover your individuality.

Thrasymachos. Yes, if it comes to that, I suppose you're right.

Philalethes. And if by chance, after those ten thousand years have gone by, no one ever thinks of awakening you, I fancy it would be no great misfortune. You would have become quite accustomed to non-existence after so long a spell of it—following upon such a very few years of life. At any rate you may be sure you would be perfectly ignorant of the whole thing. Further, if you knew that the mysterious power which keeps you in your present state of life had never once ceased in those ten thousand years to bring forth other phenomena like yourself, and to endow them with life, it would fully console you.

Thrasymachos. Indeed! So you think you're quietly going to do me out of my individuality with all this fine talk. But I'm up to your tricks. I tell you I won't exist unless I can have my individuality. I'm not going to be put off with 'mysterious powers,' and what you call 'phenomena.' I can't do without my individuality, and I won't give it up.

Philalethes. You mean, I suppose, that your individuality is such a delightful thing, so splendid, so perfect, and beyond compare—that you can't imagine anything better. Aren't you ready to exchange your present state for one which, if we can judge by what is told us, may possibly be superior and more endurable?

Thrasymachos. Don't you see that my individuality, be it what it may, is my very self? To me it is the most important thing in the world.

For God is God and I am I.

I want to exist, *I, I*. That's the main thing. I don't care about an existence which has to be proved to be mine, before I can believe it.

Philalethes. Think what you're doing! When you say *I, I, I* want to exist, it is not you alone that says this. Everything says it, absolutely everything that has the faintest trace of consciousness. It follows, then, that this desire of yours is just the part of you that is *not individual*—the part that is common to all things without distinction. It is the cry, not of the individual, but of existence itself; it is the intrinsic element in everything that exists, nay, it is the cause of anything existing at all. This desire craves for, and so is satisfied with, nothing less than existence in general—not any definite individual existence. No! that is not its aim. It seems to be so only because this desire—this *Will*—attains consciousness only in the individual, and therefore looks as though it were concerned with nothing but the individual. There lies the illusion—an illusion, it is true, in which the individual is held fast: but, if he reflects, he can break the fetters and set himself free. It is only indirectly, I say, that the individual has this violent craving for existence. It is *the Will to Live* which is the real and direct aspirant—alike and identical in all things. Since, then, existence is the free work, nay, the mere reflection of the will, where existence is, there, too, must be will; and for the moment the will finds its satisfaction in existence itself; so far, I mean, as that which never rests, but presses forward eternally, can ever find any satisfaction at all. The will is careless of the individual: the individual is not its business; although, as I have said, this seems to be the case, because the individual has no direct consciousness of will except in himself. The effect of this is to make the individual careful to maintain his own existence; and if this were not so, there would be no surety for the preservation of the species. From all this it is clear that individuality is not a form of perfection, but rather of limitation; and so to be freed from it is not loss but gain. Trouble yourself no more about the matter. Once thoroughly recognize what you are, what your existence really is, namely, the universal will to live, and the whole question will seem to you childish, and most ridiculous!

Thrasymachos. You're childish yourself and most ridiculous, like all philosophers! and if a man of my age lets himself in for a quarter-of-an-hour's talk with such fools, it is only because it amuses me and passes the time. I've more important business to attend to, so Good-bye.

PSYCHOLOGICAL OBSERVATIONS

THERE is an unconscious propriety in the way in which, in all European languages, the word *person* is commonly used to denote a human being. The real meaning of *persona* is *a mask,* such as actors were accustomed to wear on the ancient stage; and it is quite true that no one shows himself as he is, but wears his mask and plays his part. Indeed, the whole of our social arrangements may be likened to a perpetual comedy; and this is why a man who is worth anything finds society so insipid, while a blockhead is quite at home in it.

    •   •   •   •   •   •

Reason deserves to be called a prophet; for in showing us the consequence and effect of our actions in the present, does it not tell us what the future will be? This is precisely why reason is such an excellent power of restraint in moments when we are possessed by some base passion, some fit of anger, some covetous desire, that will lead us to do things whereof we must presently repent.

    •   •   •   •   •

Hatred comes from the heart; *contempt* from the head; and neither feeling is quite within our control. For we cannot alter our heart; its basis is determined by motives; and our head deals with objective facts, and applies to them rules which are immutable. Any given individual is the union of a particular heart with a particular head.

Hatred and contempt are diametrically opposed and mutually exclusive. There are even not a few cases where hatred of a person is rooted in nothing but forced esteem for his qualities. And besides, if a man sets out to hate all the miserable creatures he meets, he will not have much energy left for anything else; whereas he can despise them, one and all, with the greatest ease. True, genuine contempt is just the reverse of true, genuine pride; it keeps quite quiet and gives no sign of its existence. For if a man shows that he despises you, he signifies at least this much regard for you, that he wants to let you know how little he appreciates you; and his wish is dictated by hatred, which cannot exist with real contempt. On the contrary, if it is genuine, it is simply the conviction that the object of it is a man of no value at all. Contempt is not incompatible with indulgent and kindly treatment, and for the sake of one's own peace and safety, this should not be omitted; it will prevent irritation; and there is no one who cannot do harm if he is roused to it. But if this pure, cold, sincere contempt ever shows itself, it will be met with the most truculent hatred; for the despised person is not in a position to fight contempt with its own weapons.

.   .   .   .   .   .

Melancholy is a very different thing from bad humor, and of the two, it is not nearly so far removed from a gay and happy temperament. Melancholy attracts, while bad humor repels.

Hypochondria is a species of torment which not only makes us unreasonably cross with the things of the present; not only fills us with groundless anxiety on the score of future misfortunes entirely of our own manufacture; but also leads to unmerited self-reproach for what we have done in the past.

Hypochondria shows itself in a perpetual hunting after things that vex and annoy, and then brooding over them. The cause of it is an inward morbid discontent, often coexisting with a naturally restless temperament. In their extreme form, this discontent and this unrest lead to suicide.

Any incident, however trivial, that rouses disagreeable emotion, leaves an after-effect in our mind, which for the time it lasts, prevents our taking a clear objective view of the things about us, and tinges all our thoughts: just as a small object held close to the eye limits and distorts our field of vision.

.   .   .   .   .   .

What makes people *hard-hearted* is this, that each man has, or fancies he has, as much as he can bear in his own troubles. Hence, if a man suddenly finds himself in an unusually happy position, it will in most cases result in his being sympathetic and kind. But if he has never been in any other than a happy position, or this becomes his permanent state, the effect of it is often just the contrary: it so far removes him from suffering that he is incapable of feeling any more sympathy with it. So it is the poor often show themselves more ready to help than the rich.

.   .   .   .   .   .

At times it seems as though we both wanted and did not want the same thing, and felt at once glad and sorry about it. For instance, if on some fixed date we are going to be put to decisive test about anything in which it would be a great advantage to us to come off victorious, we shall be anxious for it to take place at once, and at the same time we shall tremble at the thought of its approach. And if, in the meantime, we hear that, for once in a way, the date has been postponed, we shall experience a feeling both of pleasure and of annoyance; for the news is disappointing, but nevertheless it affords us momentary relief. It is just the same thing if we are expecting some important letter carrying a definite decision, and it fails to arrive.

In such cases there are really two different motives at work in us; the stronger but more distant of the two being the desire to stand the test and to have the decision given in our favor; and the weaker, which touches us more nearly, the wish to be left for the present in peace and quiet, and accordingly in further enjoyment of the advantage which at any rate attaches to a state of hopeful uncertainty, compared with the possibility that the issue may be unfavorable.

.   .   .   .   .   .

In my head there is a permanent opposition-party; and whenever I take any step or come to any decision—though I may have given the matter mature consideration—it afterwards attacks what I have done, without, however, being each time necessarily in the right. This is, I suppose, only a form of rectification on the part of the spirit of scrutiny; but it often reproaches me when I do not deserve it. The same thing, no doubt, happens to many others as well; for where is the man who can help thinking that, after all, it were better not to have done something that he did with great deliberation:

> *Quid tam dextro pede concipic ut te*
> *Conatus non poeniteat votique peracti?*

.   .   .   .   .   .

Why is it that *common* is an expression of contempt? and *uncommon, extraordinary, distinguished,* denote approbation? Why is everything that is common contemptible?

Common in its original meaning denotes that which is peculiar to all men, *i. e.,* shared equally by the whole species, and therefore an inherent part of its nature. Accordingly, if an individual possesses no qualities beyond those which attach to mankind in general, he is a *common man. Ordinary* is a much milder word, and refers rather to intellectual character; whereas *common* has more of a moral application.

What value can a creature have that is not a whit different from millions of its kind? Millions, do I say? nay, an infinitude of creatures which, century after century, in never-ending flow, Nature sends bubbling up from her inexhaustible springs; as generous with them as the smith with the useless sparks that fly around his anvil.

It is oviously quite right that a creature which has no qualities except those of the species, should have to confine its claim to an existence entirely within the limits of the species, and live a life conditioned by those limits.

In various passages of my works,[1] I have argued that whilst a lower animal possesses nothing more than the generic character of its species, man is the only being which can lay claim to possess an individual character. But in most men this individual character comes to very little in reality; and they may be almost all ranged under certain classes: *ce sont des espèces.* Their thoughts and desires, like their faces, are those of the species, or, at any rate, those of the class to which they belong; and so, they are of a trivial, every-day, common character, and exist by the thousand. You can usually tell beforehand what they are likely to do and say. They have no special stamp or mark to distinguish them; they are like manufactured goods, all of a piece.

If, then, their nature is merged in that of the species, how shall their existence go beyond it? The curse of vulgarity puts men on a par with lower animals, by allowing them none but a generic nature, a generic form of existence.

Anything that is high or great or noble, must then, as a matter of course, and by its very nature, stand alone in a world where no better expression can be found to denote what is base and contemptible than that which I have mentioned as in general use, namely, *common.*

. . . . . .

Will, as the *thing-in-itself,* is the foundation of all being; it is part and parcel of every creature, and the permanent element in everything. Will, then, is that which we possess in common with all men, nay, with all animals, and even

[1] *Grundprobleme der Ethik,* p. 48; *Welt als Wille und Vorstellung,* vol. i. p. 338.

with lower forms of existence; and in so far we are akin to everything—so far, that is, as everything is filled to overflowing with will. On the other hand, that which places one being over another, and sets differences between man and man, is intellect and knowledge; therefore in every manifestation of self we should, as far as possible, give play to the intellect alone; for, as we have seen, the will is the *common* part of us. Every violent exhibition of will is common and vulgar; in other words, it reduces us to the level of the species, and makes us a mere type and example of it; in that it is just the character of the species that we are showing. So every fit of anger is something *common*— every unrestrained display of joy, or of hate, or fear—in short, every form of emotion; in other words, every movement of the will, if it's so strong as decidedly to outweigh the intellectual element in consciousness, and to make the man appear as a being that *wills* rather than *knows*.

In giving way to emotion of this violent kind, the greatest genius puts himself on a level with the commonest son of earth. Contrarily, if a man desires to be absolutely uncommon, in other words, great, he should never allow his consciousness to be taken possession of and dominated by the movement of his will, however much he may be solicited thereto. For example, he must be able to observe that other people are badly disposed towards him, without feeling any hatred towards them himself; nay, there is no surer sign of a great mind than that it refuses to notice annoying and insulting expressions, but straightway ascribes them, as it ascribes countless other mistakes, to the defective knowledge of the speaker, and so merely observes without feeling them. This is the meaning of that remark of Gracian, that nothing is more unworthy of a man than to let it be seen that he is one—*el mayor desdoro de un hombre es dar muestras de que es hombre.*

And even in the drama, which is the peculiar province

of the passions and emotions, it is easy for them to appear common and vulgar. And this is specially observable in the works of the French tragic writers, who set no other aim before themselves but the delineation of the passions; and by indulging at one moment in a vaporous kind of pathos which makes them ridiculous, at another in epigrammatic witticisms, endeavor to conceal the vulgarity of their subject. I remember seeing the celebrated Mademoiselle Rachel as Maria Stuart: and when she burst out in fury against Elizabeth—though she did it very well—I could not help thinking of a washerwoman. She played the final parting in such a way as to deprive it of all true tragic feeling, of which, indeed, the French have no notion at all. The same part was incomparably better played by the Italian Ristori; and, in fact, the Italian nature, though in many respects very different from the German, shares its appreciation for what is deep, serious, and true in Art; herein opposed to the French, which everywhere betrays that it possesses none of this feeling whatever.

The noble, in other words, the uncommon, element in the drama—nay, what is sublime in it—is not reached until the intellect is set to work, as opposed to the will; until it takes a free flight over all those passionate movements of the will, and makes them subject of its contemplation. Shakespeare, in particular, shows that this is his general method, more especially in Hamlet. And only when intellect rises to the point where the vanity of all effort is manifest, and the will proceeds to an act of self-annulment, is the drama tragic in the true sense of the word; it is then that it reaches its highest aim in becoming really sublime.

.   .   .   .   .   .

Every man takes the limits of his own field of vision for the limits of the world. This is an error of the intellect as inevitable as that error of the eye which lets us fancy that on the horizon heaven and earth meet. This explains many things, and among them the fact that everyone measures us with his own standard—generally about as long as a tailor's tape, and we have to put up with it: as also that no one will allow us to be taller than himself—a supposition which is once for all taken for granted.

. . . . . .

There is no doubt that many a man owes his good fortune in life solely to the circumstance that he has a pleasant way of smiling, and so wins the heart in his favor.

However, the heart would do better to be careful, and to remember what Hamlet put down in his tablets—*that one may smile, and smile, and be a villain.*

. . . . . .

Everything that is really fundamental in a man, and therefore genuine works, as such, unconsciously; in this respect like the power of nature. That which has passed through the domain of consciousness is thereby transformed into an idea or picture; and so if it comes to be uttered, it is only an idea or picture which passes from one person to another.

Accordingly, any quality of mind or character that is genuine and lasting, is originally unconscious; and it is only when unconsciously brought into play that it makes a profound impression. If any like quality is consciously exercised, it means that it has been worked up; it becomes intentional, and therefore matter of affectation, in other words, of deception.

If a man does a thing unconsciously, it costs him no trouble; but if he tries to do it by taking trouble, he fails. This applies to the origin of those fundamental ideas which form the pith and marrow of all genuine work. Only that which is innate is genuine and will hold water; and every man who wants to achieve something, whether in practical life, in literature, or in art, must *follow the rules without knowing them.*

Men of very great capacity, will as a rule, find the company of very stupid people preferable to that of the common run; for the same reason the tyrant and the mob, the grandfather and the grandchildren, are natural allies.

.   .   .   .   .   .

That line of Ovid's,

Pronaque cum spectent animalia cetera terram,

can be applied in its true physical sense to the lower animals alone; but in a metaphorical and spiritual sense it is, alas! true of nearly all men as well. All their plans and projects are merged in the desire of physical enjoyment, physical well-being. They may, indeed, have personal interests, often embracing a very varied sphere; but still these latter receive their importance entirely from the relation in which they stand to the former. This is not only proved by their manner of life and the things they say, but it even shows itself in the way they look, the expression of their physiognomy, their gait and gesticulations. Everything about them cries out; *in terram prona!*

It is not to them, it is only to the nobler and more highly endowed natures—men who really think and look about them in the world, and form exceptional specimens of humanity—that the next lines are applicable;

Os homini sublime dedit coelumque tueri
Jussit et erectos ad sidera tollere vultus.

.   .   .   .   .   .

No one knows what capacities for doing and suffering he has in himself, until something comes to rouse them to activity: just as in a pond of still water, lying there like a mirror, there is no sign of the roar and thunder with which it can leap from the precipice, and yet remain what it is; or again, rise high in the air as a fountain. When water is as cold as ice, you can have no idea of the latent warmth contained in it.

Why is it that, in spite of all the mirrors in the world, no one really knows what he looks like?

A man may call to mind the face of his friend, but not his own. Here, then, is an initial difficulty in the way of applying the maxim, *Know thyself*.

This is partly, no doubt, to be explained by the fact that it is physically impossible for a man to see himself in the glass except with face turned straight towards it and perfectly motionless; where the expression of the eye, which counts for so much, and really gives its whole character to the face, is to a great extent lost. But co-existing with this physical impossibility, there seems to me to be an ethical impossibility of an analogous nature, and producing the same effect. A man cannot look upon his own reflection as though the person presented there were *a stranger* to him; and yet this is necessary if he is to take *an objective view*. In the last resort, an objective view means a deep-rooted feeling on the part of the individual, as a moral being, that that which he is contemplating is *not himself;*[1] and unless he can take this point of view, he will not see things in a really true light, which is possible only if he is alive to their actual defects, exactly as they are. Instead of that, when a man sees himself in the glass, something out of his own egotistic nature whispers to him to take care to remember that *it is no stranger, but himself, that he is looking at;* and this operates as a *noli me tangere,* and prevents him taking on objective view. It seems, indeed, as if, without the leaven of a grain of malice, such a view were impossible.

.   .   .   .   .   .

According as a man's mental energy is exerted or relaxed, will life appear to him either so short, and petty, and fleeting, that nothing can possibly happen over which it is worth his while to spend emotion; that nothing really mat-

[1] Cf. *Grundprobleme der Ethik,* p. 275.

ters, whether it is pleasure or riches, or even fame, and that in whatever way a man may have failed, he cannot have lost much—or, on the other hand, life will seem so long, so important, so all in all, so momentous and so full of difficulty that we have to plunge into it with our whole soul if we are to obtain a share of its goods, make sure of its prizes, and carry out our plans. This latter is the immanent and common view of life; it is what Gracian means when he speaks of the serious way of looking at things—*tomar muy de veras el vivir.* The former is the transcendental view, which is well expressed in Ovid's *non est tanti*—it is not worth so much trouble; still better, however, by Plato's remark that nothing in human affairs is worth any great anxiety — οὔτε τι τῶν ἀνθρωπίνων ἄξιον ἐστι μεγάλης σπουδῆς. This condition of mind is due to the intellect having got the upper hand in the domain of consciousness, where, freed from the mere service of the will, it looks upon the phenomena of life objectively, and so cannot faii to gain a clear insight into its vain and futile character. But in the other condition of mind, will predominates; and the intellect exists only to light it on its way to the attainment of its desires.

A man is great or small according as he leans to the one or the other of these views of life.

.   .   .   .   .   .

People of very brilliant ability think little of admitting their errors and weaknesses, or of letting others see them. They look upon them as something for which they have duly paid; and instead of fancying that these weaknesses are a disgrace, they consider they are doing them an honor. This is especially the case when errors are of the kind that hang together with their qualities—*conditiones sine quibus non*—or, as George Sand said, *Les défauts de ses vertus.*

Contrarily, there are people of good character and irreproachable intellectual capacity, who, far from admitting the few little weaknesses they have, conceal them with care, and show themselves very sensitive to any suggestion of their existence; and this, just because their whole merit consists in being free from error and infirmity. If these people are found to have done anything wrong, their reputation immediately suffers.

.   .   .   .   .   .

With people of only moderate ability, modesty is mere honesty; but with those who possess great talent, it is hypocrisy. Hence, it is just as becoming in the latter to make no secret of the respect they bear themselves and no disguise of the fact that they are conscious of unusual power, as it is in the former to be modest. Valerius Maximus gives some very neat examples of this in his chapter on self-confidence, *de fiducia sui.*

.   .   .   .   .   .

Not to go to the theatre is like making one's toilet without a mirror. But it is still worse to take a decision without consulting a friend. For a man may have the most excellent judgment in all other matters, and yet go wrong in those which concern himself; because here the will comes in and deranges the intellect at once. Therefore let a man take counsel of a friend. A doctor can cure everyone but himself; if he falls ill, he sends for a colleague.

.   .   .   .   .   .

In all that we do, we wish, more or less, to come to the end; we are impatient to finish and glad to be done. But the last scene of all, the general end, is something that, as a rule, we wish as far off as may be.

.   .   .   .   .   .

Every parting gives a foretaste of death; every coming together again a foretaste of the resurrection. This is why even people who were indifferent to each other, rejoice so much if they come together again after twenty or thirty years' separation.

Intellects differ from one another in a very real and fundamental way: but no comparison can well be made by merely general observations. It is necessary to come close, and to go into details; for the difference that exists cannot be seen from afar; and it is not easy to judge by outward appearances, as in the several cases of education, leisure and occupation. But even judging by these alone, it must be admitted that many a man has *a degree of existence* at least ten times as high as another—in other words, exists ten times as much.

I am not speaking here of savages whose life is often only one degree above that of the apes in their woods. Consider, for instance, a porter in Naples or Venice (in the north of Europe solicitude for the winter months makes people more thoughtful and therefore reflective); look at the life he leads, from its beginning to its end:— driven by poverty; living on his physical strength; meeting the needs of every day, nay, of every hour, by hard work, great effort, constant tumult, want in all its forms, no care for the morrow; his only comfort rest after exhaustion; continuous quarreling; not a moment free for reflection; such sensual delights as a mild climate and only just sufficient food will permit of; and then, finally, as the metaphysical element, the crass superstition of his church; the whole forming a manner of life with only a low degree of consciousness, where a man hustles, or rather is hustled, through his existence. This restless and confused dream forms the life of how many millions!

Such men *think* only just so much as is necessary to carry out their will for the moment. They never reflect upon their life as a connected whole, let alone, then, upon existence in general; to a certain extent they may be said to exist without really knowing it. The existence of the mobsman or the slave who lives on in this unthinking way, stands very much nearer than ours to that of the brute,

which is confined entirely to the present moment; but, for
that very reason, it has also less of pain in it than ours.
Nay, since all pleasure is in its nature negative, that is to
say, consists in freedom from some form of misery or need,
the constant and rapid interchange between setting about
something and getting it done, which is the permanent accompaniment of the work they do, and then again the augmented form which this takes when they go from work
to rest and the satisfaction of their needs—all this gives
them a constant source of enjoyment; and the fact that
it is much commoner to see happy faces amongst the poor
than amongst the rich, is a sure proof that it is used to
good advantage.

Passing from this kind of man, consider, next, the sober,
sensible merchant, who leads a life of speculation, thinks
long over his plans and carries them out with great care,
founds a house, and provides for his wife, his children and
descendants; takes his share, too, in the life of a community. It is obvious that a man like this has a much
higher degree of consciousness than the former, and so his
existence has a higher degree of reality.

Then look at the man of learning, who investigates, it
may be, the history of the past. He will have reached the
point at which a man becomes conscious of existence as a
whole, sees beyond the period of his own life, beyond his
own personal interests, thinking over the whole course of
the world's history.

Then, finally, look at the poet or the philosopher, in
whom reflection has reached such a height, that, instead of
being drawn on to investigate any one particular phe-
nomenon of existence, he stands in amazement *before existence itself*, this great sphinx, and makes it his problem.
In him consciousness has reached the degree of clearness at
which it embraces the world itself: his intellect has completely abandoned its function as the servant of his will,

and now holds the world before him; and the world calls
upon him much more to examine and consider it, than to
play a part in it himself. If, then, the degree of consciousness is the degree of reality, such a man will be said to exist
most of all, and there will be sense and significance in so
describing him.

Between the two extremes here sketched, and the inter-
vening stages, everyone will be able to find the place at
which he himself stands.

.   .   .   .   .   .

We know that man is in general superior to all other
animals, and this is also the case in his capacity for being
trained. Mohammedans are trained to pray with their
faces turned towards Mecca, five times a day; and they
never fail to do it. Christians are trained to cross themselves on certain occasions, to bow, and so on. Indeed, it
may be said that religion is the *chef d'œuvre* of the art
of training, because it trains people in the way they shall
think: and, as is well known, you cannot begin the process
too early. There is no absurdity so palpable but that it
may be firmly planted in the human head if you only
begin to inculcate it before the age of five, by constantly
repeating it with an air of great solemnity. For as in the
case of animals, so in that of men, training is successful
only when you begin in early youth.

Noblemen and gentlemen are trained to hold nothing
sacred but their word of honor—to maintain a zealous,
rigid, and unshaken belief in the ridiculous code of chivalry;
and if they are called upon to do so, to seal their belief by
dying for it, and seriously to regard a king as a being of
a higher order.

Again, our expressions of politeness, the compliments we
make, in particular, the respectful atttentions we pay to
ladies, are a matter of training; as also our esteem for
good birth, rank, titles, and so on. Of the same character

is the resentment we feel at any insult directed against us; and the measure of this resentment may be exactly determined by the nature of the insult. An Englishman, for instance, thinks it a deadly insult to be told that he is no gentleman, or, still worse, that he is a liar; a Frenchman has the same feeling if you call him a coward, and a German if you say he is stupid.

There are many persons who are trained to be strictly honorable in regard to one particular matter, while they have little honor to boast of in anything else. Many a man, for instance, will not steal your money; but he will lay hands on everything of yours that he can enjoy without having to pay for it. A man of business will often deceive you without the slightest scruple, but he will absolutely refuse to commit a theft.

. . . . . .

Imagination is strong in a man when that particular function of the brain which enables him to observe is roused to activity without any necessary excitement of the senses. Accordingly, we find that imagination is active just in proportion as our senses are not excited by external objects. A long period of solitude, whether in prison or in a sick room; quiet, twilight, darkness—these are the things that promote its activity; and under their influence it comes into play of itself. On the other hand, when a great deal of material is presented to our faculties of observation, as happens on a journey, or in the hurly-burly of the world, or, again, in broad daylight, the imagination is idle, and, even though call may be made upon it, refuses to become active, as though it understood that was not its proper time.

However, if the imagination is to yield any real product, it must have received a great deal of material from the external world. This is the only way in which its storehouse can be filled. The phantasy is nourished much in the same way as the body, which is least capable of any work and enjoys doing nothing just in the very moment when it receives its food which it has to digest. And yet it is to this very food that it owes the power which it afterwards puts forth at the right time.

. . . . . .

Opinion is like a pendulum and obeys the same law. If it goes past the centre of gravity on one side, it must go a like distance on the other; it is only after a certain time that it finds the true point at which it can remain at rest.

. . . . . .

By a process of contradiction, distance in space makes things look small, and therefore free from defect. This is why a landscape looks so much better in a contracting mirror or in a *camera obscura*, than it is in reality. The same effect is produced by distance in time. The scenes and events of long ago, and the persons who took part in them, wear a charming aspect to the eye of memory, which sees only the outlines and takes no note of disagreeable details. The present enjoys no such advantage, and so it always seems defective.

And again, as regards space, small objects close to us look big, and if they are very close, we may be able to see nothing else, but when we go a little way off, they become minute and invisible. It is the same again as regards time. The little incidents and accidents of every day fill us with emotion, anxiety, annoyance, passion, as long as they are close to us, when they appear so big, so important, so serious; but as soon as they are borne down the restless stream of time, they lose what significance they had; we think no more of them and soon forget them altogether. They were big only because they were near.

. . . . . .

Joy and *sorrow* are not ideas of the mind, but affections of the will, and so they do not lie in the domain of memory. We cannot recall our joys and sorrows; by which I mean that we cannot renew them. We can recall only the *ideas* that accompanied them; and, in particular, the things we were led to say; and these form a gauge of our feelings at the time. Hence our memory of joys and sorrows is always imperfect, and they become a matter of indifference to us as soon as they are over. This explains the vanity of the attempt, which we sometimes make, to revive the pleasures and the pains of the past. Pleasure and pain are essentially an affair of the will; and the will, as such, is not possessed of memory, which is a function of the intellect; and this in its turn gives out and takes in nothing but thoughts and ideas, which are not here in question.

It is a curious fact that in bad days we can vividly recall the good time that is now no more; but in good days, we have only a very cold and imperfect memory of the bad.

.   .   .   .   .   .

We have a much better memory of actual objects or pictures than for mere ideas. Hence a good imagination makes it easier to learn languages; for by its aid, the new word is at once united with the actual object to which it refers; whereas, if there is no imagination, it is simply put on a parallel with the equivalent word in the mother tongue.

Mnemonics should not only mean the art of keeping something indirectly in the memory by the use of some direct pun or witticism; it should, rather, be applied to a systematic theory of memory, and explain its several attributes by reference both to its real nature, and to the relation in which these attributes stand to one another.

.   .   .   .   .   .

There are moments in life when our senses obtain a higher and rarer degree of clearness, apart from any particular occasion for it in the nature of our surroundings; and explicable, rather, on physiological grounds alone, as the result of some enhanced state of susceptibility, working from within outwards. Such moments remain indelibly impressed upon the memory, and preserve themselves in their individuality entire. We can assign no reason for it, nor explain why this among so many thousand moments like it should be specially remembered. It seems as much a matter of chance as when single specimens of a whole race of animals now extinct are discovered in the layers of a rock; or when, on opening a book, we light upon an insect accidently crushed within the leaves. Memories of this kind are always sweet and pleasant.

.   .   .   .   .   .

It occasionally happens that, for no particular reason, long-forgotten scenes suddenly start up in the memory. This may in many cases be due to the action of some hardly perceptible odor which accompanied those scenes and now recurs exactly the same as before. For it is well known that the sense of smell is specially effective in awakening memories, and that in general it does not require much to rouse a train of ideas. And I may say, in passing, that the sense of sight is connected with the understanding,[1] the sense of hearing with the reason,[2] and, as we see in the present case, the sense of smell with the memory. Touch and Taste are more material and dependent upon contact. They have no ideal side.

.   .   .   .   .   .

It must also be reckoned among the peculiar attributes of memory that a slight state of intoxication often so greatly enhances the recollection of past times and scenes, that all the circumstances connected with them come back much more clearly than would be possible in a state of sobriety; but that, on the other hand, the recollection of what one said or did while the intoxication lasted, is more than usually imperfect; nay, that if one has been absolutely tipsy, it is gone altogether. We may say, then,

[1] *Vierfache Wurzel* § 21.
[2] *Parerga* vol. ii., § 311.

that whilst intoxication enhances the memory for what is past, it allows it to remember little of the present.

· · · · · ·

Men need some kind of external activity, because they are inactive within. Contrarily, if they are active within, they do not care to be dragged out of themselves; it disturbs and impedes their thoughts in a way that is often most ruinous to them.

· · · · · ·

I am not surprised some people are bored when they find themselves alone; for they cannot laugh if they are quite by themselves. The very idea of it seems folly to them.

Are we, then to look upon laughter as merely a signal for others—a mere sign, like a word? What makes it impossible for people to laugh when they are alone is nothing but want of imagination, dullness of mind generally—ἀναισθησία καὶ βραδυτὴς ψυχῆς, as Theophrastus has it.[3] The lower animals never laugh, either alone or in company. Myson, the misanthropist, was once surprised by one of these people as he was laughing to himself. *Why do you laugh?* he asked; *there is no one with you. That is just why I am laughing,* said Myson.

· · · · · ·

Natural *gesticulation*, such as commonly accompanies any lively talk, is a language of its own, more widespread, even, than the language of words—so far, I mean, as it is independent of words and alike in all nations. It is true that nations make use of it in proportion as they are vivacious, and that in particular cases, amongst the Italians, for instance, it is supplemented by certain peculiar gestures which are merely conventional, and therefore possessed of nothing more than a local value.

In the universal use made of it, gesticulation has some analogy with logic and grammar, in that it has to do with

[3] *Characters,* e. 27.

the form, rather than with the matter of conversation; but on the other hand it is distinguishable from them by the fact that it has more of a moral than of an intellectual bearing; in other words, it reflects the movements of the will. As an accompaniment of conversation it is like the bass of a melody; and if, as in music, it keeps true to the progress of the treble, it serves to heighten the effect.

In a conversation, the gesture depends upon the form in which the subject-matter is conveyed; and it is interesting to observe that, whatever that subject-matter may be, with a recurrence of the form, the very same gesture is repeated. So if I happen to see—from my window, say—two persons carrying on a lively conversation, without my being able to catch a word, I can, nevertheless, understand the general nature of it perfectly well; I mean, the kind of thing that is being said and the form it takes. There is no mistake about it. The speaker is arguing about something, advancing his reasons, then limiting their application, then driving them home and drawing the conclusion in triumph; or he is recounting his experiences, proving, perhaps, beyond the shadow of a doubt, how much he has been injured, but bringing the clearest and most damning evidence to show that his opponents were foolish and obstinate people who would not be convinced; or else he is telling of the splendid plan he laid, and how he carried it to a successful issue, or perhaps failed because the luck was against him; or, it may be, he is saying that he was completely at a loss to know what to do, or that he was quick in seeing some traps set for him, and that by insisting on his rights or by applying a little force, he succeeded in frustrating and punishing his enemies; and so on in hundreds of cases of a similar kind.

Strictly speaking, however, what I get from gesticulation alone is an abstract notion of the essential drift of what is being said, and that, too, whether I judge from a moral or an intellectual point of view. It is the quintessence, the true substance of the conversation, and this remains identical, no matter what may have given rise to the conversation, or what it may be about; the relation between the two being that of a general idea or class-name to the individuals which it covers.

As I have said, the most interesting and amusing part of the matter is the complete identity and solidarity of the gestures used to denote the same set of circumstances, even though by people of very different temperament; so that the gestures become exactly like words of a language, alike for every one, and subject only to such small modifications as depend upon variety of accent and education. And yet there can be no doubt but that these standing gestures, which every one uses, are the result of no convention or collusion. They are original and innate—a true language of nature; consolidated, it may be, by imitation and the influence of custom.

It is well known that it is part of an actor's duty to make a careful study of gesture; and the same thing is true, to a somewhat smaller degree, of a public speaker. This study must consist chiefly in watching others and imitating their movements, for there are no abstract rules fairly applicable to the matter, with the exception of some very general leading principles, such as—to take an example —that the gesture must not follow the word, but rather come immediately before it, by way of announcing its approach and attracting the hearer's attention.

Englishmen entertain a peculiar contempt for gesticulatios, and look upon it as something vulgar and undignified. This seems to me a silly prejudice on their part, and the outcome of their general prudery. For here we have a language which nature has given to every one; which every one understands; and to do away with and forbid it for no better reason than it is opposed to that much-lauded thing, gentlemanly feeling, is a very questionable proceeding.

ON EDUCATION

THE human intellect is said to be so constituted that *general ideas* arise by abstraction from *particular observations,* and therefore come after them in point of time. If this is what actually occurs, as happens in the case of a man who has to depend solely upon his own experience for what he learns—who has no teacher and no book,—such a man knows quite well which of his particular observations belong to and are represented by each of his general ideas. He has a perfect acquaintance with both sides of his experience, and accordingly, he treats everything that comes in his way from a right standpoint. This might be called the *natural* method of education.

Contrarily the *artificial* method is to hear what other people say, to learn and to read, and so to get your head crammed full of general ideas before you have any sort of extended acquaintance with the world as it is, and as you may see it for yourself. You will be told that the particular observations which go to make these general ideas will come to you later on in the course of experience; but until that time arrives, you apply your general ideas wrongly, you judge men and things from a wrong standpoint, you see them in a wrong light, and treat them in a wrong way. So it is that education perverts the mind.

This explains why it so frequently happens that, after a long course of learning and reading, we enter upon the world in our youth, partly with an artless ignorance of things, partly with wrong notions about them; so that our demeanor savors at one moment of a nervous anxiety, at another of a mistaken confidence. The reason of this is simply that our head is full of general ideas which we are now trying to turn to some use, but which we hardly ever apply rightly. This is the result of acting in direct opposition to the natural development of the mind by obtaining general ideas first, and particular observations last: it is putting the cart before the horse. Instead of developing the child's own faculties of discernment, and teaching it to judge and think for itself, the teacher uses all his energies to stuff its head full of the ready-made thoughts of other people. The mistaken views of life, which spring from a false application of general ideas, have afterwards to be corrected by long years of experience; and it is seldom that they are wholly corrected. This is why so few men of learning are possessed of common-sense, such as is often to be met with in people who have had no instruction at all.

To acquire a knowledge of the world might be defined as the aim of all education; and it follows from what I have said that special stress should be laid upon beginning to acquire this knowledge *at the right end*. As I have shown, this means, in the main, that the particular observation of a thing shall precede the general idea of it; further, that narrow and circumscribed ideas shall come before ideas of a wide range. It means, therefore, that the whole system of education shall follow in the steps that must have been taken by the ideas themselves in the course of their formation. But whenever any of these steps are skipped or left out, the instruction is defective, and the ideas obtained are false; and finally, a distorted view of the world arises, peculiar to the individual himself—a view such as almost everyone entertains for some time, and most men for as long as they live. No one can look into his own mind without seeing that it was only after reaching a very mature age, and in some cases when he least expected it, that he came to a right understanding or a clear view of many

matters in his life, that, after all, were not very difficult
or complicated. Up till then, they were points in his
knowledge of the world which were still obscure, due to his
having skipped some particular lesson in those early days
of his education, whatever it may have been like—whether
artificial and conventional, or of that natural kind which is
based upon individual experience.

It follows that an attempt should be made to find out
the strictly natural course of knowledge, so that education
may proceed methodically by keeping to it; and that children may become acquainted with the ways of the world,
without getting wrong ideas into their heads, which very
often cannot be got out again. If this plan were adopted,
special care would have to be taken to prevent children
from using words without clearly understanding their meaning and application. The fatal tendency to be satisfied
with words instead of trying to understand things—to learn
phrases by heart, so that they may prove a refuge in time
of need, exists, as a rule, even in children; and the tendency
lasts on into manhood, making the knowledge of many
learned persons to consist in mere verbiage.

However, the main endeavor must always be to let particular observations precede general ideas, and not *vice
versa*, as is usually and unfortunately the case; as though
a child should come feet foremost into the world, or a
verse be begun by writing down the rhyme! The ordinary
method is to imprint ideas and opinions, in the strict sense
of the word, *prejudices*, on the mind of the child, before
it has had any but a very few particular observations. It
is thus that he afterwards comes to view the world and
gather experience through the medium of those ready-made
ideas, rather than to let his ideas be formed for him out
of his own experience of life, as they ought to be.

A man sees a great many things when he looks at the
world for himself, and he sees them from many sides; but

this method of learning is not nearly so short or so quick as the method which employs abstract ideas and makes hasty generalizations about everything. Experience, therefore, will be a long time in correcting preconceived ideas, or perhaps never bring its task to an end; for wherever a man finds that the aspect of things seems to contradict the general ideas he has formed, he will begin by rejecting the evidence it offers as partial and one-sided; nay, he will shut his eyes to it altogether and deny that it stands in any contradiction at all with his preconceived notions, in order that he may thus preserve them uninjured. So it is that many a man carries about a burden of wrong notions all his life long—crotchets, whims, fancies, prejudices, which at last become fixed ideas. The fact is that he has never tried to form his fundamental ideas for himself out of his own experience of life, his own way of looking at the world, because he has taken over his ideas ready-made from other people; and this it is that makes him—as it makes how many others!—so shallow and superficial.

Instead of that method of instruction, care should be taken to educate children on the natural lines. No idea should ever be established in a child's mind otherwise than by what the child can see for itself, or at any rate it should be verified by the same means; and the result of this would be that the child's ideas, if few, would be well-grounded and accurate. It would learn how to measure things by its own standard rather than by another's; and so it would escape a thousand strange fancies and prejudices, and not need to have them eradicated by the lessons it will subsequently be taught in the school of life. The child would, in this way, have its mind once for all habituated to clear views and thorough-going knowledge; it would use its own judgment and take an unbiased estimate of things.

And, in general, children should not form their notions of what life is like from the copy before they have learned it from the original, to whatever aspect of it their attention may be directed. Instead, therefore, of hastening to place *books*, and books alone, in their hands, let them be made acquainted, step by step, with *things*—with the actual circumstances of human life. And above all let care be taken to bring them to a clear and objective view of the world as it is, to educate them always to derive their ideas directly from real life, and to shape them in conformity with it—not to fetch them from other sources, such as books, fairy tales, or what people say—then to apply them ready-made to real life. For this will mean that their heads are full of wrong notions, and that they will either see things in a false light or try in vain to *remodel the world* to suit their views, and so enter upon false paths; and that, too, whether they are only constructing theories of life or engaged in the actual business of it. It is incredible how much harm is done when the seeds of wrong notions are laid in the mind in those early years, later on to bear a crop of prejudice; for the subsequent lessons, which are learned from real life in the world have to be devoted mainly to their extirpation. *To unlearn the evil* was the answer, according to Diogenes Laertius,[1] Antisthenes gave, when he was asked what branch of knowledge was most necessary; and we can see what he meant.

No child under the age of fifteen should receive instruction in subjects which may possibly be the vehicle of serious error, such as philosophy, religion, or any other branch of knowledge where it is necessary to take large views; because wrong notions imbibed early can seldom be rooted out, and of all the intellectual faculties, judgment is the last to arrive at maturity. The child should give its attention either to subjects where no error is possible at all, such as mathematics, or to those in which there is no par-

[1] vi. 7.

ticular danger in making a mistake, such as languages, natural science, history and so on. And in general, the branches of knowledge which are to be studied at any period of life should be such as the mind is equal to at that period and can perfectly understand. Childhood and youth form the time for collecting materials, for getting a special and thorough knowledge of the individual and particular things. In those years it is too early to form views on a large scale; and ultimate explanations must be put off to a later date. The faculty of judgment, which cannot come into play without mature experience, should be left to itself; and care should be taken not to anticipate its action by inculcating prejudice, which will paralyze it for ever.

On the other hand, the memory should be specially taxed in youth, since it is then that it is strongest and most tenacious. But in choosing the things that should be committed to memory the utmost care and forethought must be exercised; as lessons well learnt in youth are never forgotten. This precious soil must therefore be cultivated so as to bear as much fruit as possible. If you think how deeply rooted in your memory are those persons whom you knew in the first twelve years of your life, how indelible the impression made upon you by the events of those years, how clear your recollection of most of the things that happened to you then, most of what was told or taught you, it will seem a natural thing to take the susceptibility and tenacity of the mind at that period as the groundwork of education. This may be done by a strict observance of method, and a systematic regulation of the impressions which the mind is to receive.

But the years of youth allotted to a man are short, and memory is, in general, bound within narrow limits; still more so, the memory of any one individual. Since this is the case, it is all-important to fill the memory with what is essential and material in any branch of knowledge, to the exclusion of everything else. The decision as to what is essential and material should rest with the master-minds in every department of thought; their choice should be made after the most mature deliberation, and the outcome of it fixed and determined. Such a choice would have to proceed by sifting the things which it is necessary and important for a man to know in general, and then, necessary and important for him to know in any particular business or calling. Knowledge of the first kind would have to be classified, after an encyclopædic fashion, in graduated courses, adapted to the degree of general culture which a man may be expected to have in the circumstances in which he is placed; beginning with a course limited to the necessary requirements of primary education, and extending upwards to the subjects treated of in all the branches of philosophical thought. The regulation of the second kind of knowledge would be left to those who had shown genuine mastery in the several departments into which it is divided; and the whole system would provide an elaborate rule or canon for intellectual education, which would, of course, have to be revised every ten years. Some such arrangement as this would employ the youthful power of the memory to best advantage, and supply excellent working material to the faculty of judgment, when it made its appearance later on.

A man's knowledge may be said to be mature, in other words, it has reached the most complete state of perfection to which he, as an individual, is capable of bringing it, when an exact correspondence is established between the whole of his abstract ideas and the things he has actually perceived for himself. This will mean that each of his abstract ideas rests, directly or indirectly, upon a basis of observation, which alone endows it with any real value; and also that he is able to place every observation he makes under the right abstract idea which belongs to it. Maturity is the work of experience alone; and therefore it requires time. The knowledge we derive from our own observation is usually distinct from that which we acquire through the medium of abstract ideas; the one coming to us in the natural way, the other by what people tell us, and the course of instruction we receive, whether it is good or bad. The result is, that in youth there is generally very little agreement or correspondence between our abstract ideas, which are merely phrases in the mind, and that real knowledge which we have obtained by our own observation. It is only later on that a gradual approach takes place between these two kinds of knowledge, accompanied by a mutual correction of error; and knowledge is not mature until this coalition is accomplished. This maturity or perfection of knowledge is something quite independent of another kind of perfection, which may be of a high or a low order—the perfection, I mean, to which a man may bring his own individual faculties; which is measured, not by any correspondence between the two kinds of knowledge, but by the degree of intensity which each kind attains.

For the practical man the most needful thing is to acquire an accurate and profound knowledge of *the ways of the world*. But this, though the most needful, is also the most wearisome of all studies, as a man may reach a great age without coming to the end of his task; whereas, in the domain of the sciences, he masters the more important facts when he is still young. In acquiring that knowledge of the world, it is while he is a novice, namely, in boyhood and in youth, that the first and hardest lessons are put before him; but it often happens that even in later years there is still a great deal to be learned.

The study is difficult enough in itself; but the difficulty is doubled by *novels*, which represent a state of things in life and the world, such as, in fact, does not exist. Youth is credulous, and accepts these views of life, which then become part and parcel of the mind; so that, instead of a merely negative condition of ignorance, you have positive error—a whole tissue of false notions to start with; and at a later date these actually spoil the schooling of experience, and put a wrong construction on the lessons it teaches. If, before this, the youth had no light at all to guide him, he is now misled by a will-o'-wisp; still more often is this the case with a girl. They have both had a false view of things foisted on them by reading novels; and expectations have been aroused which can never be fulfilled. This generally exercises a baneful influence on their whole life. In this respect those whose youth has allowed them no time or opportunity for reading novels—those who work with their hands and the like—are in a position of decided advantage. There are a few novels to which this reproach cannot be addressed—nay, which have an effect the contrary of bad. First and foremost, to give an example, *Gil Blas*, and the other works of Le Sage (or rather their Spanish originals); further, *The Vicar of Wakefield*, and, to some extent Sir Walter Scott's novels. *Don Quixote* may be regarded as a satirical exhibition of the error to which I am referring.

OF WOMEN

SCHILLER's poem in honor of women, *Würde der Frauen,* is the result of much careful thought, and it appeals to the reader by its antithetic style and its use of contrast; but as an expression of the true praise, which should be accorded to them, it is, I think, inferior to these few words of Jouy's: *Without women, the beginning of our life would be helpless; the middle, devoid of pleasure; and the end, of consolation.* The same thing is more feelingly expressed by Byron in *Sardanapalus:*

> *The very first*
> *Of human life must spring from woman's breast,*
> *Your first small words are taught you from her lips,*
> *Your first tears quench'd by her, and your last sighs*
> *Too often breathed out in a woman's hearing,*
> *When men have shrunk from the ignoble care*
> *Of watching the last hour of him who led them.*
>
> (Act I. Scene 2.)

These two passages indicate the right standpoint for the appreciation of women.

You need only look at the way in which she is formed, to see that woman is not meant to undergo great labor, whether of the mind or of the body. She pays the debt of life not by what she does, but by what she suffers; by the pains of child-bearing and care for the child, and by submission to her husband, to whom she should be a patient and cheering companion. The keenest sorrows and joys are not for her, nor is she called upon to display a great deal of strength. The current of her life should be more gentle, peaceful and trivial than man's, without being essentially happier or unhappier.

Women are directly fitted for acting as the nurses and

280

teachers of our early childhood by the fact that they are themselves childish, frivolous and short-sighted; in a word, they are big children all their life long—a kind of intermediate stage between the child and the full-grown man, who is man in the strict sense of the word. See how a girl will fondle a child for days together, dance with it and sing to it; and then think what a man, with the best will in the world, could do if he were put in her place.

With young girls Nature seems to have had in view what, in the language of the drama, is called *a striking effect;* as for a few years she dowers them with a wealth of beauty and is lavish in her gift of charm, at the expense of all the rest of their life; so that during those years they may capture the fantasy of some man to such a degree that he is hurried away into undertaking the honorable care of them, in some form or other, as long as they live—a step for which there would not appear to be any sufficient warranty if reason only directed his thoughts. Accordingly, Nature has equipped woman, as she does all her creatures, with the weapons and implements requisite for the safeguarding of her existence, and for just as long as it is necessary for her to have them. Here, as elsewhere, Nature proceeds with her usual economy; for just as the female ant, after fecundation, loses her wings, which are then superfluous, nay, actually a danger to the business of breeding; so, after giving birth to one or two children, a woman generally loses her beauty; probably, indeed, for similar reasons.

And so we find that young girls, in their hearts, look upon domestic affairs or work of any kind as of secondary importance, if not actually as a mere jest. The only business that really claims their earnest attention is love, making conquests, and everything connected with this—dress, dancing, and so on.

The nobler and more perfect a thing is, the later and

slower it is in arriving at maturity. A man reaches the maturity of his reasoning powers and mental faculties hardly before the age of twenty-eight; a woman at eighteen. And then, too, in the case of woman, it is only reason of a sort—very niggard in its dimensions. That is why women remain children their whole life long; never seeing anything but what is quite close to them, cleaving to the present moment, taking appearance for reality, and preferring trifles to matters of the first importance. For it is by virtue of his reasoning faculty that man does not live in the present only, like the brute, but looks about him and considers the past and the future; and this is the origin of prudence, as well as of that care and anxiety which so many people exhibit. Both the advantages and the disadvantages which this involves, are shared in by the woman to a smaller extent because of her weaker power of reasoning. She may, in fact, be described as intellectually short-sighted, because, while she has an intuitive understanding of what lies quite close to her, her field of vision is narrow and does not reach to what is remote; so that things which are absent, or past, or to come, have much less effect upon women than upon men. This is the reason why women are more often inclined to be extravagant, and sometimes carry their inclination to a length that borders upon madness. In their hearts, women think that it is men's business to earn money and theirs to spend it—if possible during their husband's life, but, at any rate, after his death. The very fact that their husband hands them over his earnings for purposes of housekeeping, strengthens them in this belief.

However many disadvantages all this may involve, there is at least this to be said in its favor; that the woman lives more in the present than the man, and that, if the present is at all tolerable, she enjoys it more eagerly. This is the source of that cheerfulness which is peculiar to women, fitting her to amuse man in his hours of recreation, and, in case of need, to console him when he is borne down by the weight of his cares.

It is by no means a bad plan to consult women in matters of difficulty, as the Germans used to do in ancient times; for their way of looking at things is quite different from ours, chiefly in the fact that they like to take the shortest way to their goal, and, in general, manage to fix their eyes upon what lies before them; while we, as a rule, see far beyond it, just because it is in front of our noses. In cases like this, we need to be brought back to the right standpoint, so as to recover the near and simple view.

Then, again, women are decidedly more sober in their judgment than we are, so that they do not see more in things than is really there; whilst, if our passions are aroused, we are apt to see things in an exaggerated way, or imagine what does not exist.

The weakness of their reasoning faculty also explains why it is that women show more sympathy for the unfortunate than men do, and so treat them with more kindness and interest; and why it is that, on the contrary, they are inferior to men in point of justice, and less honorable and conscientious. For it is just because their reasoning power is weak that present circumstances have such a hold over them, and those concrete things, which lie directly before their eyes, exercise a power which is seldom counteracted to any extent by abstract principles of thought, by fixed rules of conduct, firm resolutions or, in general, by consideration for the past and the future, or regard for what is absent and remote. Accordingly, they possess the first and main elements that go to make a virtuous character, but they are deficient in those secondary qualities which are often a necessary instrument in the formation of it.[1]

[1] In this respect they may be compared to an animal organism which contains a liver but no gall-bladder. Here let me refer to what I have said in my treatise on *The Foundation of Morals*, § 17.

Hence, it will be found that the fundamental fault of the female character is that it has *no sense of justice*. This is mainly due to the fact, already mentioned, that women are defective in the powers of reasoning and deliberation; but it is also traceable to the position which Nature has assigned to them as the weaker sex. They are dependent, not upon strength, but upon craft; and hence their instinctive capacity for cunning, and their ineradicable tendency to say what is not true. For as lions are provided with claws and teeth, and elephants and boars with tusks, bulls with horns, and cuttle fish with its clouds of inky fluid, so Nature has equipped woman, for her defence and protection, with the arts of dissimulation; and all the power which Nature has conferred upon man in the shape of physical strength and reason, has been bestowed upon women in this form. Hence, dissimulation is innate in woman, and almost as much a quality of the stupid as of the clever. It is as natural for them to make use of it on every occasion as it is for those animals to employ their means of defence when they are attacked; they have a feeling that in doing so they are only within their rights. Therefore a woman who is perfectly truthful and not given to dissimulation is perhaps an impossibility, and for this very reason they are so quick at seeing through dissimulation in others that it is not a wise thing to attempt it with them. But this fundamental defect which I have stated, with all that it entails, gives rise to falsity, faithlessness, treachery, ingratitude, and so on. Perjury in a court of justice is more often committed by women than by men. It may, indeed, be generally questioned whether women ought to be sworn in at all. From time to time one finds repeated cases everywhere of ladies, who want for nothing, taking things from shop-counters when no one is looking, and making off with them.

Nature has appointed that the propagation of the species

shall be the business of men who are young, strong and handsome; so that the race may not degenerate. This is the firm will and purpose of Nature in regard to the species, and it finds its expression in the passions of women. There is no law that is older or more powerful than this. Woe, then, to the man who sets up claims and interests that will conflict with it; whatever he may say and do, they will be unmercifully crushed at the first serious encounter. For the innate rule that governs women's conduct, though it is secret and unformulated, nay, unconscious in its working, is this: *We are justified in deceiving those who think they have acquired rights over the species by paying little attention to the individual, that is, to us. The constitution and, therefore, the welfare of the species have been placed in our hands and committed to our care, through the control we obtain over the next generation, which proceeds from us; let us discharge our duties conscientiously.* But women have no abstract knowledge of this leading principle; they are conscious of it only as a concrete fact; and they have no other method of giving expression to it than the way in which they act when the opportunity arrives. And then their conscience does not trouble them so much as we fancy; for in the darkest recesses of their heart, they are aware that in committing a breach of their duty towards the individual, they have all the better fulfilled their duty towards the species, which is infinitely greater.[2]

And since women exist in the main solely for the propagation of the species, and are not destined for anything else, they live, as a rule, more for the species than for the individual, and in their hearts take the affairs of the species more seriously than those of the individual. This

[2] A more detailed discussion of the matter in question may be found in my chief work, *Die Welt als Wille und Vorstellung,* vol. ii. ch. 44.

gives their whole life and being a certain levity; the general bent of their character is in a direction fundamentally different from that of man; and it is this to which produces that discord in married life which is so frequent, and almost the normal state.

The natural feeling between men is mere indifference, but between women it is actual enmity. The reason of this is that trade-jealousy—*odium figulinum*—which, in the case of men does not go beyond the confines of their own particular pursuit; but, with women, embraces the whole sex; since they have only one kind of business. Even when they meet in the street, women look at one another like Guelphs and Ghibellines. And it is a patent fact that when two women make first acquaintance with each other, they behave with more constraint and dissimulation than two men would show in a like case; and hence it is that an exchange of compliments between two women is a much more ridiculous proceeding than between two men. Further, whilst a man will, as a general rule, always preserve a certain amount of consideration and humanity in speaking to others, even to those who are in a very inferior position, it is intolerable to see how proudly and disdainfully a fine lady will generally behave towards one who is in a lower social rank (I do not mean a woman who is in her service), whenever she speaks to her. The reason of this may be that, with women, differences of rank are much more precarious than with us; because, while a hundred considerations carry weight in our case, in theirs there is only one, namely, with which man they have found favor; as also that they stand in much nearer relations with one another than men do, in consequence of the one-sided nature of their calling. This makes them endeavor to lay stress upon differences of rank.

It is only the man whose intellect is clouded by his sexual impulses that could give the name of *the fair sex* to that under-sided, narrow-shouldered, broad-hipped, and short-legged race; for the whole beauty of the sex is bound up with this impulse. Instead of calling them beautiful, there would be more warrant for describing women as the unæsthetic sex. Neither for music, nor for poetry, nor for fine art, have they really and truly any sense or susceptibility; it is a mere mockery if they make a pretence of it in order to assist their endeavor to please. Hence, as a result of this, they are incapable of taking a *purely objective interest* in anything; and the reason of it seems to me to be as follows. A man tries to acquire *direct* mastery over things, either by understanding them, or by forcing them to do his will. But a woman is always and everywhere reduced to obtaining this mastery *indirectly*, namely, through a man; and whatever direct mastery she may have is entirely confined to him. And so it lies in woman's nature to look upon everything only as a means for conquering man; and if she takes an interest in anything else, it is simulated—a mere roundabout way of gaining her ends by coquetry, and feigning what she does not feel. Hence, even Rousseau declared: *Women have, in general, no love for any art; they have no proper knowledge of any; and they have no genius.*[3]

No one who sees at all below the surface can have failed to remark the same thing. You need only observe the kind of attention women bestow upon a concert, an opera, or a play—the childish simplicity, for example, with which they keep on chattering during the finest passages in the greatest masterpieces. If it is true that the Greeks excluded women from their theatres they were quite right in what they did; at any rate you would have been able to hear what was said upon the stage. In our day, besides, or in lieu of saying, *Let a woman keep silence in the church*, it would be much to the point to say *Let a woman keep silence in*

[3] Lettre à d'Alembert. Note xx.

the theatre. This might, perhaps, be put up in big letters on the curtain.

And you cannot expect anything else of women if you consider that the most distinguished intellects among the whole sex have never managed to produce a single achievement in the fine arts that is really great, genuine, and original; or given to the world any work of permanent value in any sphere. This is most strikingly shown in regard to painting, where mastery of technique is at least as much within their power as within ours—and hence they are diligent in cultivating it; but still, they have not a single great painting to boast of, just because they are deficient in that objectivity of mind which is so directly indispensable in painting. They never get beyond a subjective point of view. It is quite in keeping with this that ordinary women have no real susceptibility for art at all; for Nature proceeds in strict sequence—*non facit saltum.* And Huarte[4] in his *Examen de ingenios para las scienzias*—a book which has been famous for three hundred years—denies women the possession of all the higher faculties. The case is not altered by particular and partial exceptions; taken as a whole, women are, and remain, thoroughgoing Philistines, and quite incurable. Hence, with that absurd arrangement which allows them to share the rank and title of their husbands they are a constant stimulus to his ignoble ambitions. And, further, it is just because they are Philistines that modern society, where they take the lead and set the tone, is in such a bad way. Napoleon's saying—that *women have no rank*—should be adopted as the right standpoint in determining their position in society; and as regards their other qualities Chamfort[5] makes the very true remark: *They are made to trade with*

[4] *Translator's Note.*—Juan Huarte (1520?-1590) practised as a physician at Madrid. The work cited by Schopenhauer is well known, and has been translated into many languages.

[5] *Translator's Note.*—See *Counsels and Maxims,* p. 12, Note.

our own weaknesses and our follies; but not with our reason. The sympathies that exist between them and men are skin-deep only, and do not touch the mind or the feelings or the character. They form the *sexus sequior*—the second sex, inferior in every respect to the first; their infirmities should be treated with consideration; but to show them great reverence is extremely ridiculous, and lowers us in their eyes. When Nature made two divisions of the human race, she did not draw the line exactly through the middle. These divisions are polar and opposed to each other, it is true; but the difference between them is not qualitative merely, it is also quantitative.

This is just the view which the ancients took of woman, and the view which people in the East take now; and their judgment as to her proper position is much more correct than ours, with our old French notions of gallantry and our preposterous system of reverence—that highest product of Teutonico-Christian stupidity. These notions have served only to make women more arrogant and overbearing; so that one is occasionally reminded of the holy apes in Benares, who in the consciousness of their sanctity and inviolable position, think they can do exactly as they please.

But in the West, the woman, and especially the *lady*, finds herself in a false position; for woman, rightly called by the ancients, *sexus sequior*, is by no means fit to be the object of our honor and veneration, or to hold her head higher than man and be on equal terms with him. The consequences of this false position are sufficiently obvious. Accordingly, it would be a very desirable thing if this Number-Two of the human race were in Europe also relegated to her natural place, and an end put to that lady nuisance, which not only moves all Asia to laughter, but would have been ridiculed by Greece and Rome as well. It is impossible to calculate the good effects which such a change would bring about in our social, civil and political arrangements. There would be no necessity for the Salic law: it would be a superfluous truism. In Europe the *lady,* strictly so-called, is a being who should not exist at all; she should be either a housewife or a girl who hopes to become one; and she should be brought up, not to be arrogant, but to be thrifty and submissive. It is just because there are such people as *ladies* in Europe that the women of the lower classes, that is to say, the great majority of the sex, are much more unhappy than they are in the East. And even Lord Byron says: *Thought of the state of women under the ancient Greeks—convenient enough. Present state, a remnant of the barbarism of the chivalric and the feudal ages—artificial and unnatural. They ought to mind home—and be well fed and clothed—but not mixed in society. Well educated, too, in religion—but to read neither poetry nor politics—nothing but books of piety and cookery. Music—drawing—dancing—also a little gardening and ploughing now and then. I have seen them mending the roads in Epirus with good success. Why not, as well as hay-making and milking?*

The laws of marriage prevailing in Europe consider the woman as the equivalent of the man—start, that is to say, from a wrong position. In our part of the world where monogamy is the rule, to marry means to halve one's rights and double one's duties. Now, when the laws gave women equal rights with man, they ought to have also endowed her with a masculine intellect. But the fact is, that just in proportion as the honors and privileges which the laws accord to women, exceed the amount which nature gives, is there a diminution in the number of women who really participate in these privileges; and all the remainder are deprived of their natural rights by just so much as is given to the others over and above their share. For the institution of monogamy, and the laws of marriage which it entails, bestow upon the woman an unnatural position of privilege, by considering her throughout as the full equivalent of the man, which is by no means the case; and seeing this, men who are shrewd and prudent very often scruple to make so great a sacrifice and to acquiesce in so unfair an arrangement.

Consequently, whilst among polygamous nations every woman is provided for, where monogamy prevails the number of married women is limited; and there remains over a large number of women without stay or support, who, in the upper classes, vegetate as useless old maids, and in the lower succumb to hard work for which they are not suited; or else become *filles de joie*, whose life is as destitute of joy as it is of honor. But under the circumstances they become a necessity; and their position is openly recognized as serving the special end of warding off temptation from those women favored by fate, who have found, or may hope to find, husbands. In London alone there are 80,000 prostitutes. What are they but the women, who, under the institution of monogamy have come off worse? Theirs is a dreadful fate: they are human sacrifices offered up on the altar of monogamy. The women whose wretched position is here described are the inevitable set-off to the European lady with her arrogance and pretension. Polygamy is therefore a real benefit to the female sex if it is taken as a whole. And, from another point of view, there is no true reason why a man whose wife suffers from chronic illness, or remains barren, or has gradually become too old for him, should not take a second. The motives which induce so many people to become converts to Mormonism[6] appear to be just those which militate against the unnatural institution of monogamy.

Moreover, the bestowal of unnatural rights upon women has imposed upon them unnatural duties, and, nevertheless,

[6] *Translator's Note.*—The Mormons have recently given up polygamy, and received the American franchise in its stead.

a breach of these duties makes them unhappy. Let me explain. A man may often think that his social or financial position will suffer if he marries, unless he makes some brilliant alliance. His desire will then be to win a woman of his own choice under conditions other than those of marriage, such as will secure her position and that of the children. However fair, reasonable, fit and proper these conditions may be, and the woman consents by foregoing that undue amount of privilege which marriage alone can bestow, she to some extent loses her honor, because marriage is the basis of civic society; and she will lead an unhappy life, since human nature is so constituted that we pay an attention to the opinion of other people which is out of all proportion to its value. On the other hand, if she does not consent, she runs the risk either of having to be given in marriage to a man whom she does not like, or of being landed high and dry as an old maid; for the period during which she has a chance of being settled for life is very short. And in view of this aspect of the institution of monogamy, Thomasius' profoundly learned treatise, *de Concubinatu,* is well worth reading; for it shows that, amongst all nations and in all ages, down to the Lutheran Reformation, concubinage was permitted; nay, that it was an institution which was to a certain extent actually recognized by law, and attended with no dishonor. It was only the Lutheran Reformation that degraded it from this position. It was seen to be a further justification for the marriage of the clergy; and then, after that, the Catholic Church did not dare to remain behind-hand in the matter.

There is no use arguing about polygamy; it must be taken as *de facto* existing everywhere, and the only question is as to how it shall be regulated. Where are there, then, any real monogamists? We all live, at any rate, for a time, and most of us, always, in polygamy. And so, since every man needs many women, there is nothing fairer than to allow him, nay, to make it incumbent upon him, to provide for many women. This will reduce woman to her true and natural position as a subordinate being; and the *lady*—that monster of European civilization and Teutonico-Christian stupidity—will disappear from the world, leaving only *women,* but no more *unhappy women,* of whom Europe is now full.

In India, no woman is ever independent, but in accordance with the law of Manu,[7] she stands under the control of her father, her husband, her brother or her son. It is, to be sure, a revolting thing that a widow should immolate herself upon her husband's funeral pyre; but it is also revolting that she should spend her husband's money with her paramours—the money for which he toiled his whole life long, in the consoling belief that he was providing for his children. Happy are those who have kept the middle course—*medium tenuere beati.*

The first love of a mother for her child is, with the lower animals as with men, of a purely *instinctive* character, and so it ceases when the child is no longer in a physically helpless condition. After that, the first love should give way to one that is based on habit and reason; but this often fails to make its appearance, especially where the mother did not love the father. The love of a father for his child is of a different order, and more likely to last; because it has its foundation in the fact that in the child he recognizes his own inner self; that is to say, his love for it is metaphysical in its origin.

In almost all nations, whether of the ancient or the modern world, even amongst the Hottentots,[8] property is inherited by the male descendants alone; it is only in Europe that a departure has taken place; but not amongst the

[7] Ch. V., v. 148.

[8] Leroy, *Lettres philosophiques sur l'intelligence et la perfectibilité des animaux, avec quelques lettres sur l'homme,* p. 298, Paris, 1802.

nobility, however. That the property which has cost men long years of toil and effort, and been won with so much difficulty, should afterwards come into the hands of women, who then, in their lack of reason, squander it in a short time, or otherwise fool it away, is a grievance and a wrong as serious as it is common, which should be prevented by limiting the right of women to inherit. In my opinion, the best arrangement would be that by which women, whether widows or daughters, should never receive anything beyond the interest for life on property secured by mortgage, and in no case the property itself, or the capital, except where all male descendants fail. The people who make money are men, not women; and it follows from this that women are neither justified in having unconditional possession of it, nor fit persons to be entrusted with its administration. When wealth, in any true sense of the word, that is to say, funds, houses or land, is to go to them as an inheritance they should never be allowed the free disposition of it. In their case a guardian should always be appointed; and hence they should never be given the free control of their own children, wherever it can be avoided. The vanity of women, even though it should not prove to be greater than that of men, has this much danger in it, that it takes an entirely material direction. They are vain, I mean, of their personal beauty, and then of finery, show and magnificence. That is just why they are so much in their element in society. It is this, too, which makes them so inclined to be extravagant, all the more as their reasoning power is low. Accordingly we find an ancient writer describing woman as in general of an extravagant nature—Γυνη τὸ σὐνολον ἐστι δαπανηρὸν Φύσει.[9] But with men vanity often takes the direction of non-material advantages, such as intellect, learning, courage.

[9] Brunck's *Gnomici poetae graeci*, v. 115.

In the *Politics*[10] Aristotle explains the great disadvantage which accrued to the Spartans from the fact that they conceded too much to their women, by giving them the right of inheritance and dower, and a great amount of independence; and he shows how much this contributed to Sparta's fall. May it not be the case in France that the influence of women, which went on increasing steadily from the time of Louis XIII., was to blame for that gradual corruption of the Court and the Government, which brought about the Revolution of 1789, of which all subsequent disturbances have been the fruit? However that may be, the false position which women occupy, demonstrated as it is, in the most glaring way, by the institution of the *lady*, is a fundamental defect in our social scheme, and this defect, proceeding from the very heart of it, must spread its baneful influence in all directions.

. . . . . .

That woman is by nature meant to obey may be seen by the fact that every woman who is placed in the unnatural position of complete independence, immediately attaches herself to some man, by whom she allows herself to be guided and ruled. It is because she needs a lord and master. If she is young, it will be a lover; if she is old, a priest.

[10] Bk. I., ch. 9.

ON NOISE

KANT wrote a treatise on *The Vital Powers*. I should prefer to write a dirge for them. The super-abundant display of vitality, which takes the form of knocking, hammering, and tumbling things about, has proved a daily torment to me all my life long. There are people, it is true—nay, a great many people—who smile at such things, because they are not sensitive to noise; but they are just the very people who are also not sensitive to argument, or thought, or poetry, or art, in a word, to any kind of intellectual influence. The reason of it is that the tissue of their brains is of a very rough and coarse quality. On the other hand, noise is a torture to intellectual people. In the biographies of almost all great writers, or wherever else their personal utterances are recorded, I find complaints about it; in the case of Kant, for instance, Goethe, Lichtenberg, Jean Paul; and if it should happen that any writer has omitted to express himself on the matter, it is only for want of an opportunity.

This aversion to noise I should explain as follows: If you cut up a large diamond into little bits, it will entirely lose the value it had as a whole; and an army divided up into small bodies of soldiers, loses all its strength. So a great intellect sinks to the level of an ordinary one, as soon as it is interrupted and disturbed, its attention distracted and drawn off from the matter in hand: for its superiority depends upon its power of concentration—of bringing all its strength to bear upon one theme, in the same way as a concave mirror collects into one point all the rays of light that strike upon it. Noisy interruption is a hindrance to this concentration. That is why distinguished minds have always shown such an extreme dislike to disturbance in any form, as something that breaks in upon and distracts their thoughts. Above all have they been averse to that violent interruption that comes from noise. Ordinary people are not much put out by anything of the sort. The most sensible and intelligent of all nations in Europe lays down the rule, *Never Interrupt!* as the eleventh commandment. Noise is the most impertinent of all forms of interruption. It is not only an interruption, but also a disruption of thought. Of course, where there is nothing to interrupt, noise will not be so particularly painful. Occasionally it happens that some slight but constant noise continues to bother and distract me for a time before I become distinctly conscious of it. All I feel is a steady increase in the labor of thinking—just as though I were trying to walk with a weight on my foot. At last I find out what it is.

Let me now, however, pass from genus to species. The most inexcusable and disgraceful of all noises is the cracking of whips—a truly infernal thing when it is done in the narrow resounding streets of a town. I denounce it as making a peaceful life impossible; it puts an end to all quiet thought. That this cracking of whips should be allowed at all seems to me to show in the clearest way how senseless and thoughtless is the nature of mankind. No one with anything like an idea in his head can avoid a feeling of actual pain at this sudden, sharp crack, which paralyzes the brain, rends the thread of reflection, and murders thought. Every time this noise is made, it must disturb a hundred people who are applying their minds to business of some sort, no matter how trivial it may be; while on the thinker its effect is woeful and disastrous, cutting his thoughts asunder, much as the executioner's axe severs the head from the body. No sound, be it ever so shrill, cuts so sharply into the brain as this cursed cracking of whips; you feel the sting of the lash right inside your head; and it affects the brain in the same way as touch affects a sensitive plant, and for the same length of time.

With all due respect for the most holy doctrine of utility, I really cannot see why a fellow who is taking away a wagon-load of gravel or dung should thereby obtain the right to kill in the bud the thoughts which may happen to be springing up in ten thousand heads—the number he will disturb one after another in half an hour's drive through the town. Hammering, the barking of dogs, and the crying of children are horrible to hear; but your only genuine assassin of thought is the crack of a whip; it exists for the purpose of destroying every pleasant moment of quiet thought that any one may now and then enjoy. If the driver had no other way of urging on his horse than by making this most abominable of all noises, it would be excusable; but quite the contrary is the case. This cursed cracking of whips is not only unnecessary, but even useless. Its aim is to produce an effect upon the intelligence of the horse; but through the constant abuse of it, the animal becomes habituated to the sound, which falls upon blunted feelings and produces no effect at all. The horse does not go any faster for it. You have a remarkable example of this in the ceaseless cracking of his whip on the part of a cab-driver, while he is proceeding at a slow pace on the lookout for a fare. If he were to give his horse the slightest touch with the whip, it would have much more effect. Supposing, however, that it were absolutely necessary to crack the whip in order to keep the horse constantly in mind of its presence, it would be enough to make the hundredth part of the noise. For it is a well-known fact that, in regard to sight and hearing, animals are sensitive to the faintest indications; they are alive to things we can scarcely perceive. The most surprising instances of this are furnished by trained dogs and canary birds.

It is obvious, therefore, that here we have to do with an act of pure wantonness; nay, with an impudent defiance offered to those members of the community who work with their heads by those who work with their hands. That such infamy should be tolerated in a town is a piece of barbarity and iniquity, all the more as it could easily be remedied by a police-notice to the effect that every lash shall have a knot at the end of it. There can be no harm in drawing the attention of the mob to the fact that the classes above them work with their heads, for any kind of headwork is mortal anguish to the man in the street. A fellow who rides through the narrow alleys of a populous town with unemployed post-horses or cart-horses, and keeps on cracking a whip several yards long with all his might, deserves there and then to stand down and receive five really good blows with a stick.

All the philanthropists in the world, and all the legislators, meeting to advocate and decree the total abolition of corporal punishment, will never persuade me to the contrary! There is something even more disgraceful than what I have just mentioned. Often enough you may see a carter walking along the street, quite alone, without any horses, and still cracking away incessantly; so accustomed has the wretch become to it in consequence of the unwarrantable toleration of this practice. A man's body and the needs of his body are now everywhere treated with a tender indulgence. Is the thinking mind then, to be the only thing that is never to obtain the slightest measure of consideration or protection, to say nothing of respect? Carters, porters, messengers—these are the beasts of burden amongst mankind; by all means let them be treated justly, fairly, indulgently, and with forethought; but they must not be permitted to stand in the way of the higher endeavors of humanity by wantonly making a noise. How many splendid thoughts have been lost to the world by the crack of a whip? If I had the upper hand, I should soon produce in the heads of these people an indissoluble association of ideas between cracking a whip and getting a whipping.

Let us hope that the more intelligent and refined among the nations will make a beginning in this matter, and then that the Germans may take example by it and follow suit.[1] Meanwhile, I may quote what Thomas Hood says of them[2]: *For a musical nation, they are the most noisy I ever met with.* That they are so is due to the fact, not that they are more fond of making a noise than other people—they would deny it if you asked them—but that their senses are obtuse; consequently, when they hear a noise, it does not affect them much. It does not disturb them in reading or thinking, simply because they do not think; they only smoke, which is their substitute for thought. The general toleration of unnecessary noise—the slamming of doors, for instance, a very unmannerly and ill-bred thing—is direct evidence that the prevailing habit of mind is dullness and lack of thought. In Germany it seems as though care were taken no one should ever think for mere noise—to mention one form, the way drumming goes on for no purpose at all.

Finally, as regards the literature of the subject treated of in this chapter, I have only one work to recommend, but it is a good one. I refer to a poetical epistle in *terzo rimo* by the famous painter Bronzino, entitled *De' Romori: a Messer Luca Martini.* It gives a detailed description of the torture to which people are put by the various noises of a small Italian town. Written in a tragi-comic style, it is very amusing. The epistle may be found in *Opere burlesche del Berni, Aretino ed altri,* Vol. II., p. 258; apparently published in Utrecht in 1771.

[1] According to a notice issued by the Society for the Protection of Animals in Munich, the superfluous whipping and the cracking of whips were, in December, 1858, positively forbidden in Nuremberg.

[2] In *Up the Rhine.*

A FEW PARABLES

In a field of ripening corn I came to a place which had been trampled down by some ruthless foot; and as I glanced amongst the countless stalks, every one of them alike, standing there so erect and bearing the full weight of the ear, I saw a multitude of different flowers, red and blue and violet. How pretty they looked as they grew there so naturally with their little foliage! But, thought I, they are quite useless; they bear no fruit; they are mere weeds, suffered to remain only because there is no getting rid of them. And yet, but for these flowers, there would be nothing to charm the eye in that wilderness of stalks. They are emblematic of poetry and art, which, in civic life —so severe, but still useful and not without its fruit—play the same part as flowers in the corn.

· · · · · ·

There are some really beautiful landscapes in the world, but the human figures in them are poor, and you had not better look at them.

· · · · · ·

The fly should be used as the symbol of impertinence and audacity; for whilst all other animals shun man more than anything else, and run away even before he comes near them, the fly lights upon his very nose.

· · · · · ·

Two Chinamen traveling in Europe went to the theatre for the first time. One of them did nothing but study the machinery, and he succeeded in finding out how it was worked. The other tried to get at the meaning of the piece in spite of his ignorance of the language. Here you have the Astronomer and the Philosopher.

. . . . . .

Wisdom which is only theoretical and never put into practice, is like a double rose; its color and perfume are delightful, but it withers away and leaves no seed.

No rose without a thorn. Yes, but many a thorn without a rose.

. . . . . .

A wide-spreading apple-tree stood in full bloom and behind it a straight fir raised its dark and tapering head. *Look at the thousands of gay blossoms which cover me everywhere,* said the apple-tree; *what have you to show in comparison? Dark-green needles! That is true,* replied the fir, *but when winter comes, you will be bared of your glory; and I shall be as I am now.*

. . . . . .

Once, as I was botanizing under an oak, I found amongst a number of other plants of similar height one that was dark in color, with tightly closed leaves and a stalk that was very straight and stiff. When I touched it, it said to me in firm tones: *Let me alone; I am not for your collection, like these plants to which Nature has given only a single year of life. I am a little oak.*

So it is with a man whose influence is to last for hundreds of years. As a child, as a youth, often even as a full-grown man, nay, his whole life long, he goes about among his fellows, looking like them and seemingly as unimportant. But let him alone; he will not die. Time will come and bring those who know how to value him.

. . . . . .

The man who goes up in a balloon does not feel as though he were ascending; he only sees the earth sinking deeper under him.

There is a mystery which only those will understand who feel the truth of it.

. . . . . .

Your estimation of a man's size will be affected by the distance at which you stand from him, but in two entirely opposite ways according as it is his physical or his mental stature that you are considering. The one will seem smaller, the farther off you move; the other, greater.

. . . . .

Nature covers all her works with a varnish of beauty, like the tender bloom that is breathed, as it were, on the surface of a peach or a plum. Painters and poets lay themselves out to take off this varnish, to store it up, and give it us to be enjoyed at our leisure. We drink deep of this beauty long before we enter upon life itself; and when afterwards we come to see the works of Nature for ourselves, the varnish is gone: the artists have used it up and we have enjoyed it in advance. Thus it is that the world so often appears harsh and devoid of charm, nay, actually repulsive. It were better to leave us to discover the varnish for ourselves. This would mean that we should not enjoy it all at once and in large quantities; we should have no finished pictures, no perfect poems; but we should look at all things in that genial and pleasing light in which even now a child of Nature sometimes sees them— some one who has not anticipated his æsthetic pleasures by the help of art, or taken the charms of life too early.

. . . . . .

The Cathedral in Mayence is so shut in by the houses that are built round about it, that there is no one spot from which you can see it as a whole. This is symbolic of everything great or beautiful in the world. It ought to exist for its own sake alone, but before very long it is misused to serve alien ends. People come from all directions wanting to find in it support and maintenance for themselves; they stand in the way and spoil its effect. To be sure, there is nothing surprising in this, for in a world of need and imperfection everything is seized upon which can be used to satisfy want. Nothing is exempt from this service, no, not even those very things which arise only when need and want are for a moment lost sight of—the beautiful and the true, sought for their own sakes.

This is especially illustrated and corroborated in the case of institutions—whether great or small, wealthy or poor, founded, no matter in what century or in what land, to maintain and advance human knowledge, and generally to afford help to those intellectual efforts which ennoble the race. Wherever these institutions may be, it is not long before people sneak up to them under the pretence of wishing to further those special ends, while they are really led on by the desire to secure the emoluments which have been left for their furtherance, and thus to satisfy certain coarse and brutal instincts of their own. Thus it is that we come to have so many charlatans in every branch of knowledge. The charlatan takes very different shapes according to circumstances; but at bottom he is a man who cares nothing about knowledge for its own sake, and only strives to gain the semblance of it that he may use it for his own personal ends, which are always selfish and material.

. . . . . .

Every hero is a Samson. The strong man succumbs to the intrigues of the weak and the many; and if in the end he loses all patience he crushes both them and himself. Or he is like Gulliver at Lilliput, overwhelmed by an enormous number of little men.

. . . . . .

A mother gave her children Æsop's fables to read, in the hope of educating and improving their minds; but they very soon brought the book back, and the eldest, wise beyond his years, delivered himself as follows: *This is no book for us; it's much too childish and stupid. You can't make us believe that foxes and wolves and ravens are able to talk; we've got beyond stories of that kind!*

In these young hopefuls you have the enlightened Rationalists of the future.

·   ·   ·   ·   ·

A number of porcupines huddled together for warmth on a cold day in winter; but, as they began to prick one another with their quills, they were obliged to disperse. However the cold drove them together again, when just the same thing happened. At last, after many turns of huddling and dispersing, they discovered that they would be best off by remaining at a little distance from one another. In the same way the need of society drives the human porcupines together, only to be mutually repelled by the many prickly and disagreeable qualities of their nature. The moderate distance which they at last discover to be the only tolerable condition of intercourse, is the code of politeness and fine manners; and those who transgress it are roughly told—in the English phrase—*to keep their distance*. By this arrangement the mutual need of warmth is only very moderately satisfied; but then people do not get pricked. A man who has some heat in himself prefers to remain outside, where he will neither prick other people nor get pricked himself.